Mathematics
LEVEL 7

JEAN HOLDERNESS

CAUSEWAY PRESS

Published by Causeway Press Ltd
PO Box 13, Ormskirk, Lancs L39 5HP

First published 1992
Reprinted 1993

British Library Cataloguing in Publication Data
Holderness, Jean
  Mathematics: Level 7.
  1. Mathematics
  I. Title
  510

  ISBN 0-946183-76-7

Other books in this series:
Mathematics: Levels 3 & 4 by David Alcorn
Mathematics: Level 5 by Jean Holderness
Mathematics: Level 6 by Jean Holderness
Mathematics: Level 8 by Jean Holderness
Mathematics: Levels 9 & 10 by Jean Holderness

Other titles by Jean Holderness published by
Causeway Press:
GCSE Maths: Higher Level
GCSE Maths: Intermediate Level
GCSE Maths: Foundation Level
Pure Maths in Practice

Typesetting by Alden Multimedia Ltd., Northampton
Printed by Alden Press, Oxford

Preface

Mathematics: Level 7 has been written for pupils in secondary school and it follows on from the work covered in the books *Mathematics: Level 5* and *Mathematics: Level 6*. It is based mainly on the programme of study for level 7 of the National Curriculum, but it also provides consolidation for some work of earlier levels, and some additional topics from higher levels have also been included.

For many pupils, the book could be used as a basis for a year's work, but for others there is sufficient material included for it to be used for more than a year. The teacher can decide how best to use the book with a particular class. (There are some notes for teachers on page *x*.)

As usual, my family and friends have given me support and encouragement while I have been planning and writing this book, and I would like to thank them for this. I should also like to thank those who have helped with the production of the book, Sue and Andrew, my brother Jim, and the staff at Alden Multimedia and Alden Press. From Causeway Press I have had support from everyone, and especially from David and Mike, and I thank them for all their help.

Jean Holderness

Acknowledgements

Artwork and page design Susan and Andrew Allen

Cover Andrew Allen and Jean Holderness

Photography © Jim Holderness and Andrew Allen

The Algebra factory (pp. 34 and 35). Many thanks to Adrian Grenville for allowing us to reproduce his drawing.

Copyright photographs
Ed Buziak p. 65
Popperfoto pp. 111 (bottom left), 148 (bottom right), 181 (bottom left),
                213 (top right), 213 (bottom left), 255 (top right), 263 (left), 272
Sally and Richard Greenhill pp. 1 (top right), 77 (bottom left), 111 (top right), 120 (top right), 197, 241, 285
Science Museum p. 201
Topham Picture Source pp. 1 (top left), 1 (middle left), 14, 19, 76 (top right), 77 (top left),
                77 (bottom right), 148 (bottom left), 156, 160, 168 (bottom left),
                168 (bottom right), 169, 180 (right), 213 (top left), 255 (top left),
                255 (bottom left), 255 (bottom right), 259, 262 (right), 277

Contents

Topics for Activities (included in the miscellaneous sections)

To the teacher

Mathematics: Level 7 has been planned for use in secondary schools. It follows on from the work in the books *Mathematics: Level 5* and *Mathematics: Level 6*.

It was planned to contain all the topics needed for the Programme of Study and the Attainment Targets for Level 7, together with some work from earlier levels, and a chance to make progress beyond Level 7 in some areas. When the revised National Curriculum is published, I hope that the book will still satisfy these aims.

The book follows the same pattern as the earlier books in the series. The chapters are arranged in an order which interlinks Arithmetic, Geometry, Algebra, Statistics and Probability, so that there is a variety of maths in each part of the book, but there is no need to keep to the exact order of topics.

For each chapter there is an introductory section called 'Thinking About...' You could use these sections, or parts of them, for class discussion, for group work or for individual work. They could take a brief few minutes or several lessons. You might find that by extending the ideas there you are covering the work of the chapter quite adequately and very little follow-up work will be needed.

The main part of the chapter consists of bookwork and worked examples, followed by straightforward exercises. There should be no need for most pupils to have to work through the whole of any of these exercises. They are there in case practice is needed, and to give the pupils confidence in using the mathematical techniques. It is useful to have the bookwork available for reference. If the teacher has planned a good lesson then it may be unnecessary to use the bookwork at all, but children are not always present in every lesson, and the absentees need some text to help them later.

The last exercise of each chapter is more varied, giving ideas for applications and activities of various lengths. Some are purely mathematical and some relate the mathematics of the chapter to real-life applications. The teacher can best plan how to use these activities with the class, whether to use them for individual work, group work or as a whole class activity, and deciding how much time can be spent on them. If the pupils can be allowed to make their own choice of an activity that interests them, they can produce very satisfactory work to match their own levels of ability.

The book has 18 chapters, giving roughly 6 for each term if the book is to be used for a year. After every 6 chapters there is a miscellaneous section with aural questions, revision questions and more suggestions for activities. There are puzzle questions fitted in at the ends of chapters where there is space. These are in no particular order and are there to give further interest.

The teacher should be ready to link mathematics with any topics or activities which apply directly to the interests of the class, such as studies in other subjects, or current local or national issues.

Here are some notes about particular topics:

Calculators. The references to calculators are based on scientific calculators. If pupils have them at this stage, they can get used to using them and finding out about some of the extra keys. Even scientific calculators do not all work in the same way or have similar keys, so if the pupils have different types they may need individual help at times.

Chapter 1, Numbers. Writing numbers in their prime factors gives good practice in mental arithmetic, so I have not included a tables check this time. However, the teacher should make sure that pupils can do simple arithmetic quickly and accurately, or so much time will be wasted later on.

The rules for indices have been introduced with numbers in Chapter 1 and again using algebraic letters in Chapter 3. (Numbers with negative indices have been left for Level 8.)

Chapter 2, Loci. I have linked more practice in accurate drawing with this topic. If you do not want the pupils to spend much time on accurate drawing, some of the questions of Exercise 2.2 could be answered with sketch diagrams rather than accurate ones.

Chapter 3, Algebra. Once again I have started with basic ideas of Algebra so as to give the pupils confidence. Practice in questions such as $6y - (-5y)$ are included here as they will be needed for Chapter 11, Simultaneous Equations.

Chapter 4, Calculating with decimals. This chapter also starts with basic work and leads to multiplication and division with decimals. I have included the mental calculations as required by the National Curriculum, but I think that pupils will have to do such questions as $60 \div 0.04$ confidently, using pencil and paper, before they can progress to doing them mentally.

For measurements, the possible error is half a unit either way. That is all that is needed to be understood here. (The inverse problem of how to record a measurement which appears to lie on one of these half-unit boundary points belongs to Level 9.)

Chapter 5, Statistical testing. This chapter will have to be linked to practical work and maybe it could be combined with some other subject, such as fieldwork in Geography or experiments in Science. It is worth checking the pupils' questionnaires before they start using them with people out of school. Also make sure they keep in pairs or groups, or are carefully supervised, if they go off school premises.

Chapter 9, Pythagoras' theorem. The question 'Squares and triangles' on page 106 shows one way of discovering Pythagoras' theorem.

Chapter 12, Circles and cylinders. Since I did not include this work in earlier books (previously it having been in Level 8) I have had to introduce it here.

Chapter 15, Lines of best fit. It is sufficient for pupils just to draw these 'by inspection' (Method 1). However, you might find it more satisfactory to use Method 2. This gives pupils the 'mean point' to draw their lines through, and they find this helpful. The answers for Exercise 15.2 have been worked out using regression equations and there will probably be wide variations in pupils' answers.

Computers. There are many commercially-produced programs now available which can be used to link with the mathematics in this book, and suggestions have been given of topics where they can be useful. Alternatively, you or your pupils may write your own simple programs.

Answers. I have given the answers to the straightforward questions but not always to the activities questions where it is important that the pupils make their own discoveries. The puzzle answers are not given, either. The publishers cannot publish a book without answers as well as an edition with answers as this would increase the costs. There should not be so much of a problem of pupils misusing answers by this level, but again I have arranged for the answers to begin on a right-hand page so that if you do not want the class to have them, they can be cut out of the book.

I hope you and your pupils find this book useful and interesting. Enjoy your Maths.

Jean Holderness

Tables

Time

60 seconds = 1 minute
60 minutes = 1 hour
24 hours = 1 day
7 days = 1 week
52 weeks = 1 year
365 days = 1 year
366 days = 1 leap year
12 months = 1 year

The Metric System   **British Units**

Weight

1000 mg = 1 g
100 cg = 1 g
1000 g = 1 kg
1000 kg = 1 tonne

16 ounces = 1 pound
14 pounds = 1 stone
112 pounds = 1 hundredweight
8 stones = 1 hundredweight
2240 pounds = 1 ton
20 hundredweights = 1 ton

Capacity

1000 ml = 1 ℓ
100 cl = 1 ℓ
1000 ℓ = 1 kl

8 pints = 1 gallon

1 litre = 1000 cm^3
1 litre of water weighs 1 kg
1 cm^3 of water weighs 1 g

1 pint of water weighs $1\frac{1}{4}$ lb
1 gallon of water weighs 10 lb

The Metric System   British Units

Length

The Metric System	British Units
1000 mm = 1 m	12 inches = 1 foot
100 cm = 1 m	3 feet = 1 yard
1000 m = 1 km	1760 yards = 1 mile

The approximate comparisons with the metric system which are useful are:

1 inch . . . $2\frac{1}{2}$ cm	1 cm . . . 0.4 inches
1 foot . . . 30 cm	1 m . . . 40 inches = 4 ins longer than 1 yard
1 yard . . . 0.9 m	1 km . . . $\frac{5}{8}$ mile
1 mile . . . 1.6 km	8 km . . . 5 miles
5 miles . . . 8 km	

1 lb . . . 450 g (nearly $\frac{1}{2}$ kg)	1 kg . . . 2.2 lb (just over 2 lb)
1 ton . . . 1 tonne	1 tonne . . . 1 ton

1 pint . . . just over $\frac{1}{2}$ litre	1 litre . . . $1\frac{3}{4}$ pints
1 gallon . . . $4\frac{1}{2}$ litres	1 litre . . . 0.22 gallon

To change to the metric system

Length

1 inch = 2.54 cm
1 foot = 30.48 cm
1 yard = 91.44 cm = 0.9144 m
1 mile = 1.609 km

Weight

1 oz = 28.35 g
1 lb = 453.6 g
1 ton = 1016 kg = 1.016 tonne

Capacity

1 pint = 0.568 litre
1 gallon = 4.546 litre

To change from the metric system

Length

1 cm = 0.394 in
1 m = 39.37 in = 1.094 yd
1 km = 1094 yd = 0.621 mile

Weight

1 kg = 2.205 lb
1 tonne = 0.984 ton

Capacity

1 litre = 1.76 pints = 0.220 gallons

1 Thinking about numbers

Numbers in our lives

Numbers are very important in our lives. Here are some ways in which numbers are linked to us from birth:

Date of birth
Time of birth
Weight at birth (1) in kg, (2) in lb and oz

Later on, other numbers are added. Here are some of them:
Number of house address, postcode, phone number.
National Health number, national insurance number.
Car registration number, car key number, driving licence number.
Passport number.
Bank account number, credit card number, PIN number.
Dates of family birthdays and anniversaries.
What others can you think of ?

13 is thought by some to be an unlucky number.
Can you find out any reasons for this superstition ?

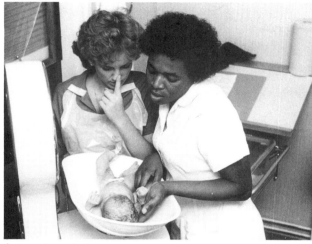

A new-born baby

House number 13

A sequence of numbers

As I was going to St Ives
I met a man with 7 wives;
Every wife had 7 sacks,
Every sack had 7 cats;
Every cat had 7 kits:
Kits, cats, sacks, and wives,
How many were there going to St Ives ?

Numbers in sports and hobbies

Show-jumping
Size of horse.
Age of rider.
Number of faults.
Time for the round.

Fishing
Date when fishing may begin.
Cost of permit.
Number of fish caught.
Weight of fish caught.

Stamp collecting
Values of stamps, foreign currency.
Date of issue.
Present price of the stamps.
Number in the collection.

Model making
Scale of model.
Cost of materials.

What numbers are used in **your** hobbies?

1 Numbers

Using index notation

$2^2 = 2 \times 2 = 4$

$2^3 = 2 \times 2 \times 2 = 8$

$3^2 = 3 \times 3 = 9$

$3^2 \times 5 = 3 \times 3 \times 5 = 9 \times 5 = 45$

$2^3 \times 3^2 \times 5 = 2 \times 2 \times 2 \times 3 \times 3 \times 5 = 8 \times 9 \times 5 = 360$

$2 \times 3 \times 5^2 \times 7 = 2 \times 3 \times 5 \times 5 \times 7 = 1050$

Prime numbers

A prime number has no factors (except itself and 1).
The first few prime numbers are 2, 3, 5, 7, 11, 13, 17, . . .

Other numbers can be expressed in **prime factors**.

$4 = 2 \times 2 = 2^2$

$6 = 2 \times 3$

$8 = 2 \times 2 \times 2 = 2^3$

$9 = 3 \times 3 = 3^2$

$10 = 2 \times 5$

$12 = 2 \times 2 \times 3 = 2^2 \times 3$

$14 = 2 \times 7$

$15 = 3 \times 5$

$16 = 2 \times 2 \times 2 \times 2 = 2^4$

$18 = 2 \times 3 \times 3 = 2 \times 3^2$

and so on.

To express a number in its prime factors

Check whether the prime numbers 2, 3, 5, . . . , in turn, are factors of the number.

If the number has a factor 2, divide by 2.
If the remaining number also has a factor 2, divide by 2 again, and repeat for as many times as possible.
Then divide by 3, as many times as possible.
Then divide by 5, as many times as possible.
Continue with the next prime numbers 7, 11, 13, . . . if necessary.
You stop dividing when you are sure that you are left with a prime number.

Examples

1 $180 = 2 \times 90$ Dividing 180 by 2
        $= 2 \times 2 \times 45$ Dividing 90 by 2
        $= 2 \times 2 \times 3 \times 15$ Dividing 45 by 3
        $= 2 \times 2 \times 3 \times 3 \times 5$ Dividing 15 by 3
        $= 2^2 \times 3^2 \times 5$

You may prefer to set the working down like this:

```
2)180
2) 90
3) 45
3) 15
    5        180 = 2² × 3² × 5
```

$$180 = 2^2 \times 3^2 \times 5$$

2 $8932 = 2 \times 4466$
        $= 2 \times 2 \times 2233$
        $= 2 \times 2 \times 7 \times 319$
        $= 2 \times 2 \times 7 \times 11 \times 29$
        $= 2^2 \times 7 \times 11 \times 29$

You can use a few short cuts if you already know some factors of a number, even if they are not prime factors.

3 $180 = 10 \times 18$
        $= 2 \times 5 \times 3 \times 6$
        $= 2 \times 5 \times 3 \times 2 \times 3$
        $= 2^2 \times 3^2 \times 5$

Note that the answer is the same as before. Whatever order you find the factors in, a number has its own prime factors and you will always find them.

4   405 = 5 × 81   You can recognise that 405 divides by 5
      = 5 × 9 × 9
      = 5 × 3 × 3 × 3 × 3
      = 3^4 × 5

5   616 = 4 × 154   You can recognise that 616 divides by 4,
                              since the last two figures (16) divide by 4

      = 2 × 2 × 2 × 77
      = 2 × 2 × 2 × 7 × 11
      = 2^3 × 7 × 11

6   1026 = 9 × 114   You can recognise that 1026 divides by 9,
                              since 1 + 0 + 2 + 6 = 9

       = 3 × 3 × 2 × 57
       = 3 × 3 × 2 × 3 × 19
       = 2 × 3^3 × 19

Finding all the factors of a number

You can use the prime factors of a number to find **all** the factors of a number.
e.g. 180 = 2^2 × 3^2 × 5
        = 2 × 2 × 3 × 3 × 5
180 will divide by 2, 3, 5, and 2 × 2 (4), 3 × 3 (9) and combinations of these, such
as 4 × 5 (20).
It will not divide by 7, 11, or any other prime numbers.
It will not divide by higher powers of 2, 3 or 5, such as 2^3 (8), 3^3 (27) or 5^2 (25).
You can find the factors in logical order.

Example

7   Find all the factors of 180.

      180 = 1 × 180
          = 2 × 90
          = 3 × 60
          = 4 × 45
          = 5 × 36
          = 6 × 30   180 does not divide by 7 or 8
          = 9 × 20
          = 10 × 18
          = 12 × 15   180 does not divide by 11, 13 or 14

      We have found all the factors, which are
      1, 2, 3, 4, 5, 6, 9, 10, 12, 15, 18, 20, 30, 36, 45, 60, 90, 180.

Exercise 1.1

1. Express these numbers using index notation.

   1 $2 \times 2 \times 2$
   2 5×5
   3 $3 \times 7 \times 7$
   4 $2 \times 2 \times 3 \times 3$
   5 $2 \times 3 \times 3 \times 3 \times 5 \times 7 \times 7$

2. Find the values of

   1 $2^2 \times 3^2$
   2 $3^3 \times 5$
   3 $2^2 \times 5^2$
   4 $2^2 \times 3 \times 7$
   5 2×5^3

3. Express these numbers in prime factors.

   1 18
   2 28
   3 38
   4 48
   5 88
   6 25
   7 45
   8 42
   9 77
   10 98

4. Express these numbers in prime factors.

   1 72
   2 162
   3 126
   4 385
   5 144
   6 160
   7 154
   8 225
   9 300
   10 171

5. Express these numbers in prime factors, and then find all the factors of the numbers.

   1 63
   2 120
   3 140
   4 84
   5 90

Indices

Multiplication

e.g. $3^2 \times 3^5 = 3 \times 3 \ \times \ 3 \times 3 \times 3 \times 3 \times 3$
$= 3^7$

Note that the indices were 2, 5 and the index in the answer is 7, because there are 7 threes to be multiplied together.

Similarly, $2^3 \times 2^6 = 2 \times 2 \times 2 \ \times \ 2 \times 2 \times 2 \times 2 \times 2 \times 2 = 2^9$

$5^2 \times 5^4 = 5 \times 5 \ \times \ 5 \times 5 \times 5 \times 5 = 5^6$

You will probably have already noticed the rule that you can find the answer by **adding** the indices.

For $7 \times 7^2 = 7 \ \times \ 7 \times 7 = 7^3$, this rule still works if you think of 7 as 7^1.

In general terms,

$$a^m \times a^n \ = \ a^{m+n}$$

where a is any number, and m and n are positive whole numbers.

(The rule is still true even if m and n are not positive whole numbers, but we are not considering other numbers at present.)

Squaring, cubing, etc.

e.g. $(7^3)^2 = 7^3 \times 7^3 = 7^6$

$(5^4)^3 = 5^4 \times 5^4 \times 5^4 = 5^{12}$

$(2^2)^5 = 2^2 \times 2^2 \times 2^2 \times 2^2 \times 2^2 = 2^{10}$

What happens to the indices ?

The general rule is

$$(a^m)^n \ = \ a^{m \times n} \quad (\text{or } a^{mn})$$

Dividing

e.g. $3^5 \div 3^2 = \dfrac{3^5}{3^2} = \dfrac{3 \times 3 \times 3 \times \cancel{3} \times \cancel{3}}{\cancel{3} \times \cancel{3}} = 3^3$

$2^7 \div 2^3 = \dfrac{2^7}{2^3} = \dfrac{2 \times 2 \times 2 \times 2 \times \cancel{2} \times \cancel{2} \times \cancel{2}}{\cancel{2} \times \cancel{2} \times \cancel{2}} = 2^4$

$5^4 \div 5 = \dfrac{5^4}{5} = \dfrac{5 \times 5 \times 5 \times \cancel{5}}{\cancel{5}} = 5^3$

What happens to the indices ? Think of 5 as 5^1.

The general rule is
$$a^m \div a^n = a^{m-n}$$
We need m greater than n (at present). a is not 0.

Here are these rules together:

$$a^m \times a^n = a^{m+n}$$
$$(a^m)^n = a^{mn}$$
$$a^m \div a^n = a^{m-n}$$

Other division using indices

e.g. $7^2 \div 7^5 = \dfrac{7^2}{7^5} = \dfrac{1}{7^3}$

$11^4 \div 11^6 = \dfrac{11^4}{11^6} = \dfrac{1}{11^2}$

$3^3 \div 3^4 = \dfrac{3^3}{3^4} = \dfrac{1}{3}$

$5^3 \div 5^3 = \dfrac{5^3}{5^3} = 1$

Note that you cannot simplify expressions such as $2^3 \times 3^4$.
e.g. $2 \times 5^3 \times 2^3 \times 5^2 = 2^4 \times 5^5$
This cannot be simplified further.

Square roots

Since $5^6 = 5^3 \times 5^3$, then (5^3) squared $= 5^6$ and the square root of 5^6 is 5^3.

Similarly, $7^4 = 7^2 \times 7^2$, and the square root of 7^4 is 7^2.

Can you find a general rule for finding square roots of numbers which are expressed in index form, if the indices are even numbers ?

One method for finding square roots of numbers which are exact squares (without using your calculator) is to write the numbers in prime factors.

Example

8 Find the square root of 2025.

First, write 2025 in its prime factors.
$$2025 = 3 \times 675$$
$$= 3 \times 3 \times 225$$
$$= 3 \times 3 \times 3 \times 75$$
$$= 3 \times 3 \times 3 \times 3 \times 25$$
$$= 3 \times 3 \times 3 \times 3 \times 5 \times 5$$
$$= 3^4 \times 5^2$$

$$\sqrt{2025} = 3^2 \times 5 \qquad \text{since the square root of } 3^4 \text{ is } 3^2 \text{ and the square root}$$
$$= 3 \times 3 \times 5 \qquad \text{of } 5^2 \text{ is } 5$$
$$= 45$$

(You can use a similar method to find the cube root of a number which is an exact cube number.

e.g. the cube root of 3^6 is 3^2, since $(3^2)^3 = 3^6$,

the cube root of 7^9 is 7^3, since $(7^3)^3 = 7^9$,

the cube root of $2^3 \times 5^6$ is 2×5^2.)

Exercise 1.2

1. Simplify, leaving in index form:

    1 $2^3 \times 2^3$ **6** $2 \times 2^3 \times 2^5$

    2 $3^2 \times 3^5$ **7** $(3^2)^4$

    3 $5^5 \div 5^2$ **8** $3^5 \div 3$

    4 $(5^3)^2$ **9** $2 \times 3^4 \times 2^2 \times 3$

    5 $7^2 \times 7^2 \times 7^2$ **10** $7^6 \div 7^3$

2. Simplify the following, and find the numerical value.

    1 $11^2 \div 11^3$ **6** $1^4 \times 1$

    2 $2^3 \div 2^5$ **7** $2 \times 5 \times 2^2 \times 5$

    3 $7^3 \div 7^3$ **8** $13^3 \div 13^2$

    4 3×3^3 **9** $(2^2)^3$

    5 $\dfrac{17^2}{17^2}$ **10** $\dfrac{3^2}{3^4}$

3. Find the square roots of these numbers, by expressing the numbers in prime factors.

1	196	**5**	1936	**8**	784
2	3025	**6**	1225	**9**	324
3	3969	**7**	9801	**10**	441
4	256				

4. Express 216 in prime factors and hence find its cube root.

Negative numbers

You will need to use negative numbers in algebraic questions so here is some revision of the methods.

Examples

$3 + 5 = 8$

$(-3) + 5 = 2$
Start at -3 on the number scale, go up 5 steps, getting to 2.

$3 - 5 = -2$
Start at 3 on the number scale, go down 5 steps, getting to -2.

$(-3) - 5 = -8$
Start at -3, go down 5 steps, getting to -8.

If there are two signs, replace them by one sign.

> Replace $++$ or $--$ by $+$
> Replace $+-$ or $-+$ by $-$

Examples

$(-4) + (+1) = (-4) + 1 = -3$
$(-4) - (-5) = (-4) + 5 = 1$
$(-4) + (-2) = (-4) - 2 = -6$
$(-4) - (+4) = (-4) - 4 = -8$

Multiplication and division

+	×	+	=	+	
−	×	−	=	+	
+	×	−	=	−	

+	÷	+	=	+	
−	÷	−	=	+	
+	÷	−	=	−	
−	÷	+	=	−	

Examples

$(+4) \times (+5) = 20$ $(+18) \div (+6) = 3$
$(-4) \times (-5) = 20$ $(-18) \div (-6) = 3$
$(+4) \times (-5) = -20$ $(+18) \div (-6) = -3$
$(-18) \div (+6) = -3$

Exercise 1.3

Work out the answers to these questions.

1.
1 $5 - 3$
2 $(-1) + 1$
3 $3 - 5$
4 $0 - 3$
5 $(-3) - 2$
6 $(+2) - 6$
7 $(-7) + 10$

8 $(-2) + 0$
9 $2 - 4$
10 $(-6) - 3$
11 $(-4) + 6$
12 $4 - 7$
13 $(-3) + 3$
14 $(-6) + 3 + 4$

15 $(-5) + 7$
16 $8 - 5 - 3$
17 $3 - 8$
18 $(-1) - 2 - 3$
19 $7 - 3$
20 $(-5) + 4 - 2$

2.
1 $3 + (+4)$
2 $(-3) - (-5)$
3 $4 + (-5)$
4 $0 + (-3)$
5 $(-6) - (+2)$
6 $3 + (-5)$
7 $8 - (-3)$

8 $(+2) - (-4)$
9 $7 - (+4)$
10 $(-4) - 0$
11 $5 - (-2)$
12 $(-3) + (-4)$
13 $(-3) - (-3)$
14 $(-2) - (+8)$

15 $(-2) + (-5)$
16 $(-3) - (-2)$
17 $(-3) + (+4)$
18 $0 - (-5)$
19 $(-2) - (+3)$
20 $(-3) - (-4)$

3.
1 $(+2) \times (-3)$
2 $(+12) \div (-2)$
3 $(-2) \times (-3)$
4 $(+2) \times (+5)$
5 $(-6) \times (-5)$
6 $(-6) \div (-2)$
7 $0 \times (-4)$

8 $9 \times (-3)$
9 $(-4) \div (-4)$
10 $2 \times (-7)$
11 $(-18) \div 9$
12 $(+8) \times 0$
13 $(-24) \div (-3)$
14 $(-8) \div (-4)$

15 $0 \div (-1)$
16 $1 \times (-1) \times (-1)$
17 $(-14) \div (+2)$
18 $(-3) \times (-1) \times (+2)$
19 $(-6) \div (-1)$
20 $(-5)^2$

Exercise 1.4   Applications and Activities

1.   **The pattern 1 2 3 4 5 6 7 8 9 0 1 2 3 . . .**

2, 3 and 4 all divide into 12.
5 divides into 12345.
How many figures of this pattern must be taken for the number to divide by
6, 8, 9, 10 ?
If the pattern goes on long enough, can you get a number that divides by 7,
or by 11 ?

2.   **A number pattern**
Copy and complete the pattern up to the row beginning 33333333.

$$3^2 = 9$$
$$33^2 = 1089$$
$$333^2 = \ldots$$
$$\ldots$$

Write a similar number pattern for 9^2, 99^2, . . .
Compare the two patterns and comment about them.

3.   **Common factors**
Which number, other than 1, divides into both 35 and 56 ?
This number is called a common factor of 35 and 56.
There is only one possible answer so it is the **highest common factor**, (HCF).

Which number divides into both 56 and 80 ?
If you gave the answer as 2 or 4, there is a larger number. What is it ?
This is the highest common factor.

If numbers have no other common factor then the HCF is 1, because all numbers
have a factor 1.
e.g. 21 and 25 have factors but no number divides into both 21 and 25, except 1.
So the HCF of 21 and 25 is 1.

If it is not easy to find the HCF you can use prime factors to help you.

Examples

1   Find the HCF of 84 and 98.

In prime factors, $84 = 2^2 \times 3 \times 7$
$98 = 2 \times 7^2$
(You can work these out for yourself.)
So both numbers have a factor 2 and a factor 7.
The highest common factor is $2 \times 7 = 14$.

2   Find the HCF of 60, 180 and 200.

$60 = 2^2 \times 3 \times 5$
$180 = 2^2 \times 3^2 \times 5$
$200 = 2^3 \times 5^2$

All numbers have factors 2^2 and 5. (2^3 means $2 \times 2 \times 2$ so 2^2 is a factor.)
The HCF is $2^2 \times 5 = 20$

Find the highest common factor of these numbers. You may find the answers by trial but it is good practice to check them by using their factors.

1	12, 16	**5**	77, 121	**8**	15, 30, 75
2	24, 56	**6**	18, 45, 99	**9**	48, 60
3	18, 35	**7**	12, 30, 66	**10**	6, 10, 15
4	5, 35, 45				

One use of factors is for cancelling when doing division questions or using fractions.

e.g. $36 \div 96 = \dfrac{\overset{3}{\cancel{36}}}{\underset{8}{\cancel{96}}} = \frac{3}{8}$ (Dividing numerator and denominator by 12)

You have divided by the HCF of 36 and 96, but you would get the same answer if you had divided by 3 and then 4, or by 12 in some other stages.

Simplify these division questions, writing the answers as fractions in their simplest form.

11	66 ÷ 84	**14**	48 ÷ 80
12	24 ÷ 72	**15**	36 ÷ 81
13	42 ÷ 56		

4. **Lowest common multiple**

The smallest number which is a multiple of two or more numbers is called the lowest common multiple (LCM).

Examples

1 Find the LCM of 5, 6 and 10.

The smallest number into which all these 3 numbers will divide is 30, so the LCM of 5, 6 and 10 is 30.

One way to find the LCM is to make lists of the multiples of these numbers and find the smallest number which belongs to all three.
5, 10, 15, 20, 25, 30, 35, 40, . . .
6, 12, 18, 24, 30, 36, 42, . . .
10, 20, 30, 40, . . .

If it is not easy to find the LCM you can use prime factors to help you.

2 Find the LCM of 24 and 90.

$24 = 2^3 \times 3$
$90 = 2 \times 3^2 \times 5$

Any multiple of 24 must contain 2^3 and 3.
Any multiple of 90 must contain 2, 3^2 and 5.
So the lowest common multiple must include 2^3, 3^2 and 5.
The LCM $= 2^3 \times 3^2 \times 5 = 8 \times 9 \times 5 = 360$.

Find the lowest common multiples of these numbers. You may find the answers by trial but it is good practice to check them by using their factors.

1	9, 12	5	8, 9, 36	8	44, 66
2	6, 22	6	10, 75	9	16, 32, 40
3	15, 24	7	12, 14	10	10, 30, 50
4	3, 7, 21				

5.   **Endings at darts**

There are several games played with darts
but we are considering the tournament
game, which you have probably seen on
television.

Players throw 3 darts at each turn.
They start with a total of 501 and subtract
their score each time until they end up
with 0.
They must end by hitting the bull, which
counts as 50, or a double.

Here are some examples of throws to end the game.
One throw.   14, with double 7.
Two throws.   41, with 25 (outer bull), then double 8;
              or 21 (treble 7), then double 10;
              or 3 then double 19.
Three throws. 114 with 60 (treble 20), then 14, then double 20.

A good darts player will know all these
endings. Where there are alternatives
he/she will know which one is better to
try.
Make a list of final scores which can be
scored with one throw, then others which
can be scored with 2 throws, and then
others which can be scored with 3 throws.
What is the highest possible score that it is
possible to end on, with 3 darts ?
What is the lowest score that it is not
possible to end on, with 3 darts ?
(Not 1, as if you reach a score with only
1 left, the score for that round is not counted.)
It is possible to score down from 501 to 0
using only 9 darts. Find a way of scoring
this.

John Lowe, the first player to score a
televised 9-dart finish.

6. **Painting by numbers**

Make a grid on squared paper with 19 columns and 18 rows.

There is no need to copy down these numbers, which belong to the left-hand 10 columns of the grid.

Colour each square on your copy as follows:

1   If the number in the square divides by 3, colour the square red.

2   If the number in the square is a square number, colour the square black.

3   Leave uncoloured all the other squares on the left side.

4   Complete the picture by colouring the right side of the grid to match symmetrically, i.e. column 11 is like column 9, column 12 is like column 8, and so on.

Invent a similar picture yourself, and ask your friends to colour it.

20	92	86	101	11	118	26	100	46	34
109	2	32	14	68	700	61	112	625	28
58	70	13	190	116	94	106	76	400	1
95	19	26	35	98	19	160	64	121	256
2	196	800	89	5	53	41	49	400	16
77	52	64	113	59	85	42	66	15	196
170	40	125	4	79	600	30	270	78	49
44	5	17	50	63	240	789	57	4	169
29	119	88	7	45	3	360	84	361	16
107	67	4	169	108	99	300	27	256	121
13	25	71	140	456	75	111	150	96	289
256	10	62	7	21	321	105	6	54	400
200	23	80	500	330	60	49	361	39	16
38	74	11	100	120	450	169	100	18	25
14	110	196	104	93	180	51	210	87	1
56	1	82	47	65	12	123	90	48	121
64	8	37	17	91	8	102	33	72	625
83	22	130	43	55	73	31	69	24	10

7. **Powers of 2**

There are several interesting traditional problems which are based on the sequence 2, 4, 8, 16, . . . or 1, 2, 4, 8, 16, . . .

The powers of 2 are 2^1 2^2 2^3 2^4 . . .
                       2   4   8   16

Later on you will learn a meaning for 2^0. 2^0 equals 1, so this fits in with the pattern.

2^0 2^1 2^2 2^3 2^4 . . .
1   2   4   8   16

The following problems are based on powers of 2. You may like to think about some of them before we give further details, so we suggest that you investigate the problems and we will return to the sequence further on in the book.

Folding a piece of paper

Can you fold a piece of paper in half, and in half again, and again, . . . 9 times altogether ?
If you fold it in half like that 50 times, how thick would the folded piece be ?

The blacksmith and the highwayman

The highwayman was trying to escape from justice, and he woke up the blacksmith late at night because his horse needed shoeing.
The blacksmith was not pleased at being disturbed so late, and he knew that the highwayman would have plenty of money, so he said it would cost £10 for each nail. The horseshoes had 8 nails each, so that came to £320.
The highwayman did not want to pay that amount so he tried to get it reduced.
Then the blacksmith said he would charge a farthing for the first nail, a halfpenny for the next, a penny for the next, twopence for the next, and so on, for the 32 nails.
This the highwayman agreed to pay, and the horse was shod.
Should the highwayman have been content to pay what was asked at first ?
(A farthing is $\frac{1}{4}$ of a penny. There used to be 960 farthings or 240 pence in £1.)

The chessboard problem

The legend says that the king was so
pleased with the person who invented the
game of chess that he asked him what he
would like for a reward.
The inventor asked for some wheat.
He wanted 1 grain of wheat for the 1st square,

2 grains for the 2nd square,
4 grains for the 3rd square,
8 grains for the 4th square,

and so on, for all 64 squares of the chessboard.

Did he get his reward ?

The tower of Hanoi puzzle

In this puzzle, there are 8 discs of different sizes on 1 peg, with two empty pegs.

The game is to transfer all the discs to one of the empty pegs.
Only one disc can be moved at a time. A disc can only be placed on an empty
peg or onto a larger disc, never onto a smaller one.
Make your own version of this game using circles of cardboard, and see how
many moves are needed. You may prefer to discover the pattern of moves by
starting with less than 8 discs. Notice the moves of the smallest disc.
The legend has it that in an Eastern temple there is such a tower with 64 discs on
it, with the priests working continuously at the task of transferring all the discs.
How long would it take to transfer all those discs, assuming that they make one
move every second ?

PUZZLE

1. There are numbered chairs placed evenly around a large, circular table, for a conference.
    Mrs Nelson is sitting on chair no. 5 and directly opposite her is Mrs Wilson on chair
    no. 14. How many people are taking part, if all chairs are occupied ?

2 Thinking about loci

The locus of a point

When we talk about the locus of a point, we mean the path the point will take, or lie on, if it is following fixed instructions.

Locus

The word 'locus' comes from Latin and means 'place'.
What other words can you think of, starting with LOC, which are connected with this Latin word ?

As the child slides down, sitting upright, the top of his head moves parallel to the slide.

As the roundabout turns, everyone moves in a circle whose centre is the centre of the roundabout.

As the windmill turns round according to the wind, the small wheel moves in a circular path.

n many computer games, the ball or missile is programmed to follow certain paths.

RADAR

RADAR stands for radio detection and ranging. Radio waves are sent out from a transmitter and these are reflected by other objects. These objects are then located by calculating their distances and directions, and their positions can be shown on a radar screen.

The ship in the photograph has been using radar on a foggy morning, to keep track of the positions of two other ships. As the fog finally lifts, the two ships are now visible.

2 Loci

The locus of a point is the path traced by the point as it moves so as to satisfy certain conditions.

The plural of locus is loci.

Examples

Describe the locus in each case. The diagram is there to help you, with the dotted line showing the locus.

1 The tip of the minute hand of a clock.

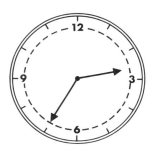

2 The saddle of a bicycle as you cycle along a straight road.

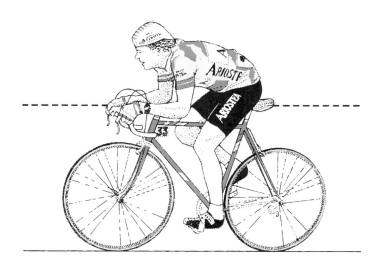

3 The edge of a flower-bed round a
rectangular lawn, where every part of the
flower-bed is not more than 1 m from the
lawn.
(Notice that there are 4 straight lines and
4 quarter-circles at the corners.)

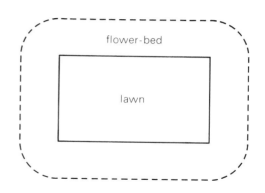

4 The path of a boy running across a
playground, keeping as far from one tree **A**
as from another tree **B**.
(This path can be said to be equidistant
from **A** and **B**.)

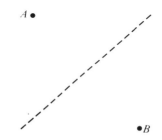

5 The path of a girl running across a field
keeping as far from the hedge as from the
fence.
(This path can be said to be equidistant
from the hedge and the fence.)

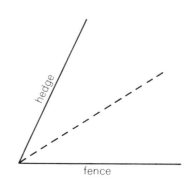

The distance measured from any point on
the locus to the hedge (or fence) would be
the shortest distance, and that is the length
of the perpendicular line from the point to
the hedge (or fence).

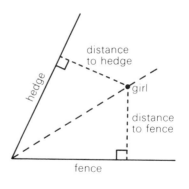

Exercise 2.1

Draw sketches showing these loci and where possible describe each locus.

1. The path of a child inside a room who runs round keeping an arm's length from any of the walls of the room.

2. The boundary of the area a horse can graze if it is tethered to a stake by a rope 4 m long.

3. The path of a boat which is passing between two rocks 50 m apart by keeping equidistant from the rocks.

4. The path of the tip of the pendulum on a clock.

5. A goat is tethered to a rail 10 m long by a chain 2 m long which can slide along the rail. Show the locus of the boundary of the part of the field it can reach. It can get to both sides of the rail.

6. A field is bounded by two straight streams, which join together in a corner of the field at an angle of 40°. A farmer wants to put a drainage ditch in the field, equidistant from the two streams. Show the path of the ditch.

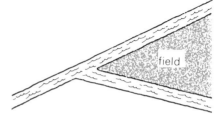

7. The locus of the knob of a door handle as the door is opened and closed.

8. Two roads cross each other at an angle of 70°. Soldiers on an exercise are told to move keeping equidistant from the roads. Show their possible paths.

9. There are two observation posts, 100 m apart. Soldiers on an exercise are told to move keeping equidistant from these posts. Show their path.

10. The path of a pedestrian who walks along the pavement, crosses the road at a pelican crossing, and then continues walking on the other pavement.

Here are some special results:

Loci

1. The locus of a point at a fixed distance *r* units from a given point *A* is a circle, centre *A*, radius *r*.

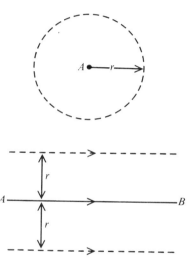

2. The locus of a point at a fixed distance *r* units from a given line *AB* is a pair of lines, each parallel to *AB*, and distance *r* from *AB*.

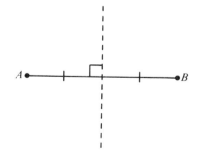

3. The locus of a point equidistant from two given points *A* and *B* is the perpendicular bisector of *AB*.

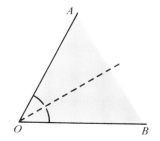

4. The locus of a point, within the shaded region, equidistant from two given lines *OA* and *OB*, is the line which bisects ∠*AOB*.

5. If two given lines are **AOC**, **BOD**, then the
    locus of a point equidistant from the two
    lines is the **pair** of lines which bisect the
    angles at **O**.
    (These lines are perpendicular to each
    other.)

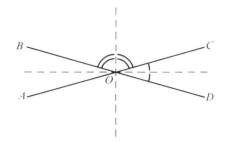

Constructions

To draw accurately a line a fixed distance from a given line

e.g. to draw a line 5 cm from **AB**.

Draw lines at right angles to **AB** at **A** and **B**
(or at any two points on **AB**).

Measure off 5 cm along these lines so that
AD = 5 cm and **BC** = 5 cm.

Join **CD**.
Then every point on **CD** is 5 cm from the
nearest point on **AB**.

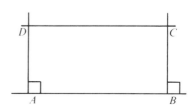

Here is a reminder of two constructions using ruler and compasses. (You can also do these constructions without compasses by using a ruler and a protractor.)

To find the perpendicular bisector of a line AB

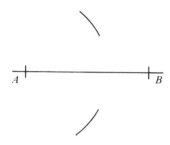

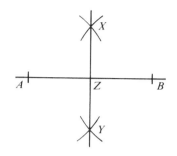

With centre A and a radius more than half of AB, draw two arcs.

With centre B and the same radius, draw two arcs to cut the first two arcs at X and Y.

Join XY, cutting AB at Z.

Then Z is the mid-point of AB, and XZY is the perpendicular bisector of AB.

To bisect an angle ACB

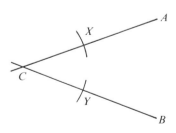

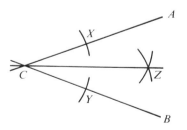

With centre C, draw arcs to cut CA and CB at X and Y.

With centres X and Y in turn, and a suitable radius, draw arcs to cut at Z.

Join CZ, which is the bisector of angle ACB.

Example

6   Draw a triangle ABC with AB = 9 cm, AC = 7 cm and $\angle BAC$ = 66°.
Find
1   the locus of points inside the triangle which are 4.5 cm from C,
2   the locus of points inside the triangle which are equidistant from AB and AC.
Mark the point P inside the triangle which is 4.5 cm from C and is as far from AB
as it is from AC.
How far is P from B ?

First, draw the triangle accurately.

For **1**, the locus of the points 4.5 cm from a point C is a circle, centre C, radius
4.5 cm.
In this question you only need the part of the circle which is inside the triangle.
Draw this locus and label it **1**.

For **2**, the locus of points inside the triangle which are equidistant from AB and AC
is the bisector of $\angle A$.
You can construct the bisector using your protractor. Since $\angle A$ = 66°, the bisector
makes angles of 33° with AB and AC. Alternatively, you can use the method for
bisecting an angle using ruler and compasses.
Draw this locus and label it **2**.

P is the point where the loci intersect.
Measure the distance PB.
(It should be 6.4 cm.)

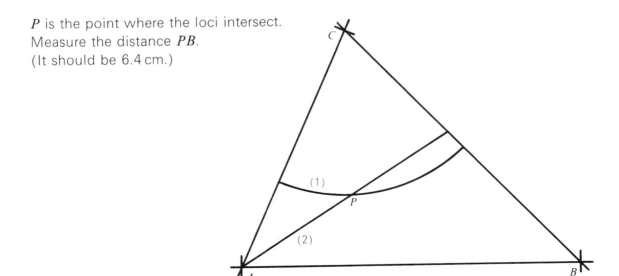

Exercise 2.2

(Squared paper is useful for questions 1 to 6.)

1. Draw a rectangle *ABCD* with *AB* = 7 cm and *BC* = 10 cm.
    Draw the locus of points inside the rectangle which are
    1 3 cm from *BC*,
    2 equidistant from *B* and *D*.

    Label each locus.
    Find a point *P* which is 3 cm from *BC* and is equidistant from *B* and *D*.
    Measure *PB* and check by measuring *PD*.

2. Draw a square *ABCD* with side 8 cm.
    Find the locus of points inside the square which are
    1 equidistant from *A* and *B*,
    2 6 cm from *D*.

    Find a point *P* which is 6 cm from *D* and is equidistant from *A* and *B*.
    Measure *PA* and check by measuring *PB*.

3. Draw a rectangle *ABCD* with *AB* = 5 cm and *BC* = 12 cm.
    Draw the locus of points inside the rectangle which are
    1 equidistant from *AB* and *BC*,
    2 2 cm from *AD*.

    Find a point *P* which is equidistant from *AB* and *BC* and 2 cm from *AD*.
    Measure *PD*.

4. Draw a triangle *ABC* with *BC* = 7.8 cm, ∠*B* = 58°, ∠*C* = 42°.
    Draw the locus of points inside the triangle which are
    1 2 cm from *BC*,
    2 6 cm from *C*.

    Find a point *P* which is 2 cm from *BC* and 6 cm from *C*.
    Measure *PA*.

5. Draw a triangle *ABC* with *BC* = 9.5 cm, *AB* = 7.5 cm, ∠*B* = 32°.
    Draw the locus of points inside the triangle which are
    1 1 cm from *BC*,
    2 equidistant from *A* and *C*.

    Find a point *P* which is 1 cm from *BC* and equidistant from *A* and *C*.
    Measure *PA* and check by measuring *PC*.

6. Draw a triangle ABC with AB = 7 cm, BC = 8 cm and $\angle B$ = 90°.
    Draw the locus of points inside the triangle which are
    1   2 cm from AB,
    2   4 cm from BC.

    Find a point P inside the triangle which is 2 cm from AB and 4 cm from BC.
    Measure PA, PB and PC.

7. Draw a triangle ABC with BC = 8.5 cm, $\angle B$ = 72°, $\angle C$ = 36°.
    Draw the locus of points inside the triangle which are
    1   4 cm from B,
    2   7 cm from C.

    Shade the region of points inside the triangle which are greater than 4 cm from
    B **and** greater than 7 cm from C.

8. Draw a triangle ABC with BC = 11 cm, AB = 7 cm and AC = 9 cm. (Begin by
    drawing BC. Use compasses to find A.)
    Draw the locus of points inside the triangle which are
    1   equidistant from AB and BC,
    2   equidistant from A and B.

    Find a point P inside the triangle which is equidistant from AB and BC, and
    equidistant from A and B.
    Shade the region of points inside the triangle which are nearer to AB than to BC
    and nearer to B than to A.

9. **The circumcircle of a triangle**

    Draw a triangle ABC with BC = 10 cm, AB = 8 cm and AC = 7.5 cm.
    Draw the locus of points which are
    1   equidistant from B and C,
    2   equidistant from A and B.

    Find a point O which is equidistant from A and B and C.
    Measure the distance OA.
    With centre O and radius OA, draw a circle. (It will also pass through B and C.)
    This circle is called the circumcircle or circumscribed circle of the triangle ABC,
    and O is called the circumcentre of the triangle.
    You can construct circumcircles of triangles of different shapes.
    Repeat the question beginning with an obtuse-angled triangle. You will find that
    O lies outside the triangle ABC.

10. **The inscribed circle of a triangle**

Draw a triangle ABC with $BC = 10$ cm, $AB = 5.5$ cm and $AC = 9$ cm.
Draw the locus of points inside the triangle which are

1 equidistant from AB and BC,
2 equidistant from BC and AC.

Find a point I which is equidistant from AB and BC and AC.
Find how far I is from these sides by drawing a line from I perpendicular to BC,
meeting BC at X. Measure the distance IX.
With centre I and radius IX, draw a circle. (It will touch BC at X and it will also
touch AB and AC.)
This circle is called the inscribed circle or in-circle of triangle ABC, and I is
called the incentre of the triangle.
You can construct the inscribed circles of triangles of different shapes.
Repeat the question using a triangle with different measurements.

Exercise 2.3   Applications and Activities

1. **1**   Make a scale drawing of a circular pond with radius 9 m.
   2   A model boat on the pond is held by a string so that as the owner walks
   round the outside of the pond the boat is always 1 m from the edge of
   the pond. Show the boat's locus on your drawing, and describe it.
   3   There is a path 1 m wide round the pond. Show the locus of the outer
   edge of the path on your drawing and describe it.

2. **1**   Make a scale drawing of this rectangular boating pool.
   Emily sails her boat on the pool.
   Show on your diagram the paths of the
   boat if Emily sends it so that:
   2   it stays equidistant from A and C,
   3   it is equidistant from BC and CD,
   4   it is 5 m from AB,
   5   it is attached to a rod 4 m long and
   the rod is held at A.

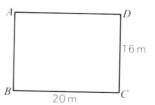

3. Draw a circle, radius 6 cm, and mark off
    radii every 30° to represent the positions
    every 5 minutes of the minute hand of a
    clock, 6 cm long.
    Imagine an insect which starts at the top
    of the clock when the hand is pointing to
    12, and travels along the hand towards
    the clock centre, moving at a steady
    speed, so that each 5 minutes it moves
    along $\frac{1}{2}$ cm.

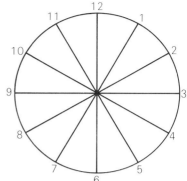

    Mark the positions the insect has reached after
    5 minutes, 10 minutes, 15 minutes, . . . 60 minutes.
    Join these points with a curve, drawn freehand, to represent the locus of the
    insect.

    You can do similar questions with the insect travelling at different speeds.

4.

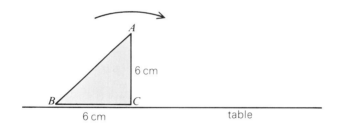

    Place your set-square with one edge, *BC*, on the table.
    Rotate it clockwise about the point *C* until *A* lies on the table. Then rotate it
    clockwise about point *A* until *B* lies on the table.
    Notice what happens to point *A*, and then repeat this and notice what happens
    to point *B*. Finally find out what happens to point *C*.
    Copy this drawing of an isosceles right-angled triangle *ABC* and as it is rotated
    similarly about *C* and then *A*, show the loci of *A*, *B* and *C* on your drawing.
    Label each locus clearly.

5. Mark a point *P* on the edge of a circle.
    Roll the circle along a straight line, without slipping.
    Sketch the locus of the point *P* as the circle rolls along the line.
    (You can use a coin, and roll it along a ruler. It may be easier to use a point on
    the circular edge of a cylindrical tin, and roll the tin along a shelf. You can use
    the valve on a bicycle wheel and wheel the bicycle along the ground, next to a
    wall.)
    The locus is a curve which is called a **cycloid**.

6. Billy rolls a tin, with radius 8 cm, down
    some steps, keeping it touching the steps
    all the time.
    Draw a scale drawing of the steps, and
    show the locus of the centre of the tin as
    it rolls.

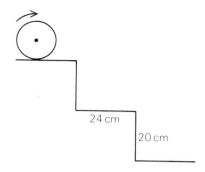

24 cm

20 cm

7. A ladder is propped up against a wall.
    The ground and the wall are both slippy,
    so the ladder slips down.
    What is the locus of the point *M*, the
    mid-point of the ladder, as the ladder
    slips ?

    Draw a rough sketch and show what you
    think the locus of *M* will look like.

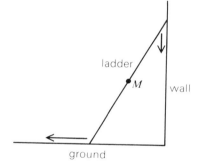

ladder

M

wall

ground

    To find the locus accurately, let the
    ladder be represented by a line 10 cm
    long.
    Then *M* is 5 cm from each end.
    Mark points *A*, *B*, *C*, . . . 1 cm apart along
    the ground, starting from *A*.
    The first position of the ladder is *AA'*.
    Mark its mid-point, with a dot.
    Then to find the position when the foot
    of the ladder is at *B*, use compasses,
    radius 10 cm, centre *B*, to find *B'* on the
    wall.

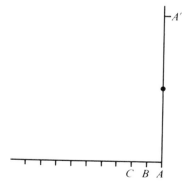

A'

C B A

    Join *BB'* and mark its midpoint.
    Then, for the foot of the ladder at *C*, find *C'*, join *CC'* and mark its mid-point.
    Continue in this way until the ladder lies on the ground.
    Join the mid-points with a smooth curve, to show the locus.

    Was your estimated guess correct ?

8.   There are local radio stations at 3 places
     A, B, C.
     Broadcasts from *A* can be heard within a
     distance of 50 km, those from *B* within a
     distance of 65 km and those from *C*
     within a distance of 45 km.

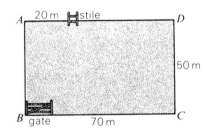

     Draw an accurate scale drawing and mark
     the loci of the boundaries of the three
     broadcast receiving areas.
     Shade in the region where all three
     stations can be heard.

9.   The diagram shows a rectangular field.
     Treasure is hidden in the field,
     1   30 m from the stile,
     2   equidistant from the hedges *CB* and
          CD.

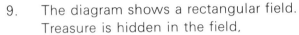

     Draw a scale drawing of the field and
     draw loci for conditions **1** and **2**.
     Mark with *T* the position of the treasure.
     How far is the treasure from the gate at
     B ?

10. On Treasure Island the treasure was
     buried,
     1   equidistant from the two hilly peaks,
     2   50 m from the spring.

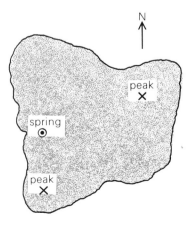

     Draw a diagram showing the peaks and
     the spring. The peaks are 100 m apart and
     one is due north-east of the other, and
     the spring is 40 m due north of one peak.
     Draw loci for conditions **1** and **2** and
     show that there are two possible
     positions of the treasure. Mark these
     positions *P* and *Q*.
     Treasure hunters dig unsuccessfully at
     one of these places. How far will they
     have to walk to get to the other place ?

PUZZLES

2. Find the missing figures in this
    multiplication question.

```
              .  .  7
      ×       2  .  .
           .  2  .  3
           .  8  .  0
     .  1  7  .  0  0
     .  2  8  .  .  3
```

3. **The portrait**
    A person, looking at a portrait, said: 'Sisters and brothers have I none, but that man's
    father was my father's son'.
    What relation was the speaker to the man in the portrait ?

4. What is the value of 9 × 8 × 7 × 6 × 5 × 4 × 3 × 2 × 1 × 0 ?

5. Mr Sharma earned £200 per week. He then got a rise of 10%. Soon afterwards, the firm
    he worked for was in financial difficulties, and all workers were told that their wages
    would have to be reduced by 10%. What would Mr Sharma earn then ?

6. How many rectangles are
    there in this diagram ?

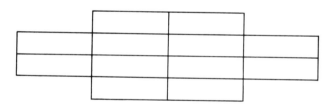

7. How many plants can be planted round the edge of a circle of circumference 12 m, at
    intervals of 25 cm ?
    How many can be planted in a line 12 m long ?

8. Copy the diagram and starting in the top
    left-hand square, draw a continuous line,
    passing through each square once only,
    and going horizontally or vertically, not
    diagonally; so that the sum of the
    numbers in each group of 4 squares
    is 20.

2	2	4	9	8	8
4	5	7	2	2	9
14	9	7	1	1	6
2	2	2	3	10	3
5	8	2	9	5	7
5	5	2	4	2	4

3 Thinking about algebra

Algebra

Algebra is a very useful branch of Mathematics. Instead of using actual numbers we can let letters represent numbers in expressions, formulae and equations.

The Algebra factory

Here is an idea from one, older, student, who decided that Algebra was so mysterious that there must be an Algebra factory somewhere, with workers producing it!
Perhaps you have your own ideas on how an Algebra factory might look.

Algebra today

Algebra has important uses in today's world, although it is more often used by the experts, such as scientists, engineers, designers, researchers, industrialists, economists, statisticians, rather than by others who benefit from the work they do.

3 Algebra

Here are some examples to remind you of the rules of algebra.

Addition and subtraction

$a + a = 2a$
$5b + 3b = 8b$
$4c + 2$ cannot be simplified
$4d + 2e$ cannot be simplified
$4f + f^2$ cannot be simplified
$g^2 + g^2 = 2g^2$
$3h^2 + h^2 = 4h^2$
$j + 4k + 5j - 3k = 6j + k$
$4m - n - 3m - 2n = m - 3n$
$p^2 - p + 2p^2 + 5p = 3p^2 + 4p$

Do not confuse addition with multiplication.

Multiplication

$a \times a = a^2$
$5b \times 3b = 15b^2$
$c \times c \times c = c^3$
$4d \times 2 = 8d$
$5e \times 6f = 30ef$ (or $30fe$)

Division

$$12a \div 3a = \frac{\overset{4}{\cancel{12a}}}{\cancel{3a}} = 4 \qquad\qquad 9c \div 3 = \frac{\overset{3}{\cancel{9}}c}{\cancel{3}} = 3c$$

$$7b \div 7b = \frac{\cancel{7b}}{\cancel{7b}} = 1 \qquad\qquad 4d \div 5e = \frac{4d}{5e}$$

Making expressions

Examples

1   If a man buys a picture for £a and sells it
    making a profit of £b, how much does he
    sell it for ?

    If he bought it for £50 and sold it making a
    profit of £20, the selling price is £70, that is,
    £(50 + 20). So in the question above, he
    sells it for £$(a + b)$.

2   A pump can fill a water tank in h hours. If p similar pumps were working together,
    how long would it take to fill the tank ?

    If a pump could fill the tank in 12 hours, then if there were 4 pumps working, they
    would each fill $\frac{1}{4}$ of the amount, and the time taken would be 3 hours, that is,
    (12 ÷ 4) hours or $\frac{12}{4}$ hours.

    In the question above, the time taken is $\dfrac{h}{p}$ hours.

Simplifying expressions involving brackets

Examples

$$4(a + 3) = 4a + 12$$
$$b(3c - 2) = 3bc - 2b$$
$$3d(d - 1) = 3d^2 - 3d$$
$$3(e + 4) + 2(3e - 5) = 3e + 12 + 6e - 10 = 9e + 2$$
$$7(f + 2g) - 4(3f - g) = 7f + 14g - 12f + 4g = 18g - 5f$$
$$12 - (h + 4) = 12 - h - 4 = 8 - h$$

Remember that if there is a minus sign immediately in front of a bracket, then when
the bracket is removed all the signs from inside the bracket are changed, + to − and
− to +.

Simple equations

Example

Solve the equation $5(x - 3) = 2(10 - x)$

Remove the brackets
$$5x - 15 = 20 - 2x$$
Add $2x$ to both sides
$$7x - 15 = 20$$
Add 15 to both sides
$$7x = 35$$
Divide both sides by 7
$$x = 5$$

To check the answer, substitute $x = 5$ into both sides of the equation separately.
LHS $= 5(x - 3) = 5 \times (5 - 3) = 5 \times 2 = 10$
RHS $= 2(10 - x) = 2 \times (10 - 5) = 2 \times 5 = 10$
Both sides are equal, both 10, so the equation checks and the solution $x = 5$ is correct.

Exercise 3.1

Simplify these expressions.

1. **1** $3a + 6a$ **6** $8f - 8f$
    2 $b + b$ **7** $4g - 7g + 4g$
    3 $9c - 4c$ **8** $8hj - 3hj$
    4 $2d + 5d - d$ **9** $10k + k$
    5 $8e - 7e$ **10** $5mn - mn$

2. **1** $a^2 + a^2$ **6** $h - \frac{3}{4}h + \frac{1}{4}h$
    2 $b + b + c$ **7** $5j^2 - 4j^2$
    3 $3d^2 + 2d^2$ **8** $3k^2 + 2k + k^2 - k$
    4 $4 + 3e - 6e$ **9** $2m + 5n - 3m + 2n$
    5 $f + 3g - g - 3f$ **10** $7p - q + 5p - 4q$

3. **1** $2a \times 3b$ **6** $15h \div 5$
    2 $4c \times 2c$ **7** $7j \div j$
    3 $2d \times 2d \times 2d$ **8** $3k \div 9$
    4 $8e \times 5$ **9** $8mn \div 4m$
    5 $7f \times 2g$ **10** $18p \div 12q$

4. Find expressions for the following.

   1 I cycle for $5a$ km and then I walk another $2a$ km. How far have I travelled altogether ?

   2 A rod is b metres long. The two ends, each for a length of c metres, are painted white. What length is unpainted ?

   3 Write down 3 consecutive numbers, of which d is the middle one.

   4 Mary buys 10 sweaters at £e each and sells them at £f each. How much profit does she make ?

   5 A 5-litre can of oil costs £g. What is the cost of 1 litre of oil, in £'s ? What is this cost, in pence ?

5. Remove the brackets, and simplify when possible.

1	$2(a + 5b)$	**6**	$2(h + j) + 3(h - j)$
2	$3(4c - d)$	**7**	$6k - 2(k + m)$
3	$4(e + 3) + 3(e - 3)$	**8**	$(n - 1) - (3 - n)$
4	$3(2f - 1) + 5(4f - 3)$	**9**	$8(p + 5q) - 3(p - 7q)$
5	$5(g - 1) - 3(2g + 1)$	**10**	$(1 - 2r) - (2 - 7r)$

6. Solve these equations.

1	$2x + 7 = 13$	**6**	$6 = 15 - 2x$
2	$4 = 4x - 14$	**7**	$4(2x - 5) + 7x = 0$
3	$3 + 5x = 11 + x$	**8**	$5(x - 3) = 3(x - 5)$
4	$7 + 2x = 13 - 3x$	**9**	$2 - 9x = 5(7 - 4x)$
5	$3x + 1 = 17 - x$	**10**	$4(3x - 7) - x = 5(x + 4)$

Multiplying powers

$a^3 \times a^5 = a \times a \times a \times a \times a \times a \times a \times a = a^8$

This rule can be expressed generally as

$a^m \times a^n = a^{m+n}$, where m and n are positive whole numbers.

$(a^5)^3 = a^5 \times a^5 \times a^5 = a^{15}$

This rule can be expressed generally, as

$(a^m)^n = a^{mn}$

Examples

$$3b^3 \times 2b^4 = 3 \times b^3 \times 2 \times b^4 = 6b^7$$

$$(4c^4)^2 = 4c^4 \times 4c^4 = 16c^8$$

$a^2 b^3$ cannot be simplified

$$a \times 3b \times a \times 2b^3 = a \times 3 \times b \times a \times 2 \times b^3 = 6a^2 b^4$$

Dividing powers

$$a^5 \div a^3 = \frac{a \times a \times a \times a \times a}{a \times a \times a} = a^2$$

This rule can be expressed generally as

$a^m \div a^n = a^{m-n}$,   where m and n are positive whole numbers,
and m is greater than n. a is not 0.

Examples

$$14b^4 \div 2b = \frac{\overset{7}{\cancel{14}} \times \overset{b^3}{\cancel{b^4}}}{\cancel{2} \times \cancel{b}} = 7b^3$$

$$\frac{2e^2}{3e^3} = \frac{2 \times \cancel{e^2}}{3 \times \underset{e}{\cancel{e^3}}} = \frac{2}{3e}$$

$$12c^5 \div 4c^3 = \frac{\overset{3}{\cancel{12}} \times \overset{c^2}{\cancel{c^5}}}{\cancel{4} \times \cancel{c^3}} = 3c^2$$

$\dfrac{h^2}{j^2}$ cannot be simplified

$$d^2 \div d^5 = \frac{\overset{1}{\cancel{d^2}}}{\underset{d^3}{\cancel{d^5}}} = \frac{1}{d^3}$$

$$\frac{14fg^3}{7f^2g} = \frac{\overset{2}{\cancel{14}} \times \cancel{f} \times \overset{g^2}{\cancel{g^3}}}{\cancel{7} \times \underset{f}{\cancel{f^2}} \times \cancel{g}} = \frac{2g^2}{f}$$

Exercise 3.2

Simplify these expressions.

1. **1** $a^2 \times a^3$ **6** $d^3 \div d^2$
    2 $b^3 \times b^4$ **7** $e^5 \div e^3$
    3 $c \times c^7$ **8** $f^7 \div f$
    4 $c^3 \times c$ **9** $g^4 \div g^3$
    5 $(d^3)^2$ **10** $h^4 \div h^4$

2.
  1 $a^5 \times a^4$
  2 $b^{10} \times b^2$
  3 $(c^4)^3$
  4 $3d^4 \times 2d^3$
  5 $e \times e^2 \times e^2$

  6 $f^3 \times f \times g^4 \times g$
  7 $(5h^3)^2$
  8 $4j^4 \times 5j^5$
  9 $3k \times 2k^2 \times 4k^4$
  10 $4m^2 \times n^3 \times 2m \times 3n^2$

3.
  1 $a^8 \div a^4$
  2 $b^5 \div b^4$
  3 $c^3 \div c^3$
  4 $\dfrac{3def}{2de}$
  5 $\dfrac{4g^5}{g^2}$

  6 $\dfrac{2h^2}{8h^2}$
  7 $40j^2k \div 30jk$
  8 $6m^4 \div m^2$
  9 $\dfrac{6pq^2r}{3pr}$
  10 $\dfrac{35s^7}{5s^5}$

Negative numbers in Algebra

Imagine the number ladder is a ladder of x's, or y's, or whatever letter you are using.

Examples

$3x - 5x = -2x$
Start at $3x$ and go down $5x$, getting to $-2x$

$(-4x) + x = -3x$
Start at $-4x$ and go up x, getting to $-3x$

$(-2y) - 3y = -5y$
Start at $-2y$ and go down $3y$, getting to $-5y$

$(-3y) + 7y = 4y$
Start at $-3y$ and go up $7y$, getting to $4y$

If there are two signs, replace them by one sign.

Replace $++$ or $--$ by $+$
Replace $+-$ or $-+$ by $-$

$5x$	$5y$
$4x$	$4y$
$3x$	$3y$
$2x$	$2y$
x	y
0	0
$-x$	$-y$
$-2x$	$-2y$
$-3x$	$-3y$
$-4x$	$-4y$
$-5x$	$-5y$

Examples

$$3x - (+5x) = 3x - 5x = -2x$$
$$(-4x) + (+x) = (-4x) + x = -3x$$
$$(-2y) + (-3y) = (-2y) - 3y = -5y$$
$$(-3y) - (-7y) = (-3y) + 7y = 4y$$

Replace ++ or −− by +
Replace +− or −+ by −

Multiplication

Examples

$$(-2x) \times 3x = -6x^2$$
$$(-5x) \times (-7y) = 35xy$$
$$(-3) \times 4x = -12x$$
$$5 \times (-x^2) = -5x^2$$
$$(-x) \times (-x) = x^2$$

$$+ \times + = +$$
$$- \times - = +$$
$$+ \times - = -$$

Division

Examples

$$(-3) \div 2x = -\frac{3}{2x}$$

$$x^2 \div (-x) = -\frac{x^2}{x} = -x$$

$$(-15y) \div (-5) = \frac{15y}{5} = 3y$$

$$+ \div + = +$$
$$- \div - = +$$
$$+ \div - = -$$
$$- \div + = -$$

Substitution

Example

When $x = -2$ and $y = -3$

$$2x + 3y = 2 \times (-2) + 3 \times (-3)$$
$$= (-4) - 9$$
$$= -13$$

$$5x - y = 5 \times (-2) - (-3)$$
$$= (-10) + 3$$
$$= -7$$

$$x^2 = (-2)^2$$
$$= (-2) \times (-2)$$
$$= 4$$

Exercise 3.3

Simplify these expressions.

1. **1** $3a - 5a$
    2 $b - 6b$
    3 $(-3c) + 2c$
    4 $4d - 4d$

    5 $(-2e) + 5e$
    6 $(-3f) - f$
    7 $2g - 3g$

    8 $(-5h) + h$
    9 $4j - 5j$
    10 $(-k) + 4k - 3k$

2. **1** $5a - (+a)$
    2 $b + (-4b)$
    3 $(-c) + (+3c)$
    4 $3d - (+3d)$

    5 $2e - (-3e)$
    6 $(-2f) - (-f)$
    7 $(-g) + (-4g)$

    8 $4h - (+4h)$
    9 $(-10j) - (-6j)$
    10 $(-6k) + (+2k)$

3. **1** $a \times (-b)$
    2 $(-c) \times (-d)$
    3 $(+2e) \div (-2)$
    4 $(-4g) \div g$

    5 $(-6h) \div (-3)$
    6 $jk \times (-j)$
    7 $0 \times (-3m)$

    8 $(-n^2) \div n$
    9 $(-2p) \times (+3p)$
    10 $4q \div (-2q)$

4. Find the values of these expressions when $a = 3$, $b = -4$ and $c = -1$.

    1 $a + b$
    2 $2a - b$
    3 $a - 2b + c$
    4 $3b - 2c$

    5 $5 + 2a - 3c$
    6 $a^2 + b^2$
    7 $\dfrac{a - 5c}{b}$

    8 $2c^2$
    9 $\dfrac{b}{a - c}$
    10 $\dfrac{b + c}{a + b}$

5. Solve these equations (which have negative solutions).

    1 $11 + 4x = 5 + 2x$
    2 $5x + 7 - 3x = 5$
    3 $4x + 3 + 2x = 0$
    4 $4x + 1 = 2x - 9$
    5 $8 - 3x = 18 + 7x$

    6 $3(x - 2) = 4x$
    7 $8(x - 1) = 6x - 11$
    8 $4(3x - 4) = 2(9x - 2)$
    9 $5(x - 6) = 7(x - 4)$
    10 $9x = 7 - 5(3 - x)$

Sequences

Write down the next 3 terms of each of these sequences.
1, 3, 5, 7, . . .
1, 4, 9, 16, . . .
3, 6, 9, 12, . . .
By looking at the pattern we can write down an expression for the nth term.

For 2, 4, 6, 8, . . .
the 1st term is 2 × 1
the 2nd term is 2 × 2
the 3rd term is 2 × 3
the 4th term is 2 × 4
the nth term is 2 × n = 2n

For 7, 11, 15, 19, . . .
the 1st term is 4 × 1 + 3
the 2nd term is 4 × 2 + 3
the 3rd term is 4 × 3 + 3
the 4th term is 4 × 4 + 3
the nth term is 4 × n + 3 = 4n + 3

For 1, 4, 9, 16, . . .
the 1st tem is 1 × 1 = 1^2
the 2nd term is 2 × 2 = 2^2
the 3rd term is 3 × 3 = 3^2
the 4th term is 4 × 4 = 4^2
the nth term is n × n = n^2

To find the expression for the nth term if the terms of the sequence increase by a constant number.

e.g. 3, 8, 13, 18, . . . goes up by 5 each time.
The nth term will include a term 5n.
In fact, it is 5n − 2.

If the sequence decreases by a constant number:

e.g. 28, 25, 22, 19, . . . goes down by 3 each time.
The nth term will include a term −3n.
In fact, it is 31 − 3n.

For other sequences, look for patterns including squares, 1, 4, 9, 16; cubes, 1, 8, 27; powers, e.g. powers of 2;   2, 4, 8, 16, (2, 2^2, 2^3, 2^4); and so on.

You can use the expression for the nth term to find any terms of the sequence.

Example

The nth term of a sequence is $\dfrac{n}{2n + 1}$

The 1st term is $\dfrac{1}{(2 \times 1) + 1} = \dfrac{1}{3}$

The 2nd term is $\dfrac{2}{(2 \times 2) + 1} = \dfrac{2}{5}$

The 3rd term is $\dfrac{3}{(2 \times 3) + 1} = \dfrac{3}{7}$

The 10th term is $\dfrac{10}{(2 \times 10) + 1} = \dfrac{10}{21}$

and so on, for any term.

Exercise 3.4

1. Write down the next 3 terms in each of these sequences, and find an expression for the nth term.

    1 2, 5, 8, 11, . . .
    2 90, 80, 70, 60, . . .
    3 9, 14, 19, 24, . . .
    4 1 + 1, 4 + 1, 9 + 1, 16 + 1, . . .
    5 10, 100, 1000, 10 000, . . .

    6 1 × 2, 2 × 3, 3 × 4, 4 × 5, . . .
    7 7, 13, 19, 25, . . .
    8 2, 4, 8, 16, . . .
    9 $\frac{1}{2}, \frac{2}{3}, \frac{3}{4}, \frac{4}{5}, \ldots$
    10 1, 8, 27, 64, . . .

2. These expressions are the nth terms of sequences. By putting $n = 1$, $n = 2$, $n = 3$ and $n = 4$ in turn, write down the first 4 terms of each sequence.

    1 $5n - 2$
    2 $17 - n$
    3 $3n + 7$
    4 $100 - 5n$
    5 $\dfrac{1}{n}$

    6 $n^3 + 1$
    7 $25 - 10n$
    8 $n^2 - n$
    9 $\dfrac{n}{n + 2}$
    10 $8n + 3$

Exercise 3.5   Applications and Activities

1. The traffic capacity of a main road may be given by the formula $n = \dfrac{3600vl}{d}$

   where n = the number of vehicles per
              hour,
         v = the average speed, in m/s,
         l = the number of traffic lanes,
         d = the distance between vehicles,
              in metres.

   1 If the road has 2 lanes, the traffic
       speed is 20 m/s, and there is
       50 metres between vehicles,
       how many vehicles per hour
       can go by ?

   2 If the road was widened to make 3 lanes and the traffic speed was increased
       to 30 m/s, but the gap between vehicles was increased to 100 metres, how
       many extra vehicles per hour could then go by ?

2. A rectangle of perimeter $2a$ cm has width 10 cm.
    Find
    1 an expression for its length,
    2 an expression for its area.

    A square has the same perimeter as the rectangle.
    Find
    3 an expression for its length,
    4 an expression for its area.

3. Complete this number pattern which involves 3 consecutive odd numbers or
    3 consecutive even numbers, up to the line beginning with 9.

$n - 2$	n	$n + 2$	Product	$4n$	Product + $4n$
1	3	5	15	12	27
2	4	6	48	16	64
3	5	7	105	. .	. . .
4	6	8	. . .	. .	. . .
. . .					

Can you find a connection between the last column and the number n ?

4. If a pencil costs p pence and a ruler costs r pence, then
    1   what is the cost, in pence, of s pencils,
    2   what is the cost of one ruler and one pencil,
    3   what is the cost of x rulers and y pencils ?
    4   If 8 pencils and 10 rulers cost £5, write down an equation involving p and r.

5. Alan is three times as old as his son Bill.
    1   If Bill's age is x years, express Alan's age in terms of x.
    2   Write down an expression for Bill's age in 16 years time.
    3   Write down an expression for Alan's age in 16 years time.
    4   If in 16 years time, Alan will be twice as old as Bill, write down an equation and solve it to find x.
    5   How old are Alan and Bill now?

6. **1**   **2**   **3**

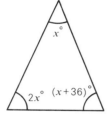 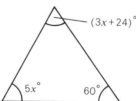 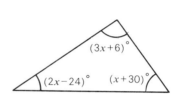

In these triangles, write down an equation involving x.
Solve it to find x, and hence find the numerical values for the sizes of the angles of the triangles.
Say what kind of triangle each one is.

PUZZLES

9. Which two consecutive months, apart from July and August, have 31 days each ?

10. A little boy lived with his parents on the 10th floor of a block of flats. When he went to school in the morning he used to take the lift from the 10th floor to the ground floor. But when he came back from school in the afternoon he went up in the lift only as far as the 5th floor and then walked up the stairs to the 10th floor where his flat was. Why ?

11. If a brick would balance on a scale with $\frac{3}{4}$ kg plus $\frac{3}{4}$ of a brick, what is the weight of the brick ?

4 Thinking about calculating with

Decimals

It is much easier to do calculations of money, weights and measures when they are based on the decimal system, whether using a calculator or not.

Decimal coinage

It was fully introduced in 1971, although the florin, which was $\frac{1}{10}$ of £1, and is now used as a 10p coin, was first issued in 1860.

Why do many countries use coins of 5, 10 and 50 units ?

Decimal coinage

The metric system

The changeover to the metric system will be almost complete by 1995, yet milk, draught beer and draught cider can still be sold in pints, goods sold loose can still be sold in pounds and ounces, and miles, yards, feet and inches can still be used for measuring distances until 1999.

Some new sayings needed...

A miss is as good as a mile.
He wants his pound of flesh.
A bushel of March dust is worth a king's ransom.
Full fathom five thy father lies.
Give him an inch and he'll take an ell.

An old petrol pump

decimals

To take a family of 2 adults and 2 children to this hotel for
10 days would cost £1000
£1100
£1129
£1128.80
Which price is best to quote ?

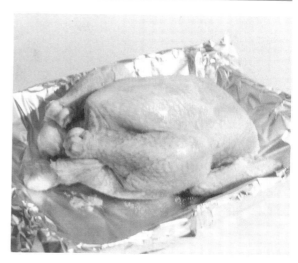

The chicken weighs 2 kg
2.4 kg
2.37 kg
2.372 kg
Which weight is best to use ?

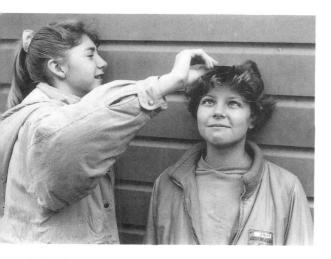

Jenny's height is 2 m
1.6 m
1.62 m
1.618 m
Which measurement is best to use ?

To fill this swimming pool with water
takes 2 000 000 litres
1 860 000 litres
1 856 237 litres
1 856 237.16 litres.
Which measurement is best to use ?

4 Calculating with decimals

Decimals

Decimals are fractions which have denominators of 10, or of powers of 10 such as 100, 1000, 10 000, . . .

The decimal point is used to separate the whole number part from the decimal part of the number.

0.6   means 6 tenths
0.07   means 7 hundredths
0.008 means 8 thousandths
0.67   means 6 tenths and 7 hundredths, or 67 hundredths
0.678 means 6 tenths, 7 hundredths and 8 thousandths, or 678 thousandths.

Working without a calculator

Although you will probably use your calculator for calculations involving decimals, this is not necessary in simple cases. You should know how to work out the answers without using a calculator, for times when it is not available, and also for doing rough checks of the answers.

Addition and subtraction
Multiplication and division by small whole numbers

Just keep the figures in their correct positions relative to the decimal point.

Examples

1   1.057 + 21.62 + 7.605 + 4.3

$$
\begin{array}{r}
1.057 \\
21.62 \\
7.605 \\
+ \ \ 4.3 \\
\hline
34.582 \\
\end{array}
$$

2   21.63 − 9.976

$$
\begin{array}{r}
21.630 \\
- \ \ 9.976 \\
\hline
11.654 \\
\end{array}
$$

3   57.6 × 4

$$\begin{array}{r} 57.6 \\ \times \quad\; 4 \\ \hline 230.4 \\ \hline \end{array}$$

4   273.62 ÷ 8

8)273.6200   Notice the two 0's written at the end
  34.2025   of the number.

5   273.62 ÷ 7, correct to 2 decimal places.

7)273.620   This will turn into a never-ending decimal,
  39.088 . . .   so we work to one more decimal place than we need.

Answer:- 39.09, correct to 2 decimal places.

Multiplying by 10, 100, 1000, . . .

To multiply by 10, 100, 1000, . . . , the numbers grow larger, so the figures move upwards (to the left) 1, 2, 3, . . . places, assuming that the decimal point is fixed. Add 0's to fill any empty places between the figures and the decimal point.

6   2.53 × 10 = 25.3
7   0.0752 × 100 = 7.52
8   18.4 × 1000 = 18 400
9   0.06 × 10 = 0.6

Dividing by 10, 100, 1000, . . .

The numbers become smaller, so the figures move downwards (to the right) 1, 2, 3, . . . places, assuming that the decimal point is fixed. Add 0's to fill any empty places between the decimal point and the figures.

10   28.9 ÷ 10 = 2.89
11   0.68 ÷ 100 = 0.0068
12   2005 ÷ 1000 = 2.005
13   3.9 ÷ 100 = 0.039

To multiply by decimal numbers

First, ignore the decimal points and multiply, then restore the decimal point in the answer, keeping as many decimal places in the answer as there were altogether in the question.

14   8 × 0.02

There are 2 decimal places altogether.
Multiply 8 by 2, making 16.
You need 2 decimal places in the answer so this is 0.16

15   0.9 × 0.8

There are 2 decimal places altogether.
Multiply 9 by 8, making 72.
You need 2 decimal places in the answer so this is 0.72

16   0.003 × 0.4

There are 4 decimal places altogether.
Multiply 3 by 4, making 12.
You need 4 decimal places in the answer, so include two 0's after the decimal point, giving 0.0012

17   0.6 × 0.05

There are 3 decimal places altogether.
Multiply 6 by 5, making 30.
You need 3 decimal places in the answer, so include a 0 after the decimal point, giving 0.030
The final 0 can be dropped after counting it, so the answer can be written as 0.03
(This is how your calculator would show the answer.)

18   70 × 0.03

There are 2 decimal places altogether.
Multiply 70 by 3, making 210.
You need 2 decimal places in the answer so this is 2.10
The final 0 can be dropped after counting it, so the answer can be written as 2.1

To divide by decimal numbers

It is easier to divide by a whole number, so the question is changed to make the number you are dividing by into a whole number.

19 $8 \div 0.02$

Write this as $\dfrac{8}{0.02}$

Multiply 0.02 by 100 to make it into the whole number 2.
So 8 must also be multiplied by 100

i.e. $\dfrac{8}{0.02} = \dfrac{8 \times 100}{0.02 \times 100} = \dfrac{800}{2} = 400$

20 $0.09 \div 0.6$

Write this as $\dfrac{0.09}{0.6}$

Multiply 0.6 by 10 to make it into the whole number 6.
So 0.09 must also be multiplied by 10

i.e. $\dfrac{0.09}{0.6} = \dfrac{0.09 \times 10}{0.6 \times 10} = \dfrac{0.9}{6} = 0.15$
$\quad \dfrac{6)0.90}{0.15}$

21 $0.6 \div 0.05$

$\dfrac{0.6}{0.05} = \dfrac{0.6 \times 100}{0.05 \times 100} = \dfrac{60}{5} = 12$

22 $20 \div 0.4$

$\dfrac{20}{0.4} = \dfrac{20 \times 10}{0.4 \times 10} = \dfrac{200}{4} = 50$

23 $0.02 \div 0.8$

$\dfrac{0.02}{0.8} = \dfrac{0.02 \times 10}{0.8 \times 10} = \dfrac{0.2}{8} = 0.025$
$\quad \dfrac{8)0.200}{0.025}$

Exercise 4.1

Try to do these questions without using your calculator, then you can use your calculator to check the answers.

1. **1** 9.46 + 8.023 + 15.6
    2 3.12 + 2.806 + 0.005
    3 0.803 + 0.042 + 0.67
    4 9.93 + 0.05 + 1.2
    5 15.5 + 2.079 + 4.32

2. **1** 41.09 − 28.32
    2 75.401 − 30.85
    3 9.67 − 5.683
    4 42.07 − 26.938
    5 20 − (15.09 + 4.56)

3. **1** 3.86 × 4
    2 0.052 × 3
    3 0.83 × 5
    4 2.9 × 8
    5 1.05 × 6

4. **1** 1.32 ÷ 8
    2 5.871 ÷ 3
    3 0.041 ÷ 4
    4 9.2 ÷ 7, to 2 dec. pl.
    5 2.05 ÷ 9, to 3 dec. pl.

5. **1** 0.076 × 10
    2 28.3 × 100
    3 3.02 × 1000
    4 49.6 × 10
    5 0.0071 × 10

6. **1** 15.6 ÷ 10
    2 1.63 ÷ 100
    3 0.7 ÷ 100
    4 7.3 ÷ 1000
    5 16.5 ÷ 100

7. **1** 0.6 × 0.6
    2 0.07 × 0.2
    3 8 × 0.04
    4 0.7 × 0.005
    5 4 × 0.3
    6 0.06 × 0.05
    7 90 × 0.7
    8 0.5 × 0.03
    9 0.001 × 0.8
    10 200 × 0.9

8. **1** 6 ÷ 0.3
    2 0.15 ÷ 0.5
    3 1 ÷ 0.08
    4 12 ÷ 0.04
    5 0.9 ÷ 0.3
    6 0.04 ÷ 0.2
    7 3.5 ÷ 0.07
    8 6.4 ÷ 0.8
    9 0.65 ÷ 0.005
    10 0.0018 ÷ 0.09

Using your calculator

These instructions are for a scientific calculator. With some calculators you may have to do some operations in a different way.

It is advisable to start every new calculation by pressing the $\boxed{C}$ key (for CLEAR), but you may find that on your calculator this is unnecessary if you have just pressed the $\boxed{=}$ key. This also works after pressing some of the other keys.

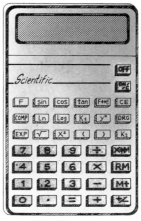

Scientific calculator

If your calculator does not seem to work in the ways shown here, read the instruction booklet and try the examples shown there.

1. When doing multiplication and division, it is better to multiply first and divide last if the division is not exact.
    e.g. For $\frac{2}{3}$ of 20, find 2 × 20 ÷ 3 instead of 2 ÷ 3 × 20.
    The answer is 13.333...

2. If the answer is not exact, or has several figures, then round it up to a sensible degree of accuracy.
    Usually 3 significant figures will be sufficient for a final numerical answer.
    Remember:- To 3 significant figures means that you should write down the first 3 figures of the number, not counting any 0's which are just filling in spaces at the beginning of the number. If the 4th figure is 5 or more you must correct up the 3rd figure. You may have to add 0's to fill in spaces.
    e.g. 279.37   = 279, to 3 sig. fig.
        279.63   = 280, to 3 sig. fig.
        58 246   = 58 200, to 3 sig. fig.
        0.006259 = 0.00626, to 3 sig. fig.

3. If you have a question involving addition or subtraction together with multiplication, the calculator will read it as if there were brackets round the multiplication part, and do that part first.
    e.g. 25.1 + 76.2 × 0.3 is read as 25.1 + (76.2 × 0.3) and the answer is 47.96.

    Similar rules work with addition or subtraction together with division.
    The calculator will do the division first.
    e.g. 5.93 − 0.86 ÷ 0.4 is read as 5.93 − (0.86 ÷ 0.4) and the answer is 3.78.

4.   If there are brackets then the part in brackets is worked out first.

      e.g. $(25.1 + 76.2) \times 0.3$
      Use the bracket keys on your calculator, or instead, you can press
      25.1 $\boxed{+}$ 76.2 $\boxed{=}$ $\boxed{\times}$ 0.3 $\boxed{=}$ so that the calculator works out the addition before
      multiplying by 0.3.
      The answer is 30.39.

      For $(5.93 - 0.86) \div 0.4$, use the bracket keys or press
      5.93 $\boxed{-}$ 0.86 $\boxed{=}$ $\boxed{\div}$ 0.4 $\boxed{=}$
      The answer is 12.675.

      $\dfrac{5.93 - 0.86}{0.4}$ is the same question, written in a different way.

5.   **Using the memory**

      e.g. $\dfrac{23.5 + 12.9}{18.1 - 6.9}$

      First find $18.1 - 6.9$ and put the answer (11.2) in the memory.
      Then press 23.5 $\boxed{+}$ 12.9 $\boxed{=}$ $\boxed{\div}$ $\boxed{RM}$ $\boxed{=}$
      The answer is 3.25
      RM stands for 'recall memory'.

      Alternatively, you could find $(23.5 + 12.9) \div (18.1 - 6.9)$, using brackets.

6.   Make a rough check of your calculation to see if the calculator answer seems to
      be about the right size.

      e.g. $25.1 + 76.2 \times 0.3$
      A rough check for 76.2×0.3 is $80 \times 0.3 = 24$
      Then $25 + 24 = 49$
      The answer 47.96 seems to be about the right size.

      $5.93 - 0.86 \div 0.4$

      For $0.86 \div 0.4$ use $\dfrac{0.8}{0.4} = \dfrac{8}{4} = 2$

      For 5.93 use 6
      $6 - 2 = 4$, so the answer 3.78 seems to be about the right size.

      $\dfrac{23.5 + 12.9}{18.1 - 6.9}$ is approximately $\dfrac{24 + 13}{18 - 7} = \dfrac{37}{11} =$ just over 3.

      The answer 3.25 seems to be about the right size.

7.   **Keys** $\boxed{\sqrt{}}$ $\boxed{x^2}$ $\boxed{y^x}$ $\boxed{\sqrt[3]{}}$

$\boxed{\sqrt{}}$ is the square root key. It must be pressed after the number.
So for $\sqrt{6}$ press 6 $\boxed{\sqrt{}}$ and you will get 2.4494...
To 3 significant figures this is 2.45

$\boxed{x^2}$ is the squaring key.
For 3.2^2 press 3.2 $\boxed{x^2}$ and you will get 10.24

$\boxed{y^x}$ or $\boxed{x^y}$ is the key for getting cubes and other powers.
For 7^3 press 7 $\boxed{y^x}$ 3 $\boxed{=}$ and you will get 343.
For 2^6 press 2 $\boxed{y^x}$ 6 $\boxed{=}$ and you will get 64.

For cube roots, use the key $\boxed{\sqrt[3]{}}$
For the cube root of 125 press 125 $\boxed{\sqrt[3]{}}$ and you will get 5.
If there is not a cube root key, use the inverse key to $\boxed{y^x}$.
This is marked $\boxed{\sqrt[x]{y}}$.
For the cube root of 125 press 125 $\boxed{\sqrt[x]{y}}$ 3 $\boxed{=}$ and you will get 5. (The 3 is to show that you want the **cube** root.)

8.   **The $\boxed{\pi}$ key**

π (pi) is the Greek letter which represents the special number 3.14159... used in circle formulae.
This number cannot be written exactly. For practical purposes it is usually sufficient to use 3.14 or 3.142 but if there is a $\boxed{\pi}$ key on your calculator it is quicker to use that. Do not leave more than 3 or 4 significant figures in the final answer.

e.g. For 6π press 6 $\boxed{\times}$ $\boxed{\pi}$ $\boxed{=}$ getting 18.849...
To 3 significant figures this is 18.8

For $\dfrac{\pi}{2}$ press $\boxed{\pi}$ $\boxed{\div}$ 2 $\boxed{=}$ getting 1.5707...

To 3 significant figures this is 1.57

9. **To find the remainder in a division sum**

e.g. Divide 961 by 23 and give the answer and remainder.

On your calculator, 961 ÷ 23 = 41.7826...
From this, the whole number answer is 41.
Leaving the answer on your calculator, subtract 41 and press $\boxed{=}$.
This leaves 0.7826...
Multiply this decimal by 23 and it gives 18. This is the remainder.
Due to rounding errors on the calculator, instead of giving 18 exactly it might
give something like 18.00000001 or 17.99999999. Count either of these as 18.

Exercise 4.2

1. Use your calculator to work out the following. Give each answer correct to
    4 significant figures.

    1 $365 - 27.65 \div 0.12$
    2 $0.761 + 0.239 \times 5.2$
    3 $693 \times 1.728 + 1.204$
    4 $63.5 \div (11.5 - 7.3)$
    5 $(25 + 3.142) \times 17.6$
    6 $15 \times 69.7 + 220 \times 1.87$

    7 $\dfrac{4 + 2.735}{23.5}$

    8 $\dfrac{15.5 - 5.25}{0.532}$

    9 $42.5 \times 13.5 - 27.8 \times 9.7$

    10 $\dfrac{3160 + 279}{23.5 \times 9.7}$

2. Work out the following. Give all answers which are not exact correct to
    3 significant figures.

    1 7.2^2
    2 0.5^3
    3 $\sqrt{1000}$
    4 $\sqrt[3]{60}$
    5 2^5
    6 $3^2 + 4^2 + 5^2$

    7 $\sqrt{40} + \sqrt{50} - \sqrt{60}$
    8 $\sqrt{22.8 \times 16.3}$
    9 $\dfrac{5.1^2 + 7.3^2}{4.9^2}$
    10 $\sqrt[3]{12} - \sqrt[3]{8}$

3. Using the π key on your calculator, work out the following, giving the answers
    correct to 3 significant figures.

    1 6.3π
    2 $\frac{3}{2}\pi$
    3 $\frac{4}{3} \times \pi \times 64$

    4 $\dfrac{6}{\pi}$

    5 $\sqrt{\dfrac{15}{\pi}}$

4. Find the whole number answer and the remainder to these division questions.

   1 $562 \div 28$ **4** $220 \div 13$

   2 $79 \div 17$ **5** $1000 \div 19$

   3 $8710 \div 35$

Reciprocals

If x is a number (not 0) then $\dfrac{1}{x}$ is called the reciprocal of x.

A number multiplied by its reciprocal equals 1.

e.g. The reciprocal of 2 is $\frac{1}{2}$ since $2 \times \frac{1}{2} = 1$

    The reciprocal of 5 is $\frac{1}{5}$ since $5 \times \frac{1}{5} = 1$

    The reciprocal of $\frac{1}{3}$ is 3 since $\frac{1}{3} \times 3 = 1$

    The reciprocal of $\frac{4}{5}$ is $\frac{5}{4}$ since $\frac{4}{5} \times \frac{5}{4} = 1$

    The reciprocal of 0.7 is $\frac{10}{7}$ since 0.7 is $\frac{7}{10}$ and $\frac{7}{10} \times \frac{10}{7} = 1$

    The reciprocal of 0.16 is $\frac{100}{16}$ (or $\frac{25}{4}$) since 0.16 is $\frac{16}{100}$ and $\frac{16}{100} \times \frac{100}{16} = 1$

    The reciprocal of 8.7 is $\frac{10}{87}$ since 8.7 is $8\frac{7}{10}$ or $\frac{87}{10}$ and $\frac{87}{10} \times \frac{10}{87} = 1$

    The reciprocal of $2\frac{3}{4}$ is $\frac{4}{11}$ since $2\frac{3}{4}$ is $\frac{11}{4}$ and $\frac{11}{4} \times \frac{4}{11} = 1$

In general, the reciprocal of $\dfrac{a}{b}$ is $\dfrac{b}{a}$.

There may be a reciprocal key on your calculator.

It will be labelled $\dfrac{1}{x}$

Press 8 $\boxed{\frac{1}{x}}$ and you will get 0.125 since $\frac{1}{8} = 0.125$

Press 1.1 $\boxed{\frac{1}{x}}$ and you will get 0.909090... since $\frac{1}{1.1} = \frac{10}{11} = 0.909090...$

What happens if you press a number then $\boxed{\frac{1}{x}}$ twice in succession ?

To find the reciprocal of a fraction using your calculator, first change the fraction to a decimal.

One use of reciprocals is to change division into multiplication.

e.g. To divide by $\frac{1}{2}$, multiply by the reciprocal of $\frac{1}{2}$, which is 2.

$16 \div \frac{1}{2} = 16 \times 2 = 32$

To divide by $\frac{2}{3}$, multiply by the reciprocal of $\frac{2}{3}$, which is $\frac{3}{2}$ or 1.5

$28 \div \frac{2}{3} = 28 \times 1.5 = 42$

To divide by $2\frac{1}{4}$, multiply by the reciprocal of $2\frac{1}{4}$, which is $\frac{4}{9}$.

$18 \div 2\frac{1}{4} = 18 \times \frac{4}{9} = 8$

Exercise 4.3

1. Write down the reciprocals of these numbers, as fractions.

1	5	**5**	$\frac{3}{11}$	**8**	$1\frac{2}{3}$
2	21	**6**	0.4	**9**	2.2
3	$\frac{1}{20}$	**7**	0.35	**10**	0.08
4	$\frac{5}{12}$				

2. Find the reciprocals of question 1 as decimals. If they are not exact, give them correct to 3 decimal places.

Accuracy of measurements

To the nearest whole number

If you are measuring a length to the nearest metre then imagine that there are boundaries on your measuring tape, marked at the 0.5 metre points.

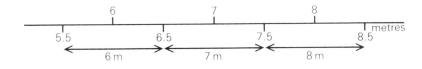

Then any measurement in the range between 5.5 m and 6.5 m will be given as 6 metres, those in the range between 6.5 m and 7.5 m will be given as 7 m, and so on.

So if you are told that a measurement is 6 m, to the nearest metre, you know that the actual measurement can be anything between 5.5 m and 6.5 m. In fact, it can be up to 0.5 m less or 0.5 m more.

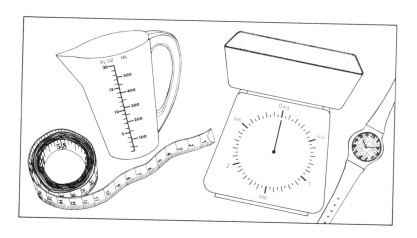

To 1 decimal place

If you are weighing an object to the nearest 0.1 kg then imagine that there are boundaries on the weighing scale marked at the 0.05 kg points.

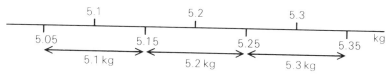

Then any weight in the range between 5.05 kg and 5.15 kg will be given as 5.1 kg, those in the range between 5.15 kg and 5.25 kg will be given as 5.2 kg, and so on.

So if you are told that a weight is 5.2 kg, to the nearest 0.1 kg, you know that the actual weight can be anything between 5.15 kg and 5.25 kg. In fact, it can be up to 0.05 kg less or 0.05 kg more.

Similar rules apply to measurements correct to 2 decimal places, 3 decimal places, to the nearest 10 units, etc.

If a length is given as 6 m, then you must assume that it has been measured to the nearest metre, and the actual length lies between 5.5 m and 6.5 m.
If the length has been measured to the nearest 0.1 m, then it is better to write it as 6.0 m. In this case the actual length lies between 5.95 m and 6.05 m.
If the length has been measured to the nearest cm (0.01 m) then it is better to write it as 6.00 m. The actual length lies between 5.995 m and 6.005 m. It could be up to 0.005 m less or 0.005 m more.

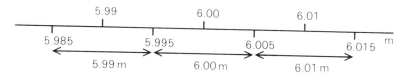

Examples

Give the limits between which these measurements must lie:
1   A line measured to the nearest mm is 4.3 cm long.
2   A time measured to the nearest minute is 2 hours 33 minutes.
3   A weight measured to the nearest gram is 5.037 kg.

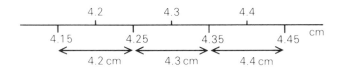

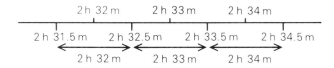

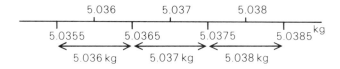

1   For 4.3 cm the actual length lies between 4.25 cm and 4.35 cm.
2   For 2 hours 33 minutes the actual time lies between 2 hours 32.5 min and
     2 hours 33.5 min.
3   For 5.037 kg the actual weight lies between 5.0365 kg and 5.0375 kg.

Exercise 4.4

1.   Give the limits between which these measurements must lie.

     1   A line 8.5 cm long, measured to the nearest mm.
     2   A weight of 2.35 kg, weighed to the nearest 0.01 kg.
     3   A capacity of 1.2 ℓ, measured to the nearest 0.1 ℓ.
     4   A time of 8 hours 20 minutes, measured to the nearest 10 minutes.
     5   A time of 2 hours 45 minutes, measured to the nearest minute.
     6   A weight of 230 kg, weighed to the nearest 10 kg.
     7   A weight of 68 kg, weighed to the nearest kg.
     8   A capacity of 350 ml, measured to the nearest 10 ml.
     9   A length of 23.6 m, measured to the nearest 0.1 m.
     10   An amount of £400, given to the nearest £100.

2. Give the limits between which these measurements must lie.

    1 A line 3.0 cm long, measured to the nearest mm.
    2 A weight of 200 g, weighed to the nearest 10 g.
    3 A time of 3 minutes 50 seconds, measured to the nearest second.
    4 A capacity of 80 ml, measured to the nearest ml.
    5 An amount of £20, given to the nearest £1.

3. Write these measurements as stated:

    1 In cm, correct to the nearest mm,
    156.92 cm, 45.89 cm, 131.121 cm, 2.8674 cm, 0.0584 cm.
    2 In metres, correct to the nearest cm,
    70.551 m, 3.288 m, 7.082 m, 0.0631 m, 0.0549 m.
    3 In kg, correct to the nearest kg,
    28.309 kg, 41.49 kg, 33.81 kg, 151.98 kg, 3.75 kg.
    4 In litres, correct to the nearest 0.1 ℓ,
    46.67 ℓ, 4.087 ℓ, 0.9235 ℓ, 8.706 ℓ, 12.098 ℓ.
    5 In minutes, correct to the nearest minute,
    21 min 53 sec, 9 min 9 sec, 2 min 35 sec, 18 min 29 sec, 27 min 30.2 sec.

4. Write these measurements as stated:

    1 3.97 m, correct to the nearest 0.1 m.
    2 47.03 sec, correct to the nearest second.
    3 1504 m, correct to the nearest 10 m.
    4 2018 ℓ, correct to the nearest 100 ℓ.
    5 15.98 kg, correct to the nearest 0.1 kg.

Exercise 4.5   Applications and Activities

1. A child's temperature rose from 37.7°C to 38.6°C. What was the rise?

2. A 5-inch nail is also measured as 12.7 cm long. What is 1 inch in cm?

3. The rainfall during 5 successive months was 7.1, 7.8, 5.5, 4.6 and 9.4 cm respectively. Find the total rainfall.

4. A book of 720 pages is 2.7 cm thick, not including the covers. What is the thickness of each sheet of the paper?

5. If £1 is worth 3.24 Dutch guilders, find the value of £8, in guilders.

6.   Each face of a hexagonal column is 0.7 m
      wide. What is the total length round the
      column ?

7.   If £1 is worth 9.72 French francs, find the value of a toy costing 30 francs, in
      £'s, to the nearest 10 p.

8.   If a train is travelling at 53 km/hour, how many metres will it travel in a minute,
      correct to the nearest 10 m ?

9.   How many buckets, each holding 9.2ℓ, can be filled from a tank containing
      1000ℓ of water, and what amount of water will be left over ?

10.   The scale of a map is '1 cm represents 5 km', and the distance on the map
      between two villages is 5.4 cm.
      How far apart are the villages ?

11.   Two parcels were weighed, each to the nearest kg, and the weights were
      recorded as 17 kg and 12 kg.
      1   Give the limits between which each of the measurements could lie.
      2   What is the sum of the recorded weights ?
      3   What is the smallest possible value of the weight of the two parcels
          together ? What is the greatest possible value of the weight of the two
          parcels together ?
      4   How much heavier is one parcel than the other, using the recorded weights ?
      5   What is the smallest possible value of the difference between the weights of
          the parcels ? What is the greatest possible value ?

12. Use your calculator to find the answers to these questions involving formulae.

1 Find the time of swing of a pendulum from the formula

$$T = 2\pi \sqrt{\frac{l}{g}},$$ where the length $l = 1.03\,\text{m}$, $g = 9.8\,\text{m/s}^2$

and T is the time, in seconds.

2 The length of chain required for a suspension bridge is L metres, where $L = 2\sqrt{(\frac{1}{2}C)^2 + \frac{4}{3}V^2}$, where C is the horizontal span, in metres, and V is the vertical height of the chain, in metres.
Find the length of the chain when $C = 50.2$ and $V = 9.3$.

Severn Bridge.

13. **Reciprocals**

Use your calculator to find the reciprocals of the whole numbers from 2 to 25, recording your answers as decimals, in a list. If an answer is a long list of figures, record it as shown on the calculator.
Make a separate list of the numbers whose reciprocals are exact decimals.
What do you notice about these numbers ?
Make a separate list of those numbers whose reciprocals have one repeating figure, e.g. the reciprocal of 12 is 0.083333...
Note that the last figure may not be the same if the number has been corrected up.
What do you notice about these numbers ?
Make a list of those numbers whose reciprocals have two repeating figures.
For the remaining numbers, can you discover anything about their reciprocals ?

14.   **Multiplying and dividing mentally**
Now that you know how to multiply simple numbers you might be able to do this in your head.
Here are some examples with possible ways to do them. If you can think of another way which you prefer, then you can use it, as long as it gives the correct answer.

Examples

1 $300 \times 60 = 3 \times 100 \times 6 \times 10$ $\left.\right\}$ (In your head)
$ = 18 \times 1000$
$ = 18\,000$

or
$300 \times 60 = 300 \times 6 \times 10$ $\left.\right\}$ (In your head)
$ = 1800 \times 10$
$ = 18\,000$

2 80×0.2 $80 \times 2 = 160$ $\left.\right\}$
$ $ Restore 1 decimal place   (In your head)
$80 \times 0.2 = 16.0$
$ = 16$

or
$80 \times 0.2 = 0.2 \times 80$ $\left.\right\}$
$ = 0.2 \times 10 \times 8$ (In your head)
$ = 2 \times 8$
$ = 16$

3 0.04×0.9 $4 \times 9 = 36$ $\left.\right\}$
 Restore 3 decimal places   (In your head)
$0.04 \times 0.9 = 0.036$

Notice that when you multiply by a decimal which is a number less than 1, the answer will be smaller than the number you are multiplying.
e.g. 80×0.2 will be smaller than 80.
 0.04×0.9 will be smaller than 0.04 and also smaller than 0.9.

Dividing simple numbers

4 $6300 \div 90 = 6300 \div 10 \div 9$ $\left.\right\}$ (In your head)
$ = 630 \div 9$
$ = 70$

5   40 ÷ 0.8 = 400 ÷ 8

         (making 0.8 into 8)   }   (In your head)

     = 50

6   3 ÷ 0.05 = 300 ÷ 5

         (making 0.05 into 5)   }   (In your head)

     = 60

7   0.06 ÷ 0.3 = 0.6 ÷ 3

         (making 0.3 into 3)   }   (In your head)

     = 0.2

Notice that when you divide by a decimal which is a number less than 1, the answer will be greater than the number you are dividing.

e.g. 40 ÷ 0.8 will be greater than 40.

   3 ÷ 0.05 will be greater than 3.

   0.06 ÷ 0.3 will be greater than 0.06

If you cannot do such questions in your head at present, do not worry too much about this. It is a skill which will improve with practice.

Try to work out the answers to these questions in your head, just writing down the answers.

1	500 × 60	**8**	30 × 0.8	**15**	0.2 ÷ 0.5
2	20 × 0.7	**9**	0.5 × 9	**16**	3.6 ÷ 0.6
3	0.6 × 0.8	**10**	10 × 0.01	**17**	0.56 ÷ 0.07
4	90 × 0.9	**11**	5500 ÷ 50	**18**	270 ÷ 0.3
5	5 × 0.05	**12**	36 ÷ 0.3	**19**	0.36 ÷ 0.4
6	70 × 40	**13**	770 ÷ 70	**20**	10 ÷ 0.1
7	0.6 × 0.2	**14**	9.6 ÷ 0.8		

PUZZLE

12.   Aruna walks from a village Kirkley towards a village Larlby. After walking for 20 minutes she stops and rests. In 5 minutes time, her friend Bakula, who left Larlby to walk to Kirkley 9 minutes after Aruna left Kirkley, reaches her. The girls walk at the same speed. How long would it have taken one of them to walk the whole distance from Kirkley to Larlby without stopping ?

5 Thinking about statistical testing

Testing statements

People think we should keep to British Summer Time (GMT + 1) in winter and double British Summer Time in summer, to keep in time with Europe.

This is a statement which may or may not be true.
You could try to find out for yourself.

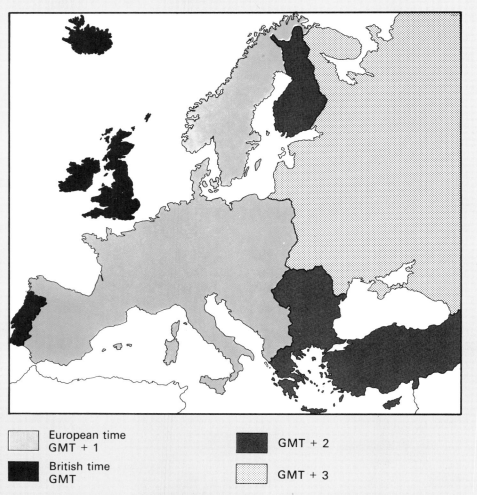

| | European time GMT + 1 | | GMT + 2 |
| | British time GMT | | GMT + 3 |

GMT stands for Greenwich Mean Time.
GMT + 1 means 1 hour ahead, so that when it is 8 am in Britain it is 9 am in most of Europe, 10 am in Greece and 11 am in Russia.
In summer, most countries move their clocks 1 hour ahead from the times shown.

Making a survey

Depending on who is involved, ask a suitable sample of people.

Do not choose too large a sample as it will take too long to carry out the survey and count the results.

Questionnaires

Keep the questionnaire short.

Keep the questions clear.

Do not ask questions which people may not be willing to answer.

Do not ask questions worded unfairly.

5 Statistical Testing

We often use Statistics to make decisions for the future. Perhaps we can think of some improvement that we would like to see adopted.

For instance, you might think that more people would use a pedestrian crossing if it was moved to a slightly different position. Your theory might be that 'More people would prefer the crossing to be moved nearer to the shops'. You would have to test this theory by asking people for their views.

If you asked a reasonable number of people and most of them agreed with you, then you would have collected enough evidence to approach the Local Authority or the Road Safety Committee and ask them to consider your idea.
This sounds a very straightforward thing to do, but there are many things to consider.

Taking a sample

You cannot ask everyone involved in crossing the road, so you will have to take a sample.

The sample should be a **random** sample. You cannot just approach the people who are crossing the road near the shops and not using the existing crossing.

The sample should try to include as many categories as possible of the people who usually cross the road.
For instance, it should include people of all ages. Perhaps the crossing is more convenient where it already is for mothers taking children to a local playgroup, and some of them should be included in your sample. Other categories might include people who live near the shops, those who live near the existing crossing, and children who use the crossing when going to school, to the park or to the shops. You can think of other categories.

The sample should be large enough to include some people of all categories. It is difficult to say how large is 'large enough', but you should aim to have at least 100 people in your sample. The larger the sample, the more accurate will be the results, but it will take you longer to do your survey.

Designing a questionnaire

To make sure you ask everyone the same questions, you will probably design a questionnaire. You can ask the questions and record the answers. (In a different situation you might find it more convenient to distribute questionnaires so that people could fill them in themselves.) You will also design a tally chart, or a similar chart, on which to classify the answers.

You could have one simple, straightforward question:
'Do you think more people would use the crossing if it was placed nearer to the shops ?'

Yes	
No	
Don't know	

You might then include another question:
'Do **you** think the crossing should be moved nearer to the shops ?'

Try not to make your questions unfair.
'The pelican crossing is no use where it is. Don't you agree that it should be moved nearer to the shops ?' is not a fair way to ask the question.

You might add a few preliminary questions to make people think about the subject of crossing the road, before you ask the main questions:
'Do you have to cross the road at all ?'
'How many times do you have to cross it ?'

Not at all	
Once or twice a week	
Once or twice a day	
Several times a day	

'Do you consider this to be a busy road for traffic ?'
'Do you normally cross at the pedestrian crossing ?'
'Do you think children should cross at the crossing ?'
'Do you think the crossing is in the best place ?'

Then you can ask the main questions.

You must also keep a check of the types of people you are asking so you would also record their categories, such as:

Male	
Female	

Child	
Adult	
Elderly person	

How to make the survey

Having designed your questionnaire you will have to decide how to do your survey.

In this example, you need to ask people who cross the road, so stopping people in that area and asking them might be the best way.
(If you are doing a survey in the street, you should check with your teacher and your parents before you go ahead. An adult should be supervising you, and you should not be alone when you approach strangers, so work with one or two friends. Be very polite when you ask people and thank them afterwards for their help. You should realise that some people may be in too much of a hurry to stop and answer your questions. Also, do be careful to keep away from the traffic on a busy road.)

In other surveys, you might decide to ask pupils and teachers in school, or your parents, friends, relatives and neighbours. It depends on what the survey is about and who is concerned. If it is a school matter it is sufficient to ask pupils, teachers and possibly parents.

A hypothesis

The theory that you are putting to the test is called a **hypothesis**.

In the example, your hypothesis is that people would like the crossing moved nearer to the shops.

Now, if you asked 100 people and 90 of them agreed with this, then you could consider that you have proved your hypothesis.
If only 30 agreed with it, then you would decide that you had not proved your hypothesis.
The difficulty is knowing whether to say you have proved your hypothesis if only about 55 people out of 100 agreed with it. With a slightly different sample of people you could have got different results, so if the result is near 50–50 you cannot be sure that your hypothesis is proved. A statistician would have further tests to use in deciding when to accept a hypothesis, but as a rough rule, for a sample of 100, only accept the hypothesis when you get at least 60 people agreeing with it.

Exercise 5.1

1.   'Pupils think we should have a school tuck-shop.'
     This is a hypothesis which you wish to test.
     1   Design a questionnaire which you could use to test this statement.
     2   Say how you would choose a suitable sample of people to ask for
     their views.

Here are some alternative statements which you may like to consider instead of, or as well as, the one above.

2.   Pupils think we should have a summer fair to raise money for charity.

3.   Parents think we should have a summer fair to raise money for extra school equipment.

4.   Older pupils think that the school uniform should be changed.

5.   Some teachers and pupils think there should be a school magazine (or a school newspaper).

Questions 6 to 10 involve local issues. Repeat question 1 for one or more of these.

6.   Parents think that there should be a new health centre built.

7.   Teenagers think that there should be better youth club provision in the area.

8.   People think that there should be a lower speed limit on the main road.

9.   Teachers think that there should be parking restrictions on the road outside the school.

10. Mothers think that there ought to be a holiday play scheme organised for younger children.

Exercise 5.2 Applications and Activities

1. For any of the questions in Exercise 5.1, carry out the survey you have planned,
    by using your questionnaire with a suitable sample of people.
    Design a data collection sheet to use to record the results of the survey. Analyse
    these results and decide whether the hypothesis is proved.
    You can comment on the results of your survey, and illustrate your answer with
    suitable statistical diagrams.
    If you consider that you have proved your hypothesis then you may like to carry
    out a further investigation.
    e.g. A school tuck-shop could not be set up without considering further
    questions such as:- Where could it be situated ? Who would be in charge of it ?
    Where would the money come from for the stock and equipment ?
    If you want other people to consider your ideas, you must show them that you
    have really thought about them.

2. 'Parents, pupils and teachers would prefer the school day to start at 8 am and
    finish at 2 pm.'
    Test this hypothesis by designing and using a questionnaire with a suitable
    sample of people, and analysing the results.
    You might like to consider such things as:
    the availability of transport,
    child-minding for mothers who work in the afternoons,
    lunch arrangements,
    extra school activities such as sports and clubs.

3. 'Parents would prefer a 4-term year instead of the 3-term year.'
    Test this hypothesis and analyse the results. You might consider such things as:
    parents' holiday arrangements from their work,
    child-minding in the holidays,
    the fact that Easter is not a fixed date,
    local arrangements for holidays, such as 'Wakes weeks', rural holidays for fruit
    picking, etc.
    the climate, saving of fuel in winter,
    the timing of national examinations.

4. If there is any other school, local, national or international issue that you would
    like to investigate, choose a suitable hypothesis and test it.
    For example, there may be an environmental issue such as 'People think that
    chemicals and pesticides should be banned because they affect our food'.

PUZZLES

13. Draw each of these figures without taking your pencil off the paper and without going along any line more than once.

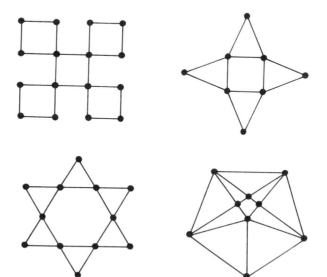

14. Arrange 16 similar coins with heads and tails alternately, like this.

    Rearrange the square so that the 1st and 3rd rows show heads and the 2nd and 4th rows show tails.

    You are not allowed to touch more than 2 coins.

15. **Jumping coins**

    Arrange 10 coins in a row.

    Now lift any coin and put it on top of another coin, but in doing so, jump over 2 coins. Then choose another coin and put this on top of a coin, again jumping over 2 coins. Continue until there are no coins left by themselves.

    Remember that a coin has always to jump over 2 others, which may be side by side or in a pile of two. You never put a 3rd coin on a pile that already contains two.

6 Thinking about areas and volumes

Area

Area is the amount of surface an object covers.

The top of the table has an area of 1.1 m².

The floor of this hall has an area of 45 m².

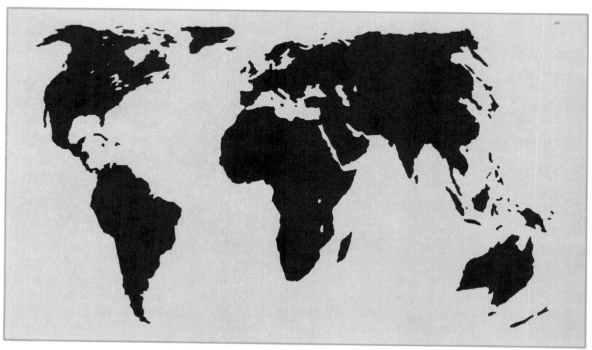

Of the Earth's surface area, 148 330 000 km² is land and 361 740 000 km² is sea.

Volume

Volume is the amount of space an object occupies.

Gold bars

Oil storage tank

At work

Think of some ways in which these people use area and/or volume in their work.

Farmer

Chemist

Areas and Volumes

Areas

When we measure area we compare it with a unit area. We use the area of a square of side 1 cm for this unit. This is called 1 square centimetre, and written as $1\,\text{cm}^2$. If we are measuring larger areas we compare them with 1 square metre ($1\,\text{m}^2$) or 1 square kilometre ($1\,\text{km}^2$).

Area formulae

Area of a rectangle = length × breadth = lb
Area of a square = (length)^2 = l^2
Area of a triangle = $\frac{1}{2}$ × base × perpendicular height = $\frac{1}{2}bh$
Area of a parallelogram = base × perpendicular height = bh
Area of a trapezium = $\frac{1}{2}$ × sum of the parallel sides × the perpendicular distance between them
$\qquad = \frac{1}{2}(a + b)h$

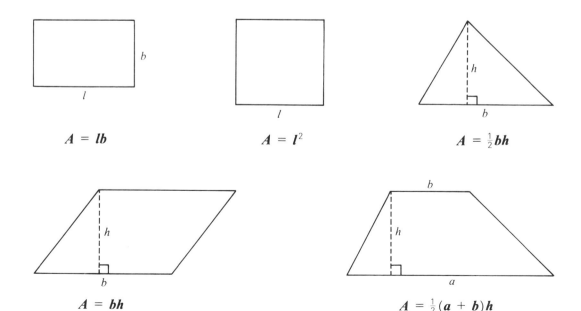

$A = lb$ $A = l^2$ $A = \frac{1}{2}bh$

$A = bh$ $A = \frac{1}{2}(a + b)h$

Examples

1   Find the area of the triangle.

$$\text{Area} = \tfrac{1}{2}bh$$
$$= \tfrac{1}{2} \times 10 \times 7 \ \text{cm}^2$$
$$= 35 \ \text{cm}^2$$

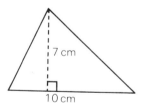

2   Find the area of the parallelogram.

$$\text{Area} = bh$$
$$= 12 \times 6 \ \text{cm}^2$$
$$= 72 \ \text{cm}^2$$

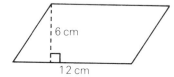

3   Find the area of the trapezium.

$$\text{Area} = \tfrac{1}{2}(a + b)h$$
$$= \tfrac{1}{2} \times (9 + 6) \times 4 \ \text{cm}^2$$
$$= 30 \ \text{cm}^2$$

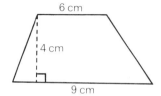

Area of a triangle

Any side of a triangle can be taken as the **base**. The perpendicular height is the height at right angles to that side.

If there is an obtuse angle, the perpendicular height meets an extension of the base line.

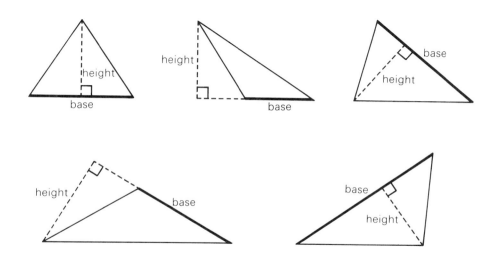

Area of a parallelogram

Any side of the parallelogram can be taken as the base. The perpendicular height is the height at right angles to that and the opposite side.

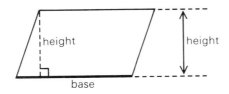 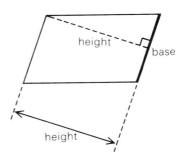

Examples

4 If $BE = 6$ cm, find the area of the triangle ABC and the length of AD.

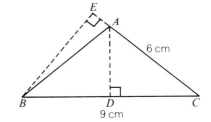

Area $= \frac{1}{2}bh$

$\quad = \frac{1}{2} \times AC \times BE$

$\quad = \frac{1}{2} \times 6 \times 6 \;\; cm^2$

$\quad = 18\,cm^2$

But, area $= \frac{1}{2} \times BC \times AD$

so, $18 = \frac{1}{2} \times 9 \times AD$ (AD in cm)

$\quad\; 36 = 9 \times AD$

$\quad\; AD = 4\,cm$

5 Find the area of the parallelogram $ABCD$ and the length of BC.

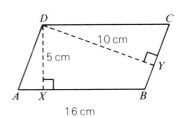

Area $= bh$

$\quad = AB \times DX$

$\quad = 16 \times 5 \;\; cm^2$

$\quad = 80\,cm^2$

But, area $= BC \times DY$

$\quad\quad 80 = BC \times 10$ (BC in cm)

$\quad\quad BC = 8\,cm$

Exercise 6.1

1. Find the areas of these figures.

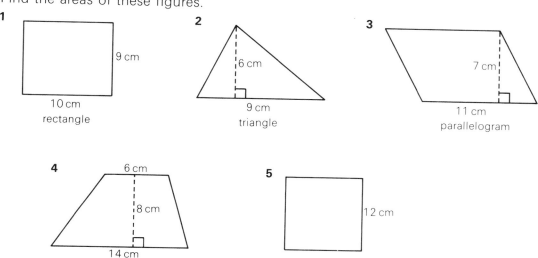

1

9 cm

10 cm

rectangle

2

6 cm

9 cm

triangle

3

7 cm

11 cm

parallelogram

4

6 cm

8 cm

14 cm

trapezium

5

12 cm

square

2. **1** Find the area of the parallelogram.
    2 Find the value of x.

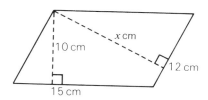

10 cm

x cm

12 cm

15 cm

3. Find the areas of these triangles.

1

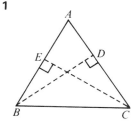

A

E D

B C

2

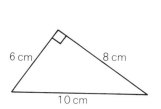

6 cm   8 cm

10 cm

3

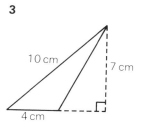

10 cm   7 cm

4 cm

$AB = \mathbf{7\,cm},\ BD = \mathbf{6\,cm},\ CE = \mathbf{5\,cm}$

4.   The inside rectangle has measurements
      8 cm by 5 cm.
      The shaded border is 1 cm wide.
      Find the area of the border.

5.   A square with edge 2 cm is cut from the
      rectangle.
      What is the area of the remaining piece ?

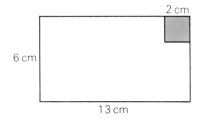

6.   Find the total area of the quadrilateral *ABCD*.

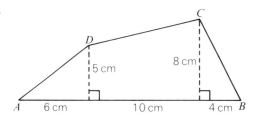

7.   *APCQ* is a parallelogram.
      Find its area.

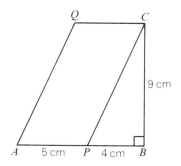

8. *ABCD* is a square of side 12 cm.
   1   Find its area.
   2   Find the areas of the shaded triangles.
   3   Hence, find the area of the
       quadrilateral *PQRS*.

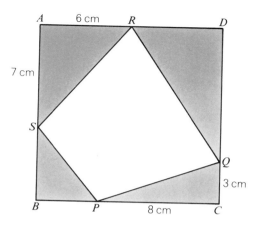

9. Construct accurately a triangle with sides 10 cm, 9 cm and 8 cm.
   By constructing another line on the diagram, find a measurement for calculating
   the area of the triangle, and find the area, correct to 0.1 cm².

Volumes

When we measure volume we compare it with a unit volume.
We use the volume of a cube of side 1 cm for the unit.
This is called 1 cubic centimetre and written as 1 cm³, sometimes as
1 cc.

If we are measuring larger volumes we compare them with 1 cubic metre (1 m³).

Volume formulae

Volume of a cuboid = length × breadth × height
               = *lbh*
Volume of a cube = (length)³ = *l*³

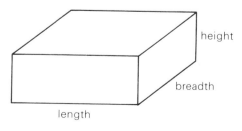

$V = lbh$

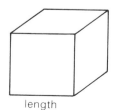

$V = l^3$

Solid figures of uniform cross-section

This figure is built with 1 cm cubes.
Its base covers an area of 6 cm^2.
When 1 layer of cubes is used, the height is
1 cm and the volume is 6 cm^3.
If there were 2 layers of cubes, the figure would
be 2 cm high and have volume 12 cm^3.
If there were 5 layers of cubes, the figure would
be 5 cm high and have
volume = 6 × 5 cm^3 = 30 cm^3.
Notice that the volume is found by multiplying
the area of the base by the height.
This formula applies to any solid figure of uniform
cross-section.
Uniform cross-section means that if you slice the
figure with parallel slices you get a surface of the same
shape and size.
All prisms are solid figures of uniform cross-section.
The height is the distance in the direction perpendicular to the cross-sectional area. It
is sometimes more convenient to call it length, depth or thickness.
e.g.

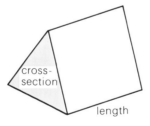
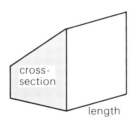
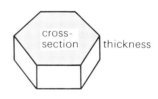

> Volume of solid of uniform cross-section
>   = area of cross-section × height

Examples

6 Find the volume of this prism.

Area of triangle = $\frac{1}{2}bh$
                    = $\frac{1}{2}$ × 7 × 6 cm^2
                    = 21 cm^2
Volume of prism = area of triangle × length
                    = 21 × 9 cm^3
                    = 189 cm^3

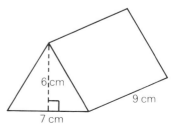

Surface area

7 Find the total surface area of this prism.

There are 5 surfaces; 2 triangles and
3 rectangles.

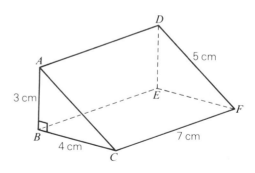

Area of triangle ABC $= \frac{1}{2}bh$
$= \frac{1}{2} \times 4 \times 3 \text{ cm}^2$
$= 6 \text{ cm}^2$
Area of triangle DEF $= 6 \text{ cm}^2$
Area of rectangle $BCFE = lb$
$= 7 \times 4 \text{ cm}^2$
$= 28 \text{ cm}^2$
Area of rectangle $ABED = 7 \times 3 \text{ cm}^2$
$= 21 \text{ cm}^2$
Area of rectangle $ACFD = 7 \times 5 \text{ cm}^2$
$= 35 \text{ cm}^2$
Total surface area $= (6 + 6 + 28 + 21 + 35) \text{ cm}^2$
$= 96 \text{ cm}^2$

Tables

If you have to change area or volume units, for example, from mm^2 to cm^2, you must
know the connection.

Area tables

Since 10 mm = 1 cm,
$100 \text{ mm}^2 = 1 \text{ cm}^2$ (10 × 10)

Since 100 cm = 1 m,
$10\,000 \text{ cm}^2 = 1 \text{ m}^2$ (100 × 100)

Since 1000 m = 1 km,
$1\,000\,000 \text{ m}^2 = 1 \text{ km}^2$ (1000 × 1000)

A unit for measuring land is a hectare, which is
an area of $10\,000 \text{ m}^2$.
So 100 hectares = 1 km²

Volume tables

Since 10 mm = 1 cm,
   $1000 \, mm^3 = 1 \, cm^3$ (10 × 10 × 10)

Since 100 cm = 1 m,
$1\,000\,000 \, cm^3 = 1 \, m^3$ (100 × 100 × 100)

Remember that 1 litre = $1000 \, cm^3$,
So   1000 litres = $1 \, m^3$

Also, $1 \, cm^3$ of water weighs 1 gram.
1 litre of water or $1000 \, cm^3$ of water weighs 1 kg.

1 cm³

Examples

8   Find the area of this rectangle.

Working in cm:
$A = lb$
   $= 155 \times 36 \; cm^2$
   $= 5580 \, cm^2$
To get the answer in m^2, divide by 10 000
   $= 0.558 \, m^2$

Or, working in metres:
$A = 1.55 \times 0.36 \; m^2$
   $= 0.558 \, m^2$

36 cm

155 cm

9   A tank is 2 m long, 1.5 m wide and 80 cm deep. How many litres of water will it hold ?

Working in cm:
Volume = lbh
          $= 200 \times 150 \times 80 \; cm^3$
          $= 2\,400\,000 \, cm^3$
To find how many litres, divide by 1000. (1 ℓ = $1000 \, cm^3$)
The tank will hold 2400 litres.

Or, working in metres:
Volume = $2 \times 1.5 \times 0.8 \; m^3$
          $= 2.4 \, m^3$
To find how many litres, multiply by 1000. (1 m^3 = 1000ℓ)
The tank will hold 2400 litres.

Exercise 6.2

1. Find the volumes of these solid figures.
    1 A rectangular box, 11 cm long, 8 cm wide and 5 cm high.
    2 A cube of edge 6 cm.
    3 A solid with uniform cross-section of area 15 cm² and height 3 cm.
    4 This triangular prism.   **5**   This 5-sided prism.

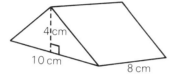
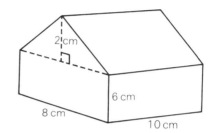

2. **1** If a cuboid has length 10 cm, width 7 cm and volume 280 cm³, what is
        its height ?
    2 If a cube has a volume of 343 cm³, what is the length of an edge ?

3. **1** Find the total surface area of a rectangular box with length 10 cm,
        width 9 cm and height 6 cm.
    2 Find the total surface area of a cube of edge 5 cm.

4. A water trough has the shape of a cuboid 2.5 m long and 80 cm wide. It is filled
    with water to a depth of 45 cm.
    Find the volume of water, **1** in cm³, **2** in m³, **3** in litres.

Exercise 6.3   Applications and Activities

1. *ABC* is a triangular field with
    measurements as shown.
    Find its area.
    A path crosses the field from *B* to the
    nearest part of the road.
    Use the area of the field to find the
    length of the path, to the nearest metre.

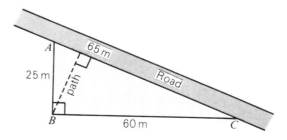

2.   A football ground is 200 m long and 160 m wide. The playing area is 108 m long
      and 90 m wide.
      1   What area is left around the pitch ?
      2   It is decided that it would be safe to allow 3 spectators for every m² of
             ground around the pitch.
             How many spectators can be accommodated, to the nearest 100 ?

3.   Barry's lawn is in the shape of a
      parallelogram.
      1   What is its area ?
      2   Barry wants to put fertilizer on the
             lawn and he needs 50 g for each
             square metre. How much fertilizer
             does he need ?
      3   He buys a 5 kg bag of fertilizer. How
             much fertilizer would be left over ?

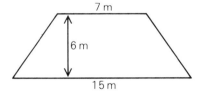

      4   The remaining fertilizer is spread over the flower-bed. How many grams/m²
             on average, to the nearest 10 g, is used there ?

4.   A railway embankment has the cross-
      sectional shape shown, and it is 400 m
      long.
      1   Find the area of the cross-section.
      2   Find the volume of material needed
             to make the embankment.

5.   Three metal cubes have edges 3 cm, 4 cm and 5 cm respectively. They are melted
      down and the metal is used to make one larger cube. How big is an edge of this
      cube ?

6.   A swimming pool is 1 m deep at the
      shallow end and 3 m deep at the deep
      end, with the bottom sloping evenly. The
      pool is 25 m long and 12 m wide.
      1   Find the area of the cross-section.
      2   Find the volume of the pool.
      3   How many litres of water are needed
             to fill the pool ?

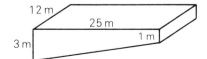

7. The diagram shows the end view of a wall of uniform cross-section with measurements as shown. The wall is 20 m long.

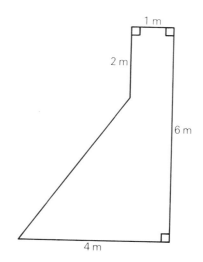

 1 Find the area of cross-section.
 2 Find the volume of the wall.
 3 The wall is made from material weighing 2.5 tonnes per m³. Find the weight of the wall, in tonnes.

8. Jim has made a stand to hold records underneath, and a fish tank on top.

He used sheets of chipboard.
The 7 pieces of chipboard used for the main part of the stand had these measurements:
1 piece is 76 cm by 34 cm,
2 pieces are 76 cm by 35 cm,
4 pieces are 34 cm by 33.5 cm.
The 4 pieces used for the hollow base had these measurements:
2 pieces are 72 cm by 11 cm,
2 pieces are 29 cm by 11 cm.
Find the total area of the 11 pieces of chipboard used, in m² to the nearest 0.1 m².

9. Design a simple bird box, rabbit hutch or something similar. Work out the amount of wood you will need.
Estimate the cost of making the object, by finding from a DIY store the cost of wood and any other materials you need.

10.   **A new garden**

This might be an imaginary garden at present, but that means you can organise it to your liking, and you do not need to worry about having to pay for it.
Decide on suitable measurements for the garden, and plan the design. You can consider having a patio, lawns, flower-beds, a vegetable plot, etc.
Design the garden and make a scale drawing of it.
Find the cost of such things as fencing, paths, lawns from seed or turf, plants and trees.
Other things to consider including are garden furniture, children's play equipment such as a swing or climbing frame, a pond and maybe goldfish in it.
Find the total cost of establishing your garden.

11.   Find the cost of decorating and furnishing a bedroom suitable for a teenager.
You can use one of the rooms in your house to give you suitable measurements. Decide what sort of bed you would have and where this would be placed. Make a scale drawing of the room and show the bedroom furniture on it.
Decide how much wallpaper would be needed to paper the walls, and how much paint would be needed to paint the woodwork and the ceiling.

Decide on the size of the carpet and the size of the curtains needed.
Decide what other furniture or fittings are needed.
Find the cost of all the items, from what is available in your local shops or in catalogues.
You can illustrate your work with drawings, or pictures cut from magazines or pamphlets.

12.   **The box problem**

You have a rectangular sheet of
cardboard, size 28 cm by 20 cm.
If you draw squares in the 4 corners, cut
along the **thick** lines and fold along the
dotted lines, you can form an open box.
(You can glue or staple the corner pieces
to the sides.)

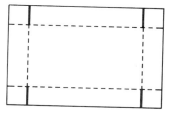

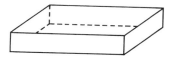

If you want the box to hold the greatest possible volume, what measurement
should you have for the sides of the squares ? If you make small squares, the
box is long and wide but not very high. If you make larger squares, the box is
taller but not so long and wide.
Investigate this problem using trial methods and give the answer correct to the
nearest mm.
Manufacturers have similar problems to consider, so that they can keep their
packaging costs down.

PUZZLES

16.   Of 100 applicants for a job it was discovered that 12 had no GSCE pass in either Maths
or Science. 74 had passed in Maths and 82 had passed in Science.
How many had GCSE passes in both Maths and Science ?

17.   Norrie caught 100 fish in 5 days, each day catching 6 more than on the previous day.
How many did he catch on each of the 5 days ?

18.   Here are some numbers in a popular quiz. Can you supply the missing words, whose
initial letters are given ?

  6 B in an O at C   15 RB in a F of S
  7 W of the W   21 'S on a D
  9 SS by a S in T   26 L in the A
10 GB (H on a W)   366 D in a LY
12 D of C   1000 M in a K

Miscellaneous Section A

Aural Practice

Often in life you will need to do quick calculations without using pencil and paper or calculator. Sometimes you will **see** the numbers written down, and sometimes you will just **hear** the questions. These aural exercises will give you some practice in **listening** to questions.

These aural exercises, A1 and A2, should be read to you, probably by your teacher or a friend, and you should write down the answers only, doing any working out in your head. You should do the 15 questions within 10 minutes.

Exercise A1

1. Write down the number which is exactly half-way between 70 and 100.

2. What is the volume of a cube of edge 3 cm ?

3. Simplify the expression $3x + 2y - 2x$.

4. What is the value of 0.8 × 0.3 ?

5. Two angles of an isosceles triangle are 35°. What size is the third angle ?

6. If the temperature is −4° and it rises by 7 degrees, what will it be then ?

7. The length of a piece of wood is given as two thousand, four hundred millimetres. Give this length in metres.

8. What is the numerical value of $2^3 × 3^2$?

9. A car does 32 miles to each gallon of petrol. How far will it travel using 5 gallons of petrol ?

10. What is the perimeter of a rectangle, 6 cm long and 5 cm wide ?

11. Find the solution of the equation $2x + 30 = 7x$.

12. A child drinks $\frac{1}{2}$ pint of milk each day. If milk costs 30 pence per pint, what is the cost for a fortnight ?

13. One representative is to be chosen at random, from 5 boys and 2 girls. What is the probability that the representative will be a girl ?

14. A metre of ribbon is cut into 4 equal pieces. How many centimetres long is each piece ?

15. Write down an approximate value for the answer to 49 × 51.

Exercise A2

1. Write down the next 2 numbers in the sequence 10, 17, 24, 31, . . .

2. Sally scores 7 out of 10 in a test. Express her score as a percentage.

3. A rope is 19.6 metres long. What length is this, to the nearest metre ?

4. What change should you get from £1 if you bought a magazine for 75 pence ?

5. Estimate the value of 2.9 × 11.1, giving the answer as a whole number.

6. If you turn up the top card of a shuffled pack of 52 cards, what is the probability that it will be a picture card, (Jack, Queen or King) ?

7. One lap of a training run is 500 metres. How many kilometres would an athlete run if he did 8 complete laps ?

8. A square has an area of 36 cm². What is the length of one side ?

9. Simplify the expression $x^3 \times x^2$.

10. What fraction of 1 kg is 200 grams ?

11. What is the name for a quadrilateral with all sides equal, but which has no right angles ?

12. How many minutes are there from five past three until quarter to four ?

13. What is the biggest number which divides exactly into both 24 and 32 ?

14. I thought of a number, multiplied it by 8, then I added on 9. The result was 25. What number did I think of ?

15. How many pieces of wire of length 0.8 metres can be cut from a roll of wire 4 metres long ?

Exercise A3   Revision

1.   Express these numbers in prime factors.
     1   75   **2**   108   **3**   132

2.   In the diagram, if $a = 42°$ and
      $b = 109°$, find the sizes of the
      angles c, d, e and f.

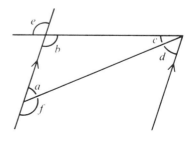

3.   Mr King's car will run for about 40 miles on one gallon of petrol, and petrol
      costs £2.20 per gallon. Find the approximate cost of the petrol needed for a
      journey of 500 miles.

4.   Without using your calculator, find the values of
      1 $0.9 + 0.4$ **4** $0.9 \div 0.4$
      2 $0.9 - 0.4$ **5** 0.9^2
      3 0.9×0.4

5.   Here are some loci drawn in ΔPQR. $PR = 10$ cm.

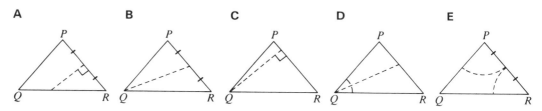

      Which diagram shows the locus of points inside the triangle satisfying these
      conditions:
      1   points equidistant from PQ and QR,
      2   points equidistant from the points P and R,
      3   points 5 cm from P or 5 cm from R ?

6.   If $a = 5$, $b = -2$ and $c = 3$, find the value of $2a^2 - 4bc$.

7.   George buys a television set which costs £360. He pays an initial payment of
      20% of the cost and arranges to pay the rest in 24 equal monthly instalments.
      What is the monthly instalment ?

8. The angles of a triangle are $(x + 18)°$, $(2x - 24)°$ and $(3x - 66)°$.
    Write down an equation involving x and solve it to find the value of x.
    Find the sizes of the 3 angles.
    What sort of triangle is it ?

9. 'Young children eat too many sweets.'
    Suppose you were testing this hypothesis, for children aged about 5, 6 or
    7 years old.
    1 Write down 5 questions you could use in a questionnaire. (You would ask
    the questions yourself and record the answers.)
    2 Say briefly how you could choose a suitable sample of children to ask.

10. Draw this parallelogram accurately.
    By drawing another line on the figure,
    find the measurements necessary to
    calculate the area of the parallelogram,
    and find the area, in cm^2, correct to
    1 decimal place.

    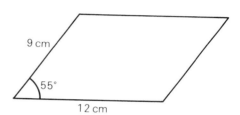

11. The distance s metres travelled by an object falling downwards is given by the
    formula $s = ut + \frac{1}{2}gt^2$, where u metres/second is the starting speed,
    t seconds is the time since the start,
    g m/s^2 is the acceleration due to gravity, and $g = 9.8$.
    An object is thrown downwards with starting speed 5.3 m/s. Use your calculator
    to find how far it has travelled in 2.5 seconds. (Put $t = 2.5$.)

12. Write down expressions for the nth terms of these sequences.

    1 20, 23, 26, 29, . . .
    2 49, 48, 47, 46, . . .
    3 3, 9, 27, 81, . . .

    4 $\frac{1}{2}, \frac{2}{3}, \frac{3}{4}, \frac{4}{5}, \ldots$

    5 $\frac{1}{2}, \frac{1}{4}, \frac{1}{8}, \frac{1}{16}, \ldots$

13. $ABCD$ is a square with diagonal AC.
    $\triangle CDE$ is isosceles with $CD = DE$.
    $\angle CDE = 40°$.
    Find the sizes of
    1 $\angle ACD$
    2 $\angle DCE$
    3 $\angle ACE$

    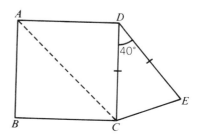

14. The bar chart shows how some money is
     divided among 3 departments A, B, C.
     The bar A is 14 cm long, B is 11 cm and
     C is 5 cm.
     If A's amount is £210, what are the
     amounts for B and C, and what is the
     total amount ?

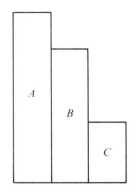

15. Simplify these expressions.

     1 $3a^3 \times 4a^4$ **4** $3d^2 \div 9d^3$

     2 $b^5 \div b^5$ **5** $e^4 + (e^2)^2$

     3 $(c^3)^4$

16. Four goats are tethered to posts at
     A, B, C and D and the boundaries of the
     regions they can graze are shown.
     Use the numbers to identify these
     regions:

     1 Which regions can be grazed both
          by goats tethered at A and by goats
          tethered at B ?

     2 Which region can be grazed by goats
          tethered at B and C only ?

     3 Which regions can be grazed by
          3 goats ?

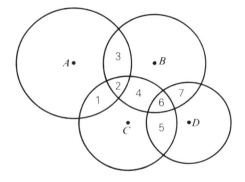

17. Parveen makes these statements.
     My height is 152 cm, to the nearest centimetre.
     My weight is 38 kg, to the nearest kg.
     My age is 12 years, to the nearest year.
     Give limits between which her height, weight and age must lie.

18. Three rods have lengths $(x + 9)$ cm, $(2x - 7)$ cm and $(6x - 5)$ cm.
     In terms of x,

     1 what is the total length of the 3 rods,

     2 what is the average length,

     3 how much longer is the 3rd rod than the 2nd one ?

19. In the diagram, find the size of ∠DAB.

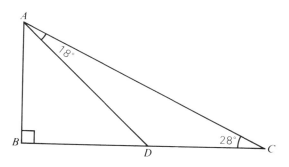

20. Water is flowing into a rectangular tank of length 50 cm and width 40 cm, at the rate of 160 cm³ per second. Find the rise in the water level in 5 minutes.

Exercise A4   Activities

1.   Designing a float for a carnival

Imagine that you and a group of friends have the chance to take part in a carnival procession. You will travel on a lorry, which you will decorate.

Decide on a theme. As a simple example, if you decided that your theme was 'There was an old woman who lived in a shoe', then one of you could be dressed as the old woman and the rest of you as her children. As scenery, you would need a large picture, or even a model, of the shoe. If your theme was 'Robin Hood', then you could have Robin, Maid Marian and the Merry Men, and the scenery would

be a picture of the forest with perhaps Nottingham Castle in the background. Draw a sketch of the scenery, and include the actual measurements which will be necessary. Draw a plan of the floor of the lorry, showing where the scenery and other items will be placed, and where certain people will sit or stand. The floor of the lorry is 5.5 m long and 2.2 m wide.

Draw sketches of the costumes to be used, and give a list of other items needed. Make a rough estimate of the costs of materials for the scenery and the costumes, and other items. You can assume that someone else will pay for hiring the lorry and for any necessary insurance.

2. **Pulleys and cogs**

In a simple pulley, you pull downwards on one side
of the rope and the load rises on the other side.
In the diagram, as you pull downwards, will the
pulley turn clockwise or anticlockwise ?
If you pull the rope downwards x metres, how far
will the load rise ?
The force needed to raise the load is equal to the
weight of the load. (This is ignoring extra force
needed to overcome the friction at the pulley.)

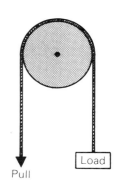

Here are some other systems of pulleys.

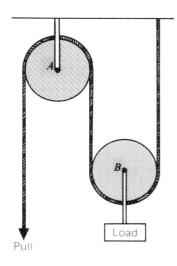

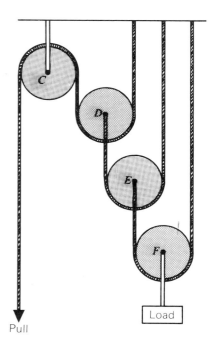

For these systems, as you pull downwards, will the pulleys turn clockwise or
anticlockwise ?
If you pull the rope down x metres, how far will the load rise ?
In the 1st arrangement, the force needed is $\frac{1}{2}$ the weight of the load.
In the 2nd arrangement, the force needed is $\frac{1}{8}$ the weight of the load.
(This is ignoring extra force needed because of friction and the weights of the
movable pulleys.)
Perhaps you can find out about other systems of pulleys and similar machines,
such as a block and tackle or a wheel and axle.

Cogs

These are used in gears.

Here is a simple gear
mechanism.

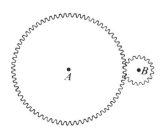

Here is a more complicated one.

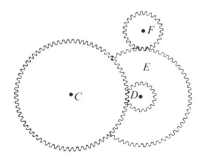

C turns *D*
D and *E* turn together
E turns *F*

If *A* and *C* turn clockwise, in which directions will the other cogs turn ?
If *A* has 60 teeth and *B* has 20 teeth, when *A* turns through 1 revolution, how
many turns will *B* make ?
If *C* has 80 teeth and *D* has 20 teeth, when *C* turns through 1 revolution how
many turns will *D* and *E* make ? If also *E* has 96 teeth and *F* has 32 teeth, how
many turns will *F* make ?
You can try to find out about the gears used on a bicycle.

3. **Ways of paying for goods and services**

Children know that to pay for something they must use money, but as you get older you learn that paying cash is not always the only option when you buy something. If you want to order something by post or phone, then it is not a good idea to send cash. What are the alternatives ?

It is not always sensible for adults to carry a large amount of cash, yet unforseen payments may be needed, for instance, if the car breaks down on a journey and has to be repaired.

Find out some details about the following methods, or any other methods you can think of, for paying for goods or services, and say what advantages or disadvantages they have over using cash:

Using cheques, using credit cards, having an account at a shop, using tokens such as TV licence stamps, paying by montly direct debit, paying by instalments, paying by COD (cash on delivery).

4. **Circumference and area of circles**

What is the relationship between the length of the diameter of a circle, or the radius, and its circumference?

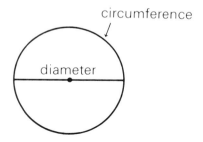

In a description of King Solomon's Temple, in Jerusalem, it is said...
'He also made the Sea of cast metal; it was round in shape, the diameter from rim to rim being ten cubits, and it took a line thirty cubits long to go round it.'
Thus it was thought that the circumference was three times as long as the diameter.

One way to investigate the relationship is to actually measure some circular objects. Choose 5 or 10 objects of different sizes, such as a coin, a tin of soft drink, a football, a bicycle wheel.
Sometimes you can measure the diameter directly. You will have to think out how to find the diameter of some things, such as a football. To measure the circumference of a tin, wrap a piece of string round it and then measure the length of the string. One way to measure the circumference of a coin is to roll it carefully, without it slipping, along the edge of a ruler. How can you measure the circumference of a bicycle wheel ?

Decide what units you are going to use, and how accurate your measurements should be. For small things you could measure in cm to the nearest mm. For larger objects you may prefer to measure to the nearest cm, or to 0.5 cm.

You are trying to find out if there is any relationship between circumference and diameter, so you need to work out circumference ÷ diameter, giving the answer correct to 2 decimal places. Set your results down in a table. One item has been given here, as an example.

Object	C	D	$\dfrac{C}{D}$ as a fraction	$\dfrac{C}{D}$ as a decimal
tin of soup	23.6 cm	7.5 cm	$\dfrac{23.6}{7.5}$	3.15

Study your results and comment on them. If the results in the last column are nearly the same, you could find the average of all these results.

Next, see if you can find out anything about the area of a circle.
You could draw circles of different sizes on graph paper and find their approximate areas by counting the small squares.
Here is another suggestion:
Draw a circle on paper and colour its circumference.
Cut it out and then cut it into 16 equal sectors.
You can find the lines to cut along by folding.
Cut it into 2 halves, then cut each half into 2, and so on.

You can rearrange the pieces, putting them point upwards and point downwards alternately. What approximate shape is made ?
How can you find its area ?
Will this help you to find a formula for the area of a circle in terms of its circumference and radius ?

Keep a copy of your work on circles as this forms an introduction to the work of Chapter 12.

5. **The regular solid figures**

The five regular solid figures are
Tetrahedron
Octahedron
Icosahedron
Cube
Dodecahedron
They were known from the days of Ancient Greece.
Later on, 4 other regular solid figures were discovered.
These are called the Kepler-Poinsot solid figures.
The 2 shown here were discovered by Kepler (1571–1630). Here are instructions for constructing them using thin cardboard.

The great stellated dodecahedron

The star points are made from this pattern.
(If you alter the measurements keep them
in the same proportion. The short lines are
0.618 × the longer lines.)
Draw the pattern on tracing paper and
transfer the main points onto cardboard by
pricking them through using the point of
your compasses.
You need 20 pieces altogether.

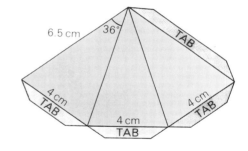

(A quicker way to get the pieces is to photocopy the pattern 3 times so that you have 4 patterns altogether. Stick these onto a sheet of A4 paper. Then use this sheet to photocopy onto A4 cardboard.)

Score along the lines, cut out, and bend the lines away from the side they were scored on.
Make the point by glueing the long tab.
To put the points together you can, if you wish, begin by making a regular icosahedron, and then glueing a point onto each face.
However, it is not necessary to use an icosahedron. Just glue 2 points together using a tab of each. Then glue a 3rd point to one of them, a 4th point to the 3rd point, and make a closed 5-pointed cluster by glueing a 5th point to the 4th point and to the 1st point.
Now you can glue more points onto the 3rd tabs left on these pieces, and build up more clusters of 5 points.
Continue in this way, completing the star.

For the last star point, alter it to make a piece like this, and glue it into its triangular hole.

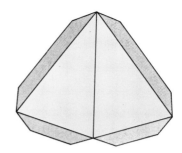

Then add a single face like this.

You will notice that there are 12 star pentagons (pentagrams) intersecting each other. Each pentagram has one parallel to it on the other side. You can paint this pair using the same colour, thus using 6 colours altogether, or you may prefer a different colour scheme.

The small stellated dodecahedron

Make this model in a similar way. Here is the pattern for a star point, and you need 12 of them.
You can make a regular dodecahedron to stick them onto, or you can just stick them together using their tabs.
A 3rd point will be fastened to both the 1st 2 points. Again, you can fix the last point in a different way.
Paint the model to match the other one.

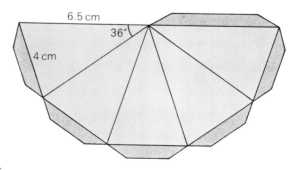

The instructions for the other two Kepler-Poinsot models will be given later.

6. **Making a slide rule**

Before the present calculators were available, about 20 years ago, the methods used as short cuts for multiplying, dividing, finding squares and square roots, etc., were to use a slide rule or tables of logarithms. Both of these were based on the rules of indices. (To multiply numbers, you add the indices, e.g. $10^3 \times 10^2 = 10^{2+3} = 10^5$. It is easier to add than to multiply, and easier to subtract than to divide.)

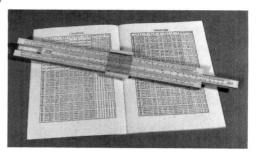

Making a simple slide rule which will add

Use two strips of cardboard, just over 20 cm long.
Label the strips from 0 to 8, with numbers 2.5 cm apart.

A	0	1	2	3	4	5	6	7	8

B	0	1	2	3	4	5	6	7	8

To add (say) 5 + 3, slide strip *B* along until its 0 is opposite the 5 of *A*. Then opposite the 3 of *B* is the answer on *A*, 8.
Practise adding some other numbers.
How would you use the slide rule to subtract ?

Making a slide rule which will multiply

We will use powers of 2.
Since $2^1 = 2$, we replace 1 on the scales above by 2.
Since $2^2 = 4$, we replace 2 on the scales above by 4.
Since $2^3 = 8$, we replace 3 on the scales above by 8, and so on.
We also replace 0 by 1.
Make new strips with these numbers.

A	1	2	4	8	16	32	64	128	256

B	1	2	4	8	16	32	64	128	256

To multiply (say) 32 × 8, slide strip **B** along until its 1 is opposite the 32 of **A**.
Then opposite the 8 of **B** is the answer on **A**, 256.
What you have done is actually

$$32 \times 8 = 2^5 \times 2^3 = 2^{5+3} = 2^8 = 256$$

Practise multiplying some more numbers shown on the scales.
Perhaps you can also use the slide rule to divide.

Now a slide rule which is only marked with powers of 2 is not much use.
The positions of the other numbers would have to be worked out. It is too
complicated at this stage to explain how to work them out but if you would like
to put more numbers on your scale you can use your calculator, and a new key
Ln, to find out how far to put any number from 1. (These distances assume that
the distance between 1 and 2 is 2.5 cm.)
First, press 2.5 ÷ 2 Ln = This gives 3.606... Put this number into the memory.
Then, for the distance of any number from 1, in cm, press RM × number Ln =
e.g. for the distance of 3 from 1, press
RM × 3 Ln = and the answer is 4.0 cm, to the nearest mm.
You can put numbers such as 3, 5, 6, 7, 9, 10, 12, 20, 25, 30, 40, 50, 60, 80,
100, 150, 200 on your scale, and then try other questions, such as 3 × 4, 12 × 5,
10 × 20.

7. **Patterns from Powers**

Copy and fill in this table for powers of numbers from 0 to 9.

n	n^2	n^3	n^4	n^5
0				
1				
...				
9				

Make another copy of the table, but write the units figures only. (These are the
remainders each time when the numbers are divided by 10.)
Look for patterns in the table, and write about them.

Make another table, leaving out the last row and this time writing the remainders
when the numbers are divided by 9. (What is a quick way to find these
remainders ?)
Look for patterns in this table, compare them with the other table, and write
about them.
You can continue this investigation by making tables for the remainders when the
numbers are divided by 8 (leaving out another row), 7, 6, 5, 4, 3 and 2, and
comparing them.

8. ## Squares and triangles

Slanted squares on squared paper

To draw the square $ABCD$, starting with
side AB:
The slope from A to B is 'down 2 units
and along 5 units'.
From B go along 2 and up 5 to find C.
From C go up 2 and backwards 5 to find D.
From D, if you go backwards 2 and
down 5 you get back to A.

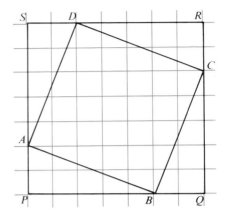

To calculate the area of the square $ABCD$, if the small squares have edge 1 cm:
area of square $PQRS$ = 7 × 7 cm^2 = 49 cm^2
area of $\triangle ABP = \frac{1}{2} × 2 × 5$ cm^2 = 5 cm^2
There are 4 congruent triangles altogether.
area of 4 triangles = 5 × 4 cm^2 = 20 cm^2
So area of square $ABCD$ = (49 − 20) cm^2 = 29 cm^2

Squares on the sides of right-angles triangles

Now draw a right-angled triangle on
squared paper, with AC = 2 cm and
AB = 5 cm.
Draw squares on each side of the triangle
and calculate their areas.
Write the results in a table.
Repeat with different right-angled
triangles, keeping the lengths of AC and
AB as whole numbers of cm.

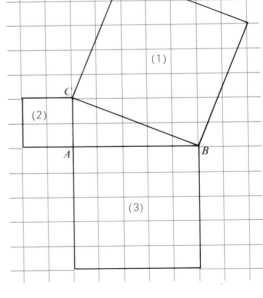

Area (1)	Area (2)	Area (3)
29	4	25

(in cm^2)

Can you discover any relationship between the areas ?

9. ## Sums of sequences

If there is a sequence of numbers which follow a mathematical rule then we can often find a pattern in the sums of terms of the sequence.

A sequence whose terms increase by a fixed number

e.g. Find the sum of the first 20 terms of the sequence 7, 10, 13, 16, . . .

The nth term is $3n + 4$
The 20th term is $(3 \times 20) + 4 = 64$
To find the sum of 20 terms:
Let the sum be s

$s = \quad 7 + 10 + 13 + 16 + \ldots + 61 + 64$
Now write the sequence backwards.
$s = \quad 64 + 61 + 58 + 55 + \ldots + 10 + \quad 7$
Now add together the last two lines, working downwards in columns.
$2s = 71 + 71 + 71 + 71 + \ldots + 71 + 71$
There are 20 terms, so
$2s = 20 \times 71 = 1420$
$\quad s = 710$

Use this method to find the sums of these sequences.

1	5, 10, 15, . . .	to 18 terms
2	1, 8, 15, . . .	to 10 terms
3	3, 7, 11, . . .	to 50 terms
4	90, 88, 86, . . .	to 40 terms
5	1, 2, 3, . . .	to 100 terms

Can you find a formula for the sum s of the 1st n whole numbers,
e.g. $1 + 2 + 3 + \ldots + n$?
You can also investigate the sum of the first n odd numbers.

10.   **Using a computer**

You probably have the use of a computer
at school, and you may also have a
computer at home. You can use a
computer in many ways to link with the
mathematics you are studying.

Nowadays there are commercial packages,
which you may have available, to give you
further practice in basic ideas, or to lead
you on to further investigations. Also, you
may write simple programs for yourself if
you are interested in programming.

Here are some suggestions for ways in which computer programs can be used in
the work of the first part of the book.

Finding the prime factors of a number.
Finding all the factors of a number.
Finding the highest common factor of two numbers.

Plotting various loci on the screen, and showing where two loci intersect.

Printing terms of a sequence, given the formula for the nth term.
Printing terms of sequences made by certain rules. You can then study these
sequences. E.g. What happens to a sequence when you begin with any two
numbers and each new term is the average of the last two preceding numbers ?

Investigating the reciprocals of whole numbers, to see which are exact decimals,
and to study the various recurring patterns of the others.

Putting a questionnaire on the screen, to be answered by pressing certain keys,
and analysing the results.

Finding areas and volumes of various figures by inputting the type of figure and
the necessary measurements.
Investigating what happens to area or volume when changes are made in the
measurements of a figure.

Here is an example of a simple program of the type you can write for yourself. It was written to find out whether any triangular numbers are also square numbers.

```
10 REM: TO FIND TRIANGULAR NUMBERS WHICH ARE SQUARES
20 INPUT N
30 LET T = 0
40 FOR C = 1 TO N
50 LET T = T + C
60 IF SQR(T) = INT(SQR(T)) THEN PRINT T
70 NEXT C
```

You can enter this program on your computer, and by putting $N = 100$ you can find out which of the first 100 triangular numbers are also square numbers.
You can alter line 60 so that the program will print all the triangular numbers, and you can do further investigations on them.

PUZZLES

19. The 11 players in a football team were on their way home late at night when their minibus broke down and they went into a hotel to get accommodation for the night. The hotel manager had only 10 empty rooms left, and each man wanted a separate room. However, the manager solved the problem in this way.
First, he put 2 men in room 1, promising that he would come back for the extra man later.
Then he put the 3rd man in room 2, the 4th man in room 3, the 5th man in room 4, the 6th man in room 5, the 7th man in room 6, the 8th man in room 7, the 9th man in room 8 and the 10th man in room 9.
Then he went back to get the extra man he had left in room 1, and put him in room 10. Everybody was happy.
Or were they ?

20. Mr Allen, Mr Barnes, Mr Curtis and Mr Dakin are an architect, a builder, a caterer and a decorator, but I can't remember who is which. One day I asked them, and to tease me they each gave me two pieces of information. When I said that their information did not seem to make sense, they admitted that they had each made one false and one true statement, but they would not tell me which was which.
Mr Allen said, 'Mr Dakin is a decorator and Mr Curtis is a caterer'.
Mr Barnes said, 'I am a builder and Mr Allen is a caterer'.
Mr Curtis said, 'Mr Allen is a decorator and and I am a builder'.
Mr Dakin said, 'I am a caterer and Mr Barnes is an architect'.

What are their professions ?

7 Thinking about estimating probabilit

Planning ahead

Always, in life, we are planning ahead. We base our plans on
(1) what is certain, or almost certain, to happen,
(2) what will probably happen,
(3) what is unlikely to happen,
(4) what is certain not to happen, or extremely unlikely to happen.

It is almost certain that Dad will get promotion at work, next year.

It is unlikely that we will visit our relations in Australia next year.

It is extremely unlikely that our house will be struck by lightning next year.

It is quite likely that my sister will get married next year

Travel and safety

In transport, appropriate safety measures have to be designed so that the probability of accidents is very small.

Railways are very safe, and there is constant research to make then even safer.

Commercial flying is also a very safe form of transport. There are strict checks on the airworthiness of planes. Air traffic control monitors all planes in the air.

The weather at sea can be unpredictable. Fog and storms are great hazards. Nowadays there is help from
  radio contact
  radar
  better design of ships
  adequate lifeboat provision

There is so much traffic on our roads nowadays that much thought is given as to how to reduce the chance of accidents.
- Seat belts
- Speed limits
- Crash helmets
- MOT tests
- Driving tests
and so on.

Estimating Probability

Probability is the likelihood of an event happening, for example, a trial being successful.

It is measured on a numerical scale from 0 to 1, and can be given as a fraction, a decimal or a percentage.

Relative frequency

If we have an ordinary die, we know that if the die is a fair one we expect each number to appear on approximately $\frac{1}{6}$ of the total number of throws. We say that the probability of each number occurring is $\frac{1}{6}$.

Maybe we suspect that the die we are using is not completely fair and does not give enough sixes. We can test whether it is fair by throwing it a large number of times and seeing how many times a six occurs.

The fraction $\dfrac{\text{number of throws giving a six}}{\text{total number of throws}}$ is called the **relative frequency** of the

number six, and gives an estimate of the probability of getting a six. To get a reliable estimate the number of throws must be quite large, at least 500 or, better still, 1000.

An experiment

Make a die for yourself which is not a perfect one.

If you make it out of wood, you can make it slightly cuboid or round some edges more than others. If you make it out of cardboard from its net, the tabs and glue which are on some edges will make it slightly uneven, and you can stick some extra weight, such as blu-tack, inside one face. Number it so that the numbers on opposite faces add up to 7.

You are trying to find the probability of each score.

Throw the die 500 times and record the results in a grid.

First, use the results to estimate the probability of throwing a six.

Make a table like this, working out the results after every 50 throws.

number of trials (n)	number of sixes (r)	fraction $\dfrac{r}{n}$	$\dfrac{r}{n}$ to 2 decimal places
50			
100			
150			
200			
. . .			
500			

You can show the results on a line-graph.

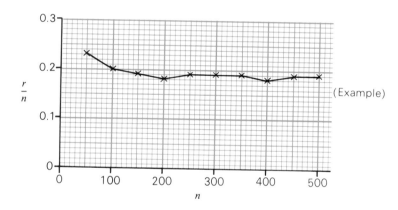

(Example)

Although the results may be erratic at first they should settle down around a certain value in the long run.

$$\text{The probability of a six} = \frac{\text{number of sixes}}{\text{total number of throws}} = \ldots$$

We can only use this definition of probability if we do enough trials to show that the fraction is settling down to a steady value. If the event is unpredictable the fraction would not settle down and we could not find a value for the probability.

Use your results to estimate the probabilities of throwing the other numbers 1, 2, 3, 4 and 5.
(What is the sum of all the probabilities ?)
Do you think your die is biased (unfair) ?

Subjective estimates

Probability may be worked out using the formula

$$\text{probability} = \frac{\text{number of successful outcomes}}{\text{number of equally likely outcomes}}$$

If it is not possible to use that formula it can be estimated by finding the relative frequency.

$$\text{Probability} = \frac{\text{number of successful trials}}{\text{total number of trials}}$$

provided that the number of trials is large, and the fraction settles down to a steady value.

But there are many times in life when we have to estimate the probability or chance of something happening, and we cannot use calculation.

e.g. What is the probability that this year there will be a White Christmas ?
(This means that there will be snow on Christmas Day.)
Now if you live in Northern Canada, you might estimate the probability as 1 (certain to happen), and if you live in the Sahara Desert you might estimate the probability as 0 (certain not to happen).

If you live in Southern England, and there has never been snow on Christmas Day for many years, you may think that there is a very slight chance, and estimate the probability as 0.1, or 0.05.

If you live in the Scottish Highlands, and most years there has been snow, you might estimate the probability as 0.8, 0.9 or 0.95.

For other parts of Britain you might make estimates at some other point on the probability scale. If you think there is an even chance, the probability will be 0.5. If it is more likely to snow than not, the probability will be over 0.5. And so on...

Some people may have a bet on an outcome such as this.

For other people, the result is more serious. Shepherds have to make sure the sheep are safe. Transport authorities have to keep their vehicles running, and people planning journeys may have to change their plans.

You learn about probability by doing simple experiments with coins, dice, cards, etc. but probability is an important subject, and affects all our lives.

Exercise 7.1

Here are some suggestions for experiments for finding probability using relative frequency.

1. Repeat the dice experiment with a properly manufactured die and decide whether it is a fair one. (If you have already collected results from throwing a die, you can use those results.)

2. What is the probability of a car, chosen at random from traffic on a main road, being less than 2 years old ?

    (Since the way you can tell the age of a car is by looking at the year letter on the number plate, and the letters change in August each year, you can adjust the time according to when you are doing the experiment.
    e.g. If doing it in March, find the probability that a car is less than 1 year 7 months old.)

You may like to make a guess first, giving the answer as a decimal.

Then collect some results from the cars on the road, recording 'new' or 'old' for every car as it passes you. Get 500 results if you can, or as many as there are in the time you have available. Ignore cars which do not have a normal number-plate.

Use the formula

$$\text{Probability} = \frac{\text{number of cars less than 2 years old}}{\text{total number of cars}}$$

Compare your answer with your guess and comment about these.

It is not easy to find the theoretical probability for this question. If you know the total number of car licences issued, and also the total number of cars sold in the last 2 years, you can estimate the proportion of new cars on the road. However, this might not match the proportion of new cars in your area.
You might think that your answer depends on when you do your surveying. There may be different proportions of newer cars in the rush-hour periods when workers are travelling to and from work, than in the middle of the day. Also the proportions may change at weekends. You can do further experiments to see if this is so.

3. What is the probability of getting 2 heads when 2 coins are tossed ?
    You may have collected results from tossing coins. If so, take them in two's, to
    represent two coins.

    H ‿ H   T ‿ H   H ‿ T   H ‿ H   T ‿ T   T ‿ H
      ✓   ✗   ✗   ✓   ✗   ✗

    If not, carry out the experiment.
    You need 500 results, if possible.
    Make a table and draw a line-graph, as in the dice experiment.

    The probability of 2 heads $= \dfrac{\text{number of times 2 heads occurs}}{\text{total number of tosses of 2 coins}}$.

    When you have carried out the experiment, work out the theoretical probability.
    Show in a table all possible equally likely outcomes when 2 coins are tossed.

    Use the formula

    $\text{Probability} = \dfrac{\text{number of successful outcomes}}{\text{total number of outcomes}}$.

    Compare the experimental result with the theoretical one, and comment about
    this.
    (Do not worry if they do not match exactly. Some results can be 'too good to be
    true'. However, if they differ widely, perhaps you are not tossing the coins fairly.)

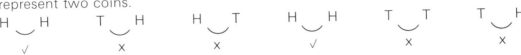

Exercise 7.2   Applications and Activities

1. Here are some more suggestions for experiments. After carrying out the
    experiment with as many trials as you have time for, work out the estimated
    probability. Then work out the theoretical probability and compare the results.

    1 Get a collection of random numbers up to 100.
        01 counts as 1, 02 as 2, etc. and count 00 as 100.
        (Use the phone book, a set of random number tables, or a computer.)
        Find the probability that a number up to 100, chosen at random, is a
        prime number.

    2 Collect a set of numbers up to 999 by looking at car number plates. If a
        number has more than 3 figures just write down the last 3.
        Find the probability that a number up to 999 is divisible by 9.
        (What is the quick way to tell if a number is divisible by 9 ?).

3 Toss sticks over a set of parallel lines.
Use the floorboards of the room if they are suitable, or make a set of parallel lines on the floor or on a table. Choose sticks all of the same length, and of length about $\frac{3}{4}$ of the distance between the lines. You can throw several sticks after each other as long as they land in different places and do not interfere with each other. They may land either across (or touching) a line, or they may land completely between the lines.
Find the probability that a stick will land across (or touching) a line.

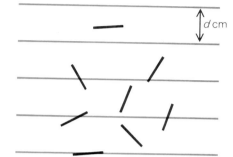

To find the theoretical probability, measure the length of a stick (s cm), and the distance between the lines (d cm). The probability is worked out using the formula

Probability $= \dfrac{2s}{\pi d}$. This is approximately $\dfrac{0.6366s}{d}$.

2. Here are some experiments where you cannot find the theoretical probability. Devise and carry out the experiments with as many trials as you have time for, and work out the estimated probability. You may like to make a guess first, and then see how close your guess was.

1 What is the probability of a car chosen at random from the cars on a main road being a Ford (or any other make you prefer, or of it being a red car) ?

2 What is the probability of the bus you normally catch to get to school being late ?

3 If you tip drawing-pins onto the floor or table from a height of $\frac{1}{2}$ metre, they can either land point upwards ⊥ or on their side ∡. What is the probability of a drawing-pin landing point upwards ?
You can also try this from different heights, as long as you do not scatter the drawing pins all over the floor, or try tipping them onto different types of surfaces, to see if the probabilities are different.

4 Get a large collection of coloured beads of which a certain (unknown) proportion are red. Put them in a bag and draw them out 10 at a time. (You should really take them out one at a time, but with a large number the result will not be affected by taking out 10 at once.) Record how many beads are red, replace them and mix them up before taking another 10 out. If you have not got any beads, use marbles, discs, cardboard squares or any collection of suitable items.
Find the probability that if a bead is drawn out of the bag at random it is red.

3.   Here are some statements. Some of them may not apply to you, or they may be
      certainties. Choose 5 statements from the rest and put them in order of likelihood.
      Then decide which probabilities are less than 0.5 and which are greater than 0.5.
      Finally, give estimated probabilities for them.

      (a) During the next month, you will do better in Maths.
      (b) During the next month, you will get some new shoes.
      (c) During the next year, you will move house.
      (d) During the next month, you will make a new friend.
      (e) For your next holiday you will go abroad.
      (f) Next weekend the weather will be fine.
      (g) During the next fortnight, you will be bitten by a dog.
      (h) During the next year, your parents will get a new car.
      (i) During the next year, you will get a new bicycle.
      (j) During the next month, you will do well in some sporting event.
      (k) Make up your own statement.

4.   **For group work**

      1   Choose 5 friends to run an obstacle
            race. Plan the obstacles they have to
            overcome. Estimate the probability of
            each one winning, as a percentage.
            (What is the total of the percentages ?)
            Then run the race and compare your
            predictions with the actual result.

      2   Choose 5 friends to enter a quiz contest. Make up some questions, and
            estimate the probability of each person winning.
            Then hold the contest and compare your predictions with the actual result.

      3   Invent a job, e.g. shop assistant. Choose 5 people to apply for the job.
            Estimate the probability of each one getting the job.
            Then interview each person and decide who would be the most suitable
            applicant. Compare your predictions with the actual choice.

5.   What is the probability of a newborn baby being a boy, or a girl ? Is it 0.5 for each ?

You could look at the births' column in the local paper for several days, or you may be able to obtain the actual figures for the district. The figures for the country are also published annually. (In 1976, in the UK there were 347 thousand boys and 328 thousand girls born.)

6.   Look in newspapers and magazines for examples of probabilities quoted.
Cut these out and arrange them on a poster, together with illustrations.

7.   Give each member of the class a random number. The numbers should be from a list of random numbers up to 100.
See how closely experimental results match theoretical ones in these and similar cases.

   1   There is a 50% chance that...
   you have a number greater than 50, or
   you have a number whose 10's figure is odd.
   Count how many of the class have numbers greater than 50.
   Then count how many of the class have numbers whose 10's figure is odd.
   See what proportion of the class are selected each time, and see how the actual results match the theoretical probability of 50%.

   2   Repeat with other probabilities, such as:
   There is a 0.3 chance that...
   you have a number between 1 and 30 inclusive, or
   you have a number ending with 7, 8 or 9, or
   you have a 2-figure number which divides by 3.

You will see the variation which can occur between the theoretical results and the actual proportions when you are using a fairly small sample (your class size).

PUZZLES

21.   The railway line from Ayling to Beeton is 48 km long.
Including Ayling and Beeton there are 9 stations at equal intervals. A train travelled from the 3rd station to the 6th station in 20 minutes. What was its average speed ?

22.   'How old are you, Grandad ?'
'Well,' said Grandad, 'if you multiply a sixth of my age by a ninth of my age you will find how old I will be in 24 years, if I should live so long.'
How old is Grandad ?

8 Thinking about inequalities and

Inequalities in life

We find that, in life, things are more often unequal than equal.

'I can't run as fast as you.'
'My dad is cleverer than your dad.'
'I get less pocket money than you do.'
'I'm bigger than you.'
'You're older than her, you should have more sense!'
'The grass is often greener on the other side of the fence.'

A small effort can move a big slab

Regions do not have equal areas, populations, temperatures, etc.

flow diagrams

Animal, vegetable or mineral ?

Choose one of these objects and let your friend discover which one by following the flow diagram. Answer the questions at each stage with 'Yes' or 'No'.

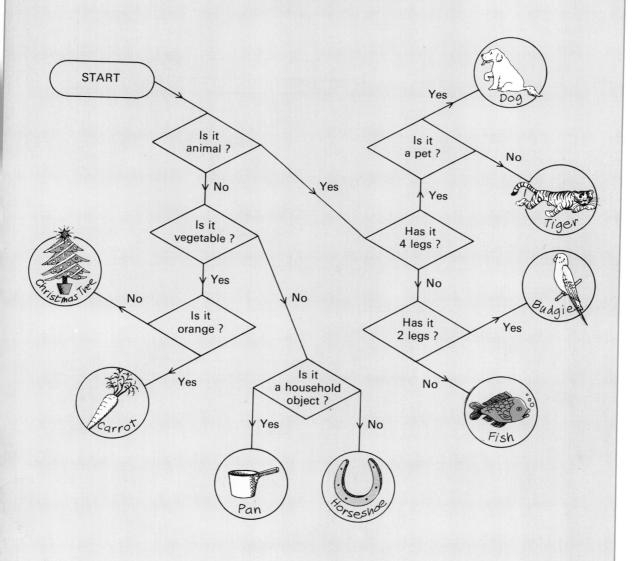

You can make a similar game for yourself.

8 Inequalities and flow diagrams

Inequalities

Here are some inequalities shown on number lines.

1 x is greater than 2
$x > 2$

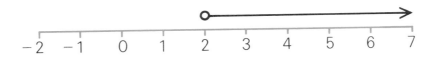

If x is a whole number, then possible values of x are 3, 4, 5, 6, 7, . . .

If x is any real number, then possible values of x include any numbers greater than 2.
One possible number is 2.00001, another is 2.00000001.
You can see that we can use numbers very close to 2, and that is why we have drawn the numbers starting from 2.
We have drawn an open circle at 2 to signify that the number 2 is not included.

2 x is greater than 2 or equal to 2
$x \geqslant 2$

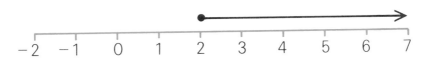

If x is a whole number, then possible values of x are 2, 3, 4, 5, 6, 7, . . .

If x is any real number, then possible values of x include any numbers from 2 upwards.
We have drawn a filled-in circle at 2 to signify that the number 2 is included.

3 x is greater than -4
$x > -4$

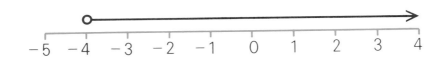

If x is a whole number, then possible values of x are -3, -2, -1, 0, 1, 2, 3, . . .

If x is any real number, then possible values of x include any numbers greater than -4.

4 x is less than 3

$x < 3$

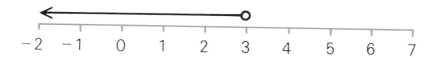

If x is a whole number, then possible values of x are 2, 1, 0, -1, -2, -3, . . .

If x is a positive whole number, then the only possible values of x are 2 and 1.

If x is any real number, then possible values of x include any numbers less than 3. One possible number is 2.999, another is 2.999999.
You can see that we can use numbers very close to 3, and that is why we have drawn the numbers starting, on the right, with 3, but with an open circle at 3 to signify that 3 is not included.

5 x is less than -1 or equal to -1

$x \leqslant -1$

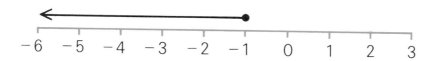

Symbols

$<$ is the symbol for 'is less than'.
$>$ is the symbol for 'is greater than'.
$\leqslant$ is the symbol for 'is less than or equal to'.
$\geqslant$ is the symbol for 'is greater than or equal to'.

Examples

1 $-2 < x < 4$

2 $x \leqslant -1$ or $x \geqslant 3$

3 If x is a whole number, what are the possible values of x if $-1 \leqslant x < 4$?

$-1 \leqslant x < 4$ means $-1 \leqslant x$ and $x < 4$, i.e. $x \geqslant -1$ **and** $x < 4$

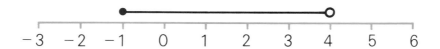

x is greater than or equal to -1
x is less than 4
The possible values of x are -1, 0, 1, 2, 3.

Exercise 8.1

1. Describe these statements in words.

    1 $x > 4$ **4** $0 < x < 3$
    2 $x \leqslant 7$ **5** $x \geqslant -2$
    3 $x < -3$

2. Write these statements in symbols.

    1 x is less than 5
    2 x is greater than or equal to -4
    3 x is greater than 0
    4 x is less than 10 but greater than -2
    5 x is less than or equal to 6

3. Show these inequalities on a number line. Draw a separate number line for each part, labelling each line from -5 to 5.

    1 $x > -2$ **6** $-3 < x < -2$
    2 $x < -3$ **7** $-4 \leqslant x \leqslant 3$
    3 $x \geqslant 0$ **8** $x < -2$ or $x > 4$
    4 $x < 4$ **9** $x \leqslant 2$ or $x \geqslant 3$
    5 $x \leqslant 3$ **10** $-3 < x < 0$

4. If x is a whole number such that $-5 \leqslant x \leqslant 5$, write down the possible values for x, for the inequalities of question 3.

5. Write a statement linking a, b, c using the symbol $<$, e.g. if $a = 3, b = -2, c = 5$ you can write $b < a < c$.

   1 $a = -3, b = 3, c = -2$
   2 $a = 4, b = 0, c = -1$
   3 $a = -2, b = 4, c = -5$
   4 $a = -2, b = 1.5, c = 1.3$
   5 $a = -4, b = 4\frac{1}{2}, c = -4\frac{1}{2}$

6. Express in symbols the inequalities shown on the number lines. O means the number is not included and ● means the number is included.

1
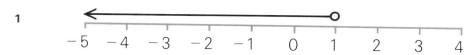

2
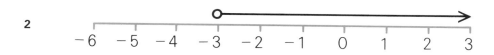

3
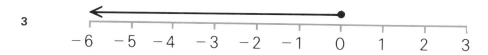

4
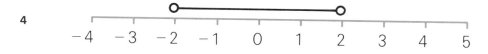

5
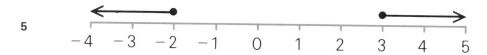

Simple inequalities

Just as we can alter equations by treating both sides alike, we can use a similar method with inequalities.

Solving simple inequalities

We can add equal numbers to both sides.
We can subtract equal numbers from both sides.
We can multiply both sides by the same **positive** number.
We can divide both sides by the same **positive** number.
In all these cases, the inequality is still true.

Examples

1   If $5x$ is greater than $3x + 12$, the statement is still true if we subtract $3x$ from both sides.
$2x$ is greater than 12
The statement will still be true if we divide both sides by 2.
x is greater than 6.

Using symbols, we have
$$5x > 3x + 12$$
$$2x > 12$$
$$x > 6$$

2 $\frac{1}{2}x + 5 \leqslant 16$

Subtract 5 from both sides
$$\frac{1}{2}x \leqslant 11$$
Multiply both sides by 2
$$x \leqslant 22$$

Note that if you multiply or divide, you must multiply or divide by a **positive** number for the inequality to be correct.
You should take care to collect the x's on the side of the equation where they will be positive.

3 $15 - 4x > x$

Do not subtract x from both sides or you will have $15 - 5x > 0$.
Then
$$-5x > -15$$
Instead, add $4x$ to both sides and you will have
$$15 > 5x$$
Divide both sides by 5
$$3 > x$$
i.e. $x < 3$

You **can** proceed from the step $-5x > -15$ if you multiply both sides by -1.
But if you multiply or divide by a **negative** number you must **reverse** the inequality sign at the same time.
So $5x < 15$, and, as above, $x < 3$.

Exercise 8.2

1. Find the set of numbers which satisfy these inequalities and show the solutions on a number line.

    1 $3x > 18$
    2 $6x + 8 < 26$
    3 $3x - 7 \geqslant 2$

    4 $10x + 6 < 11$
    5 $5x \leqslant 45$

2. If x is a whole number such that $0 \leqslant x \leqslant 10$, find the set of numbers which satisfy these inequalities.

    1 $5x \geqslant 30$
    2 $2x - 3 < 9$
    3 $3x \leqslant 4x - 5$

    4 $3x - 2 \leqslant x$
    5 $4x - 9 > 2x$

3. If x is a whole number such that $-3 \leqslant x \leqslant 3$, find the set of numbers which satisfy these inequalities.

    1 $12x < -12$
    2 $2x + 4 < 0$
    3 $4x + 6 \geqslant 6$

    4 $x < 5x - 8$
    5 $3x \geqslant x - 2$

4. Find the set of numbers which satisfy these inequalities.

    1 $2x + 3 < 23$
    2 $14 + 5x \geqslant 2 - x$
    3 $\frac{1}{2}x + 3 \geqslant 7$
    4 $36 + 4x > 0$
    5 $6 - 3x \leqslant 3x$

    6 $21 - 7x < 0$
    7 $5x + 2 > 2x - 10$
    8 $8 + 7x \geqslant 2x + 8$
    9 $\frac{1}{2}(x + 4) < 6$
    10 $4(x + 3) \leqslant 3(x + 2)$

Flow diagrams

Instead of giving instructions in a simple list, they can be arranged in a **flow diagram**.
You start by reading the box at the top, or sometimes at the left side, and follow the
direction of the arrows, reading the boxes in turn, and carrying out the instructions or
answering the questions in them.

Examples

1   To convert a measurement in litres into gallons

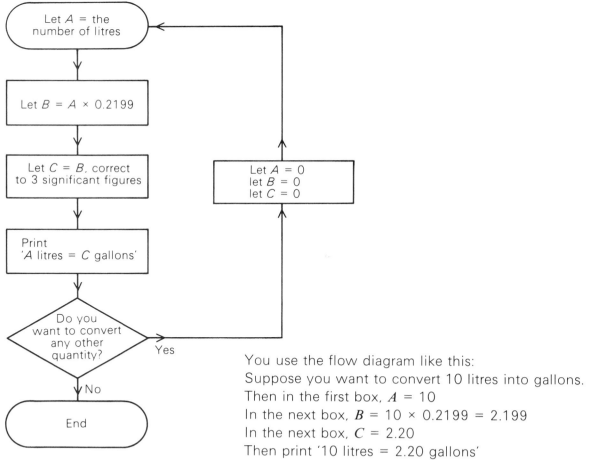

You use the flow diagram like this:
Suppose you want to convert 10 litres into gallons.
Then in the first box, $A = 10$
In the next box, $B = 10 \times 0.2199 = 2.199$
In the next box, $C = 2.20$
Then print '10 litres = 2.20 gallons'

If you do not want to convert any other quantity you reach the end of the
flow diagram.
If you want to convert another quantity, the flow diagram reduces A, B and C
temporarily to 0 (to avoid confusion) and returns to the beginning.
Use this flow diagram to convert 12 litres into gallons.

You can put all the instructions in rectangular boxes, but if you use the other shapes shown it makes the flow diagrams clearer.

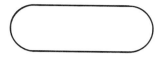

A rounded box is used at the beginning and end.

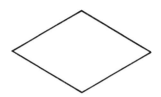

A diamond box is used for a question. The path you take from it will depend on the answer. In the example on the previous page the two paths are for the answers 'Yes' and 'No'. The path 'Yes' returns to the beginning. This is called a **loop**.

2 Here is a flow diagram which gives a sequence of numbers.

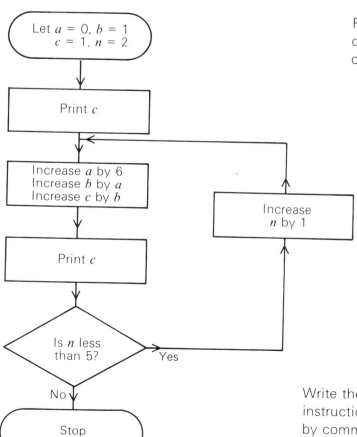

For working through the flow diagram, write down a, b, c, n in columns, which begin like this:

a	b	c	n
0	1	1	2
6	7	8	3
.	.	.	.

Write the numbers given by the instruction 'Print c' in a row, separated by commas.

What sequence of numbers is formed ?

Exercise 8.3

1. Construct a flow diagram to convert measurements in feet into measurements in metres. (1 foot = 0.3048 m)
    Use the flow diagram to convert 20 feet into metres.

2. Follow the instructions in this flow diagram to make a sequence of numbers. (For working, write down the values of x and s in two columns.)
    What is the name given to this sequence ?

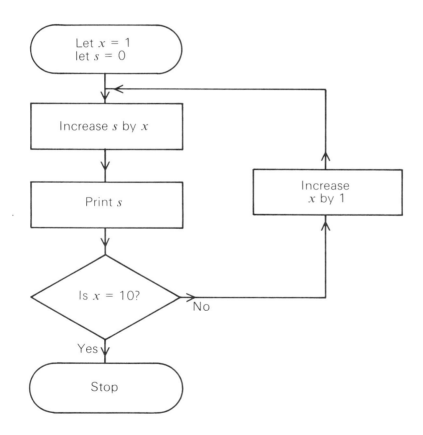

3. Construct a simple flow diagram which will print the sequence of numbers
    4, 8, 12, 16, . . . up to 40.

4. Use this flow diagram to find the largest whole number less than the cube root of 500. (Begin by putting $n = 500$.)

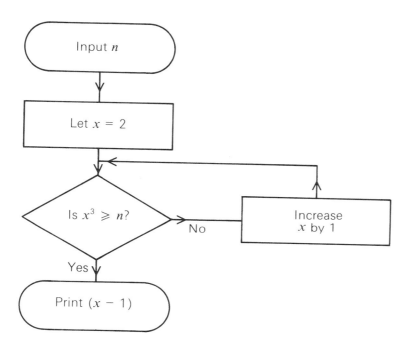

5. Construct a flow diagram to find the largest whole number less than the square root of any number n.

Exercise 8.4   Applications and Activities

1. For a party, Maria wanted to buy a packet of sweets for each child attending. She bought x packets of sweets at 15p each and y packets of sweets at 20p each.

    Express the following as mathematical statements.

    1 She bought more than 10 but not more than 18 packets of sweets.
    2 More than half of the packets bought were those at 15p.
    3 The total cost of the sweets was less than £3.

2. A market trader sells T-shirts and sweat shirts. He sells x T-shirts at £7 each and y sweat shirts at £12 each.
    Express the following as mathematical statements.

    1 He expects to sell over 100 articles altogether.
    2 He expects to take over £800 altogether.
    3 He expects to sell more than twice as many T-shirts as sweat shirts.
    4 He expects to sell at least 20 sweat shirts.

3. Two painters estimate the price they will charge for painting a building.
    The first painter, Mr Archer, says he will charge £400, and in addition, £5 for each hour the job takes.
    The second painter, Mr Barton, says he will charge £13 for each hour the job takes.

    1 If they each estimate the job will take x hours, write down expressions for the cost, if employing each painter.
    2 The customer decides that Mr Barton will do the job for less money than Mr Archer. Write down a statement expressing this.
    3 Simplify your statement to find a range of values for x, for which it is cheaper to employ Mr Barton.
    4 Which of the painters will it be cheaper to employ if the job takes 60 hours ?

4. Mrs Palmer has x 20-pence coins and y 10-pence coins and no other coins, in her purse.
    Express the following as mathematical statements.

    1 She has less than 30 of the coins.
    2 The total value of the coins is more than £3.
    3 She has more than three times as many 10-pence coins as 20-pence coins.
    4 She has at least 5 20-pence coins.

5.   Work through this flow diagram. What does your answer represent ?

Use this information
d = this year's date
b = the year in which you were born

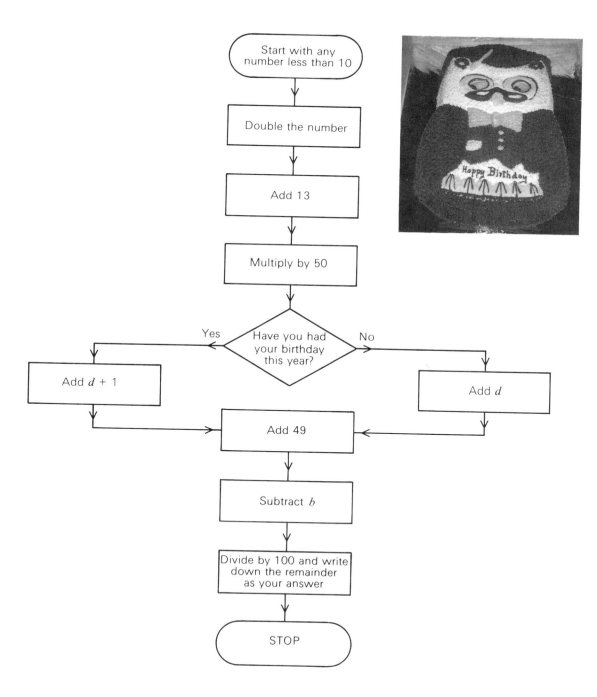

6. **1** Wendy went shopping with a £5 note. She intended to buy 5 loaves at 54p each and spend the change on bars of crispy chocolate at 28p each.
Use the flow diagram to decide how many bars of chocolate she could buy.

2 Next week, Wendy only took £2.50 with her to get 5 loaves. Work through the flow diagram again and decide what she bought.

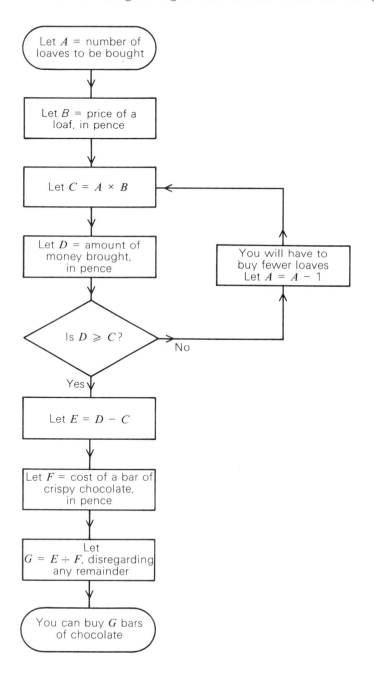

7. This flow diagram will convert °C into °F.

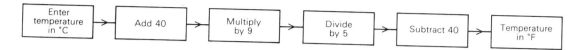

Use the flow diagram to convert 15°C into °F.

8. A cafe owner planned to buy some tables
and chairs. Tables cost £50 and chairs cost
£15 each.
If he bought t tables and c chairs, express
these statements as inequalities:

1 He wanted at least 4 tables but not more
than 7.

2 He wanted at least 4 times as many
chairs as tables, but not more than
28 chairs altogether.

3 He did not want to spend more than £600.

4 By trial, find the greatest number of tables
he can buy, satisfying these conditions,
and then find the greatest number of chairs
he can buy to go with them.

PUZZLES

23. Multiply together a half, a third and a quarter of Marcia's age, and the product will be
576.
How old is Marcia?

24. Starting at the top, how many different routes
are there to spell SQUARE, moving from a
square to one next to it each time?

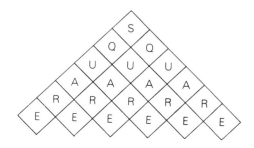

9 Thinking about Pythagoras' Theorem

Pythagoras

Pythagoras lived about 500 BC. He was very interested in numbers, and one of the interesting facts about numbers is that $3^2 + 4^2$ equals 5^2.

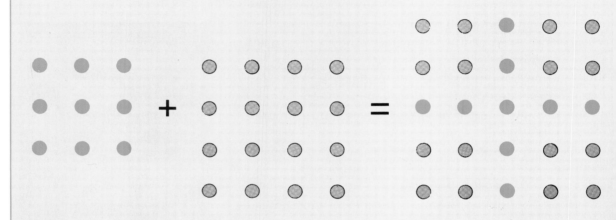

Tiling

Notice on a tiled floor or wall, how the 2 squares on the smaller sides of a right-angled triangle each have area 1 square unit and the square on the large side of the triangle has area 2 square units (from 4 half squares).

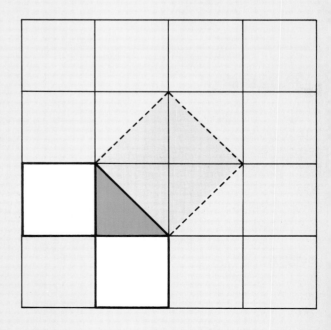

Pythagoras' Theorem

The relationship connecting the lengths of sides of a right-angled triangle is named Pythagoras' theorem.

Draw 2 squares with edges 3 units and 4 units, side by side on thin cardboard.
B is 4 units from A.
Cut out the whole outline.
Draw the dotted lines and cut along them, making 3 pieces.
Rearrange the pieces to make 1 larger square.
Notice that with the 2 smaller squares, one is the square whose side has length AB, one is the square whose side has length AC, and they are rearranged to make a square whose side has length BC.

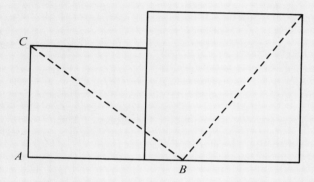

So $AB^2 + AC^2 = BC^2$, where $\triangle ABC$ is a right-angled triangle, with the right angle at A.

Egyptian rope stretchers

In Ancient Egypt, the river Nile flooded the nearby land, and this helped to irrigate and fertilize the fields. When the boundaries were washed away, the fields had to be marked out again. To make an exact right angle, a rope with sides 3 units, 4 units and 5 units was used. (This is using the reverse or **converse** of Pythagoras' theorem.) This is a method that can still be used nowadays.

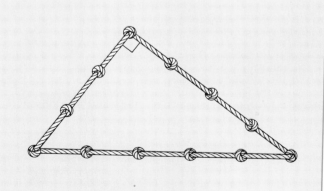

Pythagoras' Theorem

A theorem is a mathematical statement which can be proved to be true.

In a right-angled triangle, the side opposite the right angle is called the **hypotenuse**.

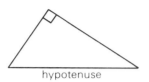
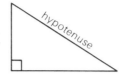
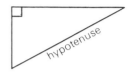

Pythagoras' theorem states that:

In a right-angled triangle, the area of the square on the hypotenuse is equal to the sum of the areas of the squares on the other two sides.

$$a^2 = b^2 + c^2$$

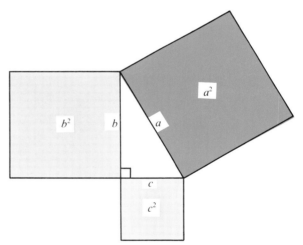

Here, because it is simpler, we have labelled the sides, using small letters, instead of labelling the vertices of the triangle.
a^2 means the area of the square with side a, and in this diagram, side a is the hypotenuse.
b^2 means the area of the square with side b.
c^2 means the area of the square with side c.

Although the result is about areas of squares on the sides of the triangles, we use it mainly for calculating lengths of sides of right-angled triangles.

Examples

1   To find a.

$$a^2 = b^2 + c^2$$
$$= 9^2 + 4^2 \quad (a \text{ in cm})$$
$$= 81 + 16$$
$$= 97$$
$$a = \sqrt{97} \text{ cm}$$
$$= 9.84 \text{ cm}$$
$$= 9.8 \text{ cm, to the nearest mm.}$$

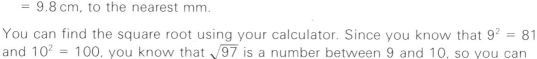

You can find the square root using your calculator. Since you know that $9^2 = 81$ and $10^2 = 100$, you know that $\sqrt{97}$ is a number between 9 and 10, so you can make a rough check of your answer.

(If you do not have to set down your working, you can do the whole calculation in one step on your calculator.
Press 9 $\boxed{x^2}$ $\boxed{+}$ 4 $\boxed{x^2}$ $\boxed{=}$ $\boxed{\sqrt{}}$ and you will get 9.84...)

We can use the result of Pythagoras' theorem to find the length of one of the other sides.

2   Find b.

Notice that c is the hypotenuse.
$$c^2 = a^2 + b^2$$
$$7^2 = 3^2 + b^2 \quad (b \text{ in cm})$$
$$49 = 9 + b^2$$
$$40 = b^2$$
$$b = \sqrt{40} \text{ cm}$$
$$= 6.3 \text{ cm, to the nearest mm.}$$

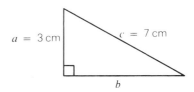

Exercise 9.1

1.   Without using your calculator, find the whole number part of the square roots of these numbers. Then use your calculator to find the square roots, correct to 1 decimal place.

1	75	**5**	41	**8**	67
2	25.5	**6**	22.1	**9**	8.2
3	99	**7**	10.6	**10**	17
4	50				

2. Use your calculator to find the square roots of these numbers. If they are not exact, give them correct to 1 decimal place.

1	189	**5**	120	**8**	360
2	216	**6**	196	**9**	525
3	476	**7**	200	**10**	1369
4	225				

3. Use Pythagoras' theorem to find the hypotenuse, a, in these triangles. If your answer is not exact, give it correct to 1 decimal place.

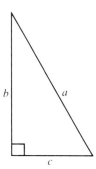

1 $b = 15$ cm, $c = 8$ cm
2 $b = 9$ cm, $c = 6$ cm
3 $b = 12$ cm, $c = 5$ cm
4 $b = 10$ cm, $c = 4$ cm
5 $b = 12$ cm, $c = 7$ cm
6 $b = 2.4$ cm, $c = 0.7$ cm
7 $b = 10.5$ cm, $c = 8.5$ cm
8 $b = 14$ cm, $c = 9$ cm
9 $b = 11.5$ cm, $c = 4.4$ cm
10 $b = \sqrt{20}$ cm, $c = 4$ cm. (Note that $b^2 = 20$)

4. Find the third side in these triangles. If your answer is not exact, give it correct to 1 decimal place.

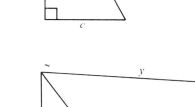

1 $c = 5$ cm, $a = 10$ cm
2 $b = 12$ cm, $a = 15$ cm
3 $b = 8$ cm, $a = 11$ cm
4 $c = 7$ cm, $a = 25$ cm
5 $c = \sqrt{13}$ cm, $a = 7$ cm
6 $b = 1.5$ cm, $a = 1.7$ cm
7 $c = 4$ cm, $a = 10$ cm
8 $b = 12$ cm, $a = 16.9$ cm
9 $b = 8$ cm, $a = 8.9$ cm
10 $c = 0.9$ cm, $a = 4.1$ cm

5. Find the length of side x and use your answer to find the length of side y.

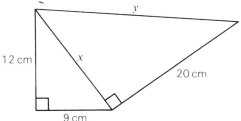

6.   Find the length of side x and use your
     answer to find the length of side y.

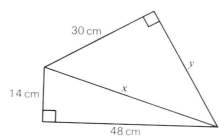

7.   Draw some right-angled triangles of
     different sizes. (Graph paper is useful.)
     Measure the sides a, b, c in cm, to the
     nearest mm. (a is the hypotenuse.)
     Set down the results in a table. Work out a^2, b^2 and c^2 in
     cm^2, correct to 2 decimal places.
     One example is shown.

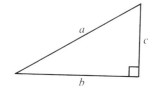

a	b	c	a^2	b^2	c^2	$b^2 + c^2$
4.6	4.2	1.9	21.16	17.64	3.61	21.25

According to Pythagoras' theorem, what should you find ?
The results may not match exactly, due to squaring approximate measurements.

8.   If you can find some ready-made right-angled triangles,
     such as set-squares, then measure their sides. If you
     cannot find triangles, find rectangles, such as a window
     pane, a door, a table, the floor of a room.
     Measure the length, breadth and a diagonal.
     Repeat the work of question 7. If the object is large,
     measure to the nearest cm, or even to the nearest 10 cm.

Triangle ABC

A triangle can have the vertices labelled by
capital letters, as usual.
In this triangle, BC is the hypotenuse.

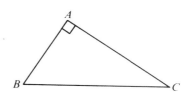

$$BC^2 = AB^2 + AC^2$$

Example

3   If, in this triangle, $AB = 5.3$ cm and $BC = 8.7$ cm, calculate AC.

Notice that the hypotenuse is BC.
$$BC^2 = AB^2 + AC^2$$
$$8.7^2 = 5.3^2 + AC^2 \quad (AC \text{ in cm})$$
$$75.69 = 28.09 + AC^2$$
$$AC^2 = 47.6$$
$$AC = \sqrt{47.6}\, \text{cm}$$
$$ = 6.9 \text{ cm, to the nearest mm.}$$

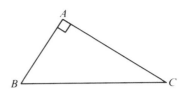

If we want to use small letters for sides, we use
a for the side opposite $\angle A$ (the side BC),
b for the side opposite $\angle B$ (the side AC),
and c for the side opposite $\angle C$ (the side AB).

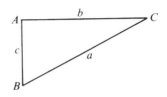

Exercise 9.2

1.   Find the third side in these triangles.
     If the answer is not exact, give it correct
     to 1 decimal place.

     1 $BC = 7$ cm, $AC = 5$ cm
     2 $BC = 5.6$ cm, $AC = 3.3$ cm
     3 $BC = 10$ cm, $AB = 12$ cm
     4 $AC = 2.8$ cm, $AB = 5.3$ cm
     5 $BC = 20.8$ cm, $AC = 10.5$ cm

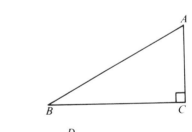

2.   Find the lengths of
     1 AB,
     2 BC,
     3 AC.

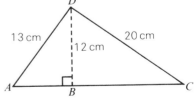

3. O is the centre of the circle. The tangent
     PT is 12 cm long. The radius is 5 cm.
     $\angle OTP = 90°$.
     1   Find the length of OP.
     2   Find the length of AP.

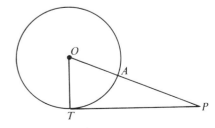

4. What is the radius of the base of a cone
    whose perpendicular height is 8 cm and
    whose slant height is 10 cm ?

5. A is the point (1, 6) and B is (13, 1).
    Use Pythagoras' theorem in triangle ABC
    to calculate the length of the line AB.

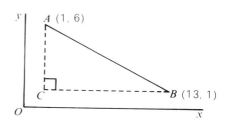

6. AB is a chord 24 cm long, in a circle
    centre O. The radius is 15 cm. C is the
    mid-point of AB.
    Find the length of OC.

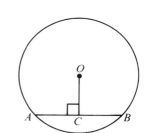

7. ABC is an equilateral triangle and
    $AB = 8$ cm.
    AD is an axis of symmetry.

    1 What is the length of BD ?
    2 What is the size of $\angle ADB$?
    3 Calculate the length of AD, correct to
       the nearest mm.

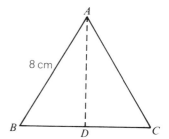

8. $ABCD$ is a square and $AB = 5$ cm.

    1 Use triangle ABC to calculate the
       length of AC, to the nearest mm.
    2 What is the length of AX, to the
       nearest mm ?

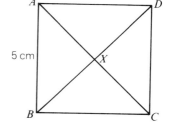

9. Find the lengths of
    1 *BD*, using triangle *ABD*,
    2 *BC*,
    3 *AC*.

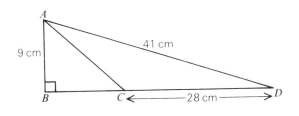

10. **1** Find the length of *AC*.
    2 Find the length of *DC*.
    3 Find the perimeter of *ABCD*.
    4 Find the area of *ABCD*.

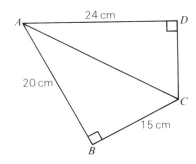

Exercise 9.3   Applications and Activities

1. A patrol boat goes 16 km South, then 12 km East. How far is it from its starting point ?

2. A gardener is making a rectangular concrete base for a greenhouse 6 feet wide and 8 feet long. Having measured out the edges he checks that it is truly rectangular by measuring both diagonals. How long should these diagonals be ?

3. A rectangular wooden box is 120 cm long, 90 cm wide and 80 cm high.
    A rod just fits inside the box.
    What is the length of the rod ?
    (Use △*ABC* to find the length of *AC*, then use △*ACD*. Is this a right-angled triangle ?)

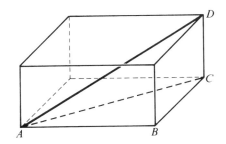

4. The diagram shows the side of a shed.
    What is the length of the sloping roof *AB*, correct to the nearest cm ?

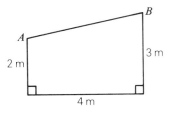

5. **Number patterns**

These sets of whole numbers which form the sides of right-angled triangles are related by a pattern.
Copy it and write down the next five lines of the pattern, working backwards from the end column.

hypotenuse	one other side	sum s	difference d	$s \times d$	3rd side
5	4	9	1	9	3
13	12	25	1	25	5
. . .	. . .	. . .	1	49	7

Here is a similar pattern, which you can copy and continue for 5 more lines.

hypotenuse	one other side	sum s	difference d	$s \times d$	3rd side
5	3	8	2	16	4
17	15	32	2	64	8
. . .	. . .	72	2	144	12

6. **A square root spiral**

This is interesting to draw, and good practice in drawing accurately.
Start with A near the centre of a large piece of paper and see how far you can get.
(Alternatively, if you have a suitable large space where you are allowed to chalk on the floor, you could draw your spiral there, using metres instead of centimetres.)

Begin by drawing the right-angled triangle ABC.
$AB = BC = 1$ cm.
$AC^2 = 1^2 + 1^2 = 1 + 1 = 2$,
so $AC = \sqrt{2}$ cm.

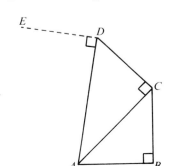

Now draw CD perpendicular to AC, 1 cm long, and join AD.
Using $\triangle ACD$, $AD^2 = 1^2 + (\sqrt{2})^2 = 1 + 2 = 3$,
so $AD = \sqrt{3}$ cm.
Now draw DE perpendicular to AD, 1 cm long, and join AE.
How long is AE ?
Carry on in a similar way.
Finally, colour the spiral, which consists of the lines AB, BC, CD, DE, . . .

7. You will have found from some of your previous work that there are certain sets of numbers where all three sides of a right-angled triangle are whole numbers.

The ones using the smallest numbers are:

(a)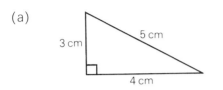

Check that $3^2 + 4^2 = 5^2$
This is called a 3, 4, 5 triangle.

Enlargements of this triangle will also use whole numbers so other groups of numbers are 6, 8, 10; 9, 12, 15; 30, 40, 50; . . .

(b)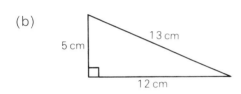

Check that $5^2 + 12^2 = 13^2$
This is called a 5, 12, 13 triangle.

State some other triangles which are enlargements of this one.

(c)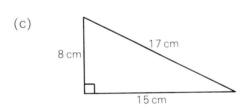

Check that $8^2 + 15^2 = 17^2$
This is an 8, 15, 17 triangle.

(d)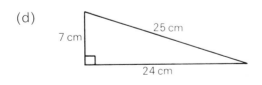

Check that $7^2 + 24^2 = 25^2$
This is a 7, 24, 25 triangle.

Since these lengths lead to whole-number answers, they are often used in made-up questions to make the working simpler.
So it is worth learning these results,
i.e. 3, 4, 5; 5, 12, 13; 8, 15, 17; 7, 24, 25.
The underlined side is the hypotenuse.
Look for such sets of numbers, or multiples or fractions of them, in questions.

Look at the measurements on these triangles and see whether they belong to any of these sets, or are multiples or fractions of such numbers, and thus find the missing lengths in the triangles.

If you cannot find an answer by recognising the set of numbers, you can use the usual method to calculate it.

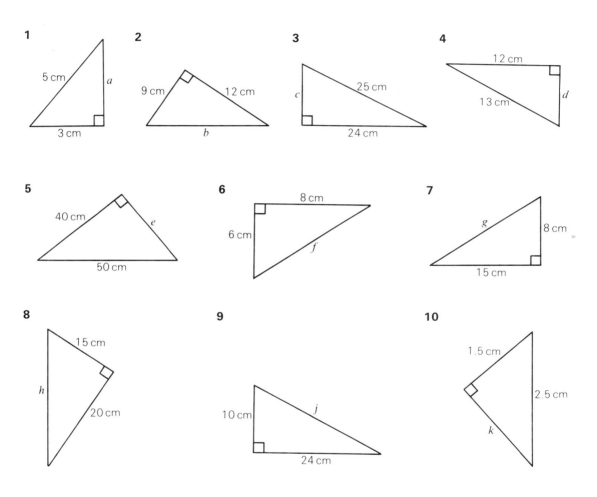

8. **Pythagoras**

Pythagoras lived about 2500 years ago and he is remembered as one of the Ancient Greek mathematicians.

Look in library books or encyclopedias and see if you can find out anything about him, his way of life, or his mathematical work, and write a short account about this.

10 Thinking about averages and

Average

We often hear the word 'average' used.

The average size of women's shoes is size 5.

The average household in the UK has 2.5 people.

In the 1991 test series against the W. Indies Graham Gooch averaged 60.00 runs per innings.

The average wage of farmworkers is £170 per week.

Mean, median, mode

Sometimes the average quoted is the mean, sometimes the median and sometimes the mode.

frequency distributions

Frequency Distributions

Make some comments about these graphs.

Distribution of men's shoe sizes

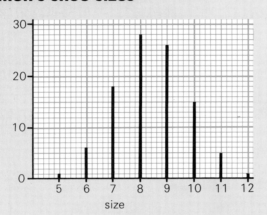

Bar-line graph to show the distribution of men's shoe sizes.

Distribution of population in 1901 and 1989

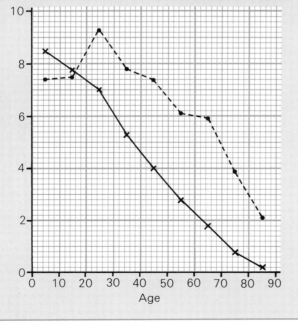

Frequency polygons showing age distribution of UK population.

x———x 1901
●--●   1989

10 Averages and frequency distributions

Averages and Range

When we have made a collection of statistical data, we often need to find an average measurement.

The average that we usually use is called the **mean**. (Its complete name is the arithmetic mean.)

The mean $\bar{x} = \dfrac{\text{sum of the items}}{\text{number of items}} = \dfrac{\Sigma x}{n}$

$\bar{x}$ is read as x bar, and is the symbol for the mean.
Instead of S, we are now using Σx.
Σ is the Greek capital letter sigma, and means 'the sum of'.
So Σx means the sum of the x-values.
n is the number of items.

There are two other kinds of average that are sometimes used, instead of the mean.

The median

When the items are arranged in order of size, the median is the value of the middle item, or the value halfway between the middle two if there is an even number of items.

The mode

This is the value which occurs most often.
(Sometimes a set of values will not have a mode, as there may not be a value which occurs more often than any of the others.)

Examples

1   The marks of 12 pupils in a test (marked out of 20) were
    19, 20, 17, 11, 19, 19, 15, 8, 15, 20, 17, 18.

    The mean mark $\bar{x} = \dfrac{\Sigma x}{n} = \dfrac{198}{12} = 16.5$

For the median mark, arrange the marks in order of size.

8   11   15   15   17   17 ↑ 18   19   19   19   20   20

middle

The median is halfway between 17 and 18, and is 17.5
The mode is the mark which occurs most often and is 19, since 3 pupils had 19 marks.

The three averages are Mean   16.5
                          Median 17.5
                          Mode   19

All these averages can be used in different circumstances.
The most usual one is the mean, as this is the one which involves all the values. If one of the values is very high or low compared to the others, this will affect the mean and in this case the median might be a better average to use. In the example, the mean has been lowered by the two low marks of 8 and 11. The median gives a better idea of the results. It tells us that half the class got less than 17.5 marks and half got more. The mode is the simplest average to find, but generally it is not as useful as the other two.

As well as finding an average value we often need to know how the values are spread out.

The range is the simplest measure of spread to find.

Range = highest value − lowest value

In the previous example, the range of marks = 20 − 8 = 12 marks.

2   The wages of 7 men were £181, £174, £159, £165, £173, £177, £185.

The mean wage $\bar{x} = \dfrac{\Sigma x}{n} = £\,\dfrac{1214}{7}$

$= £173.42...$
$= £173.40$, to the nearest 10p.

Since the wages are given in whole £'s, it is sensible to give the mean correct to 1 decimal place.

For the median wage, arrange the items in order of size.

£159   £165   £173   £174   £177   £181   £185
                         ↑
                     middle

The median wage is £174.

There is no mode wage. Each value occcurs once so there is no value which occurs more often than any of the others.

The range of wages = highest wage − lowest wage
$$= £185 − £159$$
$$= £26$$

When you have found an average, look at the figures again and see if the answer seems reasonable. In this example, answers less than £159 or greater than £185 would clearly be wrong.

Remember to give the unit of measurement, such as £, cm, kg, hours.

Do not give too many decimal places. If the data is accurate to the nearest whole number, then it is reasonable to give averages correct to 1 decimal place.

Use of a statistical calculator

Your calculator might have keys labelled DATA, Σx, n and $\bar{x}$, and you could try using these in a simple example, although it is probably just as easy to manage without using these keys.

Exercise 10.1

1.   Find the mean of these sets of numbers.

    1   2   4   7   9   10   11   12   12   14   14   15
    2   15   29   45   52   61   65   69   80   88
    3   18   6   15   8   12
    4   0.9   2.3   1.7   3.1   8.3   5.2   0.7   2.7   4.3   1.5
    5   80   90   100   100   110   120   130   150

2.   Find the median value of the sets of numbers in question 1.

3.   Find the median value of these sets of numbers.

    1   1   2   2   2   2   4   5   5   6   7   7   7   9   9   10
    2   43   37   38   42   37   43   41   35   39   37
    3   6   4   9   3   7   4   5   1   8   7   4   4   3   7   9   4   5   6   3   0
            5   8   3   2

4. Find the mode value of the sets of numbers in question 3.

5. The weights, in kg, of 10 children are
49, 36, 46, 33, 38, 43, 31, 44, 34, 36.
Find the mean, the median and the range of the weights.

6. The lengths of 5 javelin throws, in metres, are 42.4, 39.0, 41.8, 44.2, 37.3.
Find the mean, the median and the range of these distances.

7. The temperatures in a seaside town on each day of a summer week were (in °C),
25°, 25°, 28°, 29°, 28°, 27°, 27°.
Find the mean temperature and the range of temperatures.

8. The ages of 6 boys were
13y 4m, 13y 8m, 14y 0m, 14y 5m, 13y 11m, 13y 2m.
Find the mean and median ages, and the range of ages.

9. The times taken by a plumber to mend 5 bursts were
1 h 20 min, 2 h 25 min, 3 h 10 min, 1 h 10 min, 2 h 45 min.
Find the mean time taken for a job, and the range of times.

Frequency Distributions

Example

3   The numbers of children in 40 families (with at least 1 child) are as follows:

5, 4, 2, 2, 2, 6, 2, 3, 3, 2, 1, 2, 2, 1, 3, 3, 2, 1, 2, 5, 4, 3, 3, 6, 2, 2, 3, 4, 3, 2, 1, 2, 2, 2, 3, 2, 2, 2, 1, 2.

Frequency table

number of children	f
1	5
2	19
3	9
4	3
5	2
6	2
	40

f is short for **frequency**, the number of times each item occurs.

Mean

To find the mean you must first find the total number of children.

```
1 child     in  5 families =    5
2 children in 19 families =   38
3 children in  9 families =   27
4 children in  3 families =   12
5 children in  2 families =   10
6 children in  2 families =   12
            40 families = 104
```

Mean number of children per family $= \dfrac{\text{total number of children}}{\text{number of families}}$

$$= \frac{104}{40}$$

$$= 2.6$$

You could set down the working to find the mean by putting an extra column on the frequency table, and labelling the first column x.

x	f	fx
1	5	5
2	19	38
3	9	27
4	3	12
5	2	10
6	2	12
	40	104

$$\bar{x} = \frac{\Sigma fx}{\Sigma f}$$

$$= \frac{104}{40}$$

$$= 2.6$$

Note the new formula. You use the sum of the fx column divided by the sum of the f column.

To find the mode

This is the value which occurs most often. From the frequency table it is easy to see that 2 occurs most often, 19 times altogether, so the mode is 2.

To find the median

If the 40 numbers were arranged in order of size, the middle value would be halfway between the 20th and 21st numbers.

1 1 1 1 1   2 2 2 . . .   3 3 3 . . .   4 4 4 5 5 6 6

    5 1's   19 2's   9 3's

The 20th and 21st numbers are both 2, so the median is 2.

The range = highest value − lowest value
$$= 6 - 1$$
$$= 5$$

The best diagram to draw for this kind of frequency distribution is a bar-line graph. (A histogram is sometimes used.)

Bar-line graph to show the distribution of numbers of children in 40 families

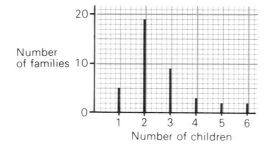

Number of families

Number of children

Exercise 10.2

1. Here is a frequency table showing the number of people in each car, for a survey of 120 cars passing along a main road.

Number of people x	1	2	3	4	5	6
Number of cars f	18	58	17	19	7	1

Find
1 the mean number of people per car,
2 the median number,
3 the mode number.
Draw a bar-line graph of the data.

2. In an experiment, 10 seeds of a particular vegetable were planted in each of 200 pots, and the number of seeds which germinated was noted for each pot. These results were obtained:

Number of seeds germinating x	0	1	2	3	4	5	6	7	8	9	10
Number of pots f	1	0	1	2	8	20	40	53	46	24	5

Find
1 the mean number of seeds germinating, per pot,
2 the median number,
3 the mode number.
Draw a bar-line graph of the distribution.

3. In a recent Golf Championship, the scores of the players for the first hole are summarized here.

Score for hole x	2	3	4	5	6	7
Frequency f	18	84	146	36	3	1

Find
1 the mean score for this hole,
2 the median score,
3 the mode score.
Draw a bar-line graph of the distribution.

Seve Ballesteros.

Grouped Frequency Distributions

Data is often put into convenient groups, called classes.

Examples

4   The distribution of examination marks of 100 pupils.

Mark	20–29	30–39	40–49	50–59	60–69	70–79	80–89
Number of pupils	3	10	21	25	22	14	5

The data can be represented by a **histogram**.

Histogram to show the distribution of examination marks

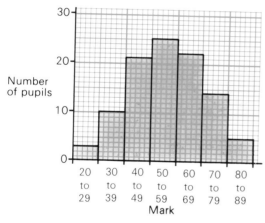

We cannot find the mode since we do not know the individual marks, but we can find the **modal class**.

The modal class is the class interval which includes the most pupils, so here it is the class 50–59 marks.

To find the mean mark, we assume that each pupil has the mark corresponding to the centre of the class interval in which it lies, e.g. the central mark of the marks 20–29 is 24.5, of 30–39 it is 34.5, and so on.

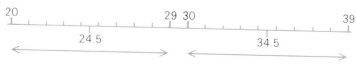

Of the 3 pupils who got between 20 and 29 marks, they could have got more or less marks than 24.5, but 24.5 is the best estimate we can make.

Use the formula $\bar{x} = \dfrac{\Sigma fx}{\Sigma f}$, taking x as the value at the centre of the interval.

marks	f	x centre of interval	fx
20–29	3	24.5	73.5
30–39	10	34.5	345.0
40–49	21	44.5	934.5
50–59	25	54.5	1362.5
60–69	22	64.5	1419.0
70–79	14	74.5	1043.0
80–89	5	84.5	422.5
	100		5600.0

$$\bar{x} = \frac{\Sigma fx}{\Sigma f}$$

$$= \frac{5600}{100}$$

$$= 56.0$$

The median will also have to be estimated.
There is a graphical method for doing this, which you will learn later. At present you will not be asked to find the median of a grouped frequency distribution.

5   The weights of a group of young men are given in this table.

Weight in kg	frequency
30 to just under 40	2
40 to just under 50	10
50 to just under 60	24
60 to just under 70	35
70 to just under 80	19
80 to just under 90	6
90 to just under 100	4
	100

The first class contains weights from 30 to 40 kg and the centre of interval is 35 kg. We rewrite the table using the centres of intervals as column x, working out a column fx, and finding the sums of columns f and fx.

Weight in kg	x centre of interval	f	fx
30–40	35	2	70
40–50	45	10	450
50–60	55	24	1320
60–70	65	35	2275
70–80	75	19	1425
80–90	85	6	510
90–100	95	4	380
		100	6430

$$\bar{x} = \frac{\Sigma fx}{\Sigma f}$$

$$= \frac{6430}{100} \text{ kg}$$

$$= 64.3 \text{ kg}$$

The mean weight is 64.3 kg.

The modal class is the class with most men in and it is 60 to 70 kg (with 35 men in).

Histogram to show the distribution of weights of 100 young men

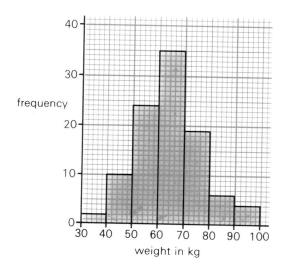

weight in kg

Exercise 10.3

1. In an examination the marks obtained by pupils were as given in this table.

Mark	20–29	30–39	40–49	50–59	60–69	70–79	80–89	90–99
Number of pupils	2	3	8	22	30	19	11	5

   1 What is the modal class of marks ?
   2 What is the centre of interval of the class 20–29 ?
   3 Make a frequency table with x as the centres of intervals. Fill in a column for fx and find an estimate for the mean mark.
   4 Draw a histogram of the distribution. Comment on its shape.

2. The table shows the distribution of runs scored by the first 5 batsmen in each team, in the 8 cricket matches played on a Sunday, in the Refuge League.

Runs	0–19	20–39	40–59	60–79	80–99	100–119
Number of batsmen	40	21	11	3	2	3

   1 What is the modal class of runs ?
   2 What is the centre of interval of the class 0–19 ?
   3 Make a frequency table with x as the centres of intervals. Fill in a column for fx and find an estimate for the mean number of runs.
   4 Draw a histogram of the distribution. Comment on its shape.

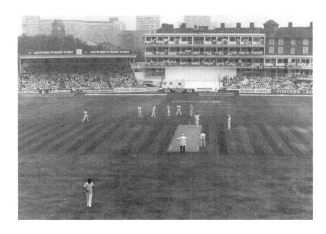

3.   The birth weights of 80 babies are recorded in this table.

Weight in lb	Number of babies
4.5 to just under 5.5	3
5.5 to just under 6.5	9
6.5 to just under 7.5	22
7.5 to just under 8.5	28
8.5 to just under 9.5	16
9.5 to just under 10.5	2

1   What is the modal class of weights ?
2   What is the centre of interval of the class 4.5–5.5 lb ?
3   Make a frequency table with x as the centres of intervals. Fill in a column for
       fx and find an estimate for the mean weight.
4   Draw a histogram of the distribution.

4.   50 leaves from an evergreen shrub were measured and these are their lengths.

Length in cm	Number of leaves
4.5 to under 5.0	1
5.0 to under 5.5	7
5.5 to under 6.0	14
6.0 to under 6.5	7
6.5 to under 7.0	10
7.0 to under 7.5	9
7.5 to under 8.0	2

1   What is the modal class of lengths ?
2   What is the centre of interval of the class 4.5–5.0 cm ?
3   Make a frequency table with x as the centres of intervals. Find an estimate for
       the mean length of leaf.
4   Draw a histogram to show the distribution of lengths.

5.   In a survey, 60 teenagers were asked how long they had watched television on
      the previous day, which was a Tuesday in term time. Here is a summary of the
      replies.

Time in hours	Number of teenagers
0 to just under 1	12
1 to just under 2	22
2 to just under 3	17
3 to just under 4	7
4 to just under 5	2

1   What is the modal class of times ?
2   What is the centre of interval of the class 0–1 hour ?
3   Make a frequency table with x as the centres of intervals, and find an estimate
      for the mean time spent watching television.
4   Draw a histogram of the distribution.

6.   The table shows the ages, in completed years, of children in a Youth
      Organisation, in a certain region.

Age	Number of members
5 or 6	590
7 or 8	2130
9 or 10	1930
11 or 12	1120
13 or 14	430
15 or 16	50

1   What is the modal class of ages ?
2   Make a frequency table with x as the centres of intervals and find an estimate
      for the mean age. (Since the ages are in completed years, the centre of
      interval of the first class is 6.0 years.)
3   Draw a histogram to show the distribution of ages and comment on its shape.
4   Suggest ways in which the Organisation might make use of some of the
      information shown here.

Frequency Polygons

A frequency polygon is an alternative diagram which is sometimes used instead of a histogram.

One use is for when two or more frequency distributions with the same total frequencies have to be compared. It is possible to draw their frequency polygons on the same graph, whereas this is not possible with histograms.

The simplest way to see how to draw a frequency polygon is to draw one on the same diagram as a histogram. It is constructed by joining the mid-points of the top lines of the histogram.

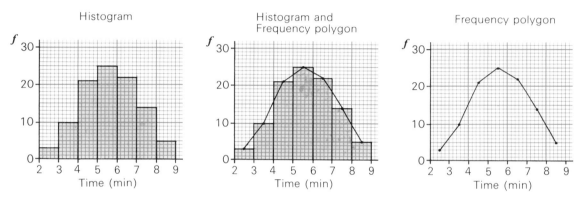

You can see that the word 'polygon' was chosen because it consists of a series of straight lines.

Some people say that the polygon should be closed, by meeting the horizontal axis on both sides.

You cannot do this if you are drawing the frequency polygon on the same diagram as a histogram, as you will not have left an empty class interval.

If you are drawing a separate frequency polygon, you can add an extra class interval on each side. These have frequency 0. Join the polygon to the mid-point of each.

Frequency polygon with extra intervals added.

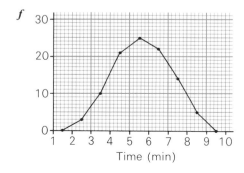

Exercise 10.4

Questions 1 to 6.
For the questions of exercise 10.3, either add a frequency polygon to the histogram that you have already drawn, or draw a separate frequency polygon of the distribution.

7.   The distributions of examination marks in two examinations are shown in this table.
     Draw frequency polygons for these distributions on the same graph and comment on them.

Mark	0–9	10–19	20–29	30–39	40–49	50–59	60–69	70–79	80–89	90–99
1st exam	6	7	7	10	15	17	18	11	6	3
2nd exam					2	4	18	47	23	6

8.   The distributions of hours of overtime worked by employees in two departments of a large firm during the last three months are shown in this table.
     Draw frequency polygons for these distributions on the same graph and comment on them.

Overtime (hours)		0–10	10–20	20–30	30–40	40–50	50–60
Number of employees	Dept A	20	43	88	61	22	6
	Dept B	8	23	45	76	48	40

Continuous data

In order to find the centre of interval it is necessary to be sure where the boundaries of the interval are.
If you record to the **completed** unit, instead of to the **nearest** unit, it makes the boundaries simpler.

e.g. If measuring lengths in cm, if you measure to the completed centimetre, then the intervals are
0 to just under 1, boundaries 0 and 1, centre of interval 0.5,
1 to just under 2, boundaries 1 and 2, centre of interval 1.5,
2 to just under 3, boundaries 2 and 3, centre of interval 2.5,
and so on.

If the measurements are then grouped, suitable groups might be
0 to just under 10, boundaries   0 and 10, centre of interval 5,
10 to just under 20, boundaries 10 and 20, centre of interval 15,
20 to just under 30, boundaries 20 and 30, centre of interval 25,
and so on.

Notice the difference in the centres of interval between exam marks, which are whole numbers, and measurements, which are continuous data.

For exam marks the classes could be
0–9, boundaries 0 and 9, centre of interval 4.5,
10–19, boundaries 10 and 19, centre of interval 14.5,
and so on.

For lengths, weights, etc. the classes could be
0–10, boundaries 0 and 10, centre of interval 5,
10–20, boundaries 10 and 20, centre of interval 15,
and so on.

If you measure to the nearest unit, you must be more careful with the boundaries. (Refer back to chapter 4 to remind yourself about these.)

e.g.
1 cm to the nearest cm, boundaries 0.5 and 1.5 cm, centre of interval is 1.0 cm.
2 cm to the nearest cm, boundaries 1.5 and 2.5 cm, centre of interval 2.0 cm.
and so on.

If you group these measurements, then
1 cm to 10 cm, boundaries 0.5 and 10.5 cm, centre of interval is 5.5 cm,
11 cm to 20 cm, boundaries 10.5 and 20.5 cm, centre of interval is 15.5 cm,
and so on.

We have avoided 0, since there can be other problems in cases where you cannot have negative readings. We will not deal with such complications at this stage.

Exercise 10.5 · Applications and Activities

1. These are the results, in order, of the 45 football matches in the Barclay's League on a particular Saturday.

1–0	1–1	2–0	2–2	2–2	2–1	1–2	3–2	3–2
1–1	1–1	0–1	0–3	3–2	1–1	1–0	2–1	0–0
0–1	2–0	0–1	1–1	2–0	0–1	1–2	2–2	2–3
1–0	2–0	2–2	0–1	0–1	2–1	0–2	1–3	1–0
0–1	0–2	0–0	3–0	3–1	3–2	2–4	0–2	0–1

    Make a list of the total number of goals in each match and show these in a frequency table.
    Find
    1 the mean number of goals per match,
    2 the median number,
    3 the range of the number of goals.
    4 Draw a bar-line graph of the distribution.

    Use the results in the most recent matches, and find their averages and draw a bar-line graph.
    Comment on any similarities or differences with the results shown here.

2. A list of surnames of 137 pupils in a year group was obtained, and the number of letters in each surname found.
    Here are the results.

Number of letters in surname	2	3	4	5	6	7	8	9	10
Frequency	1	4	14	28	35	22	17	12	4

    Find
    1 the mean number of letters in a surname,
    2 the median number,
    3 the mode,
    4 the range.
    5 Draw a bar-line graph of the data.

    Carry out your own survey using the names of pupils in your school and repeat the questions.
    Comment on any similarities or differences with the results shown here.

3. The number of words per sentence in the 1st 50 sentences of the book 'The Children of the New Forest' are recorded here.

Number of words	Number of sentences
1–10	2
11–20	9
21–30	14
31–40	7
41–50	4
51–60	8
61–70	3
71–80	2
81–90	1

1 Find the modal class of the number of words per sentence.
2 What is the centre of interval of the class 1–10 ?
3 Find an estimate for the mean number of words per sentence.
4 Draw a histogram and a frequency polygon of the data.

Choose a novel by a different author and do a similar survey.
Compare the two surveys and comment on them.
Do you think that the lengths of sentences have some effect on how easy it is to read a book ?
Does this affect your enjoyment of the story ?

4. You may have done some investigations in previous years for which you made frequency distributions and drew bar-line graphs or histograms.
If you still have the data available, you can now find the averages of these distributions.
In some cases, you may decide to do an up-to-date survey and compare it with the previous one.
You can think of ideas for new surveys for yourself. You may get ideas from the questions in this chapter, or look back to *Level 5*, chapters 7 and 18. You may think of an investigation you can do to link with a local problem, or an environmental issue.

PUZZLE

25. Jack picks 6 kg of berries in $1\frac{1}{2}$ hours, and Jill picks 3 kg in 1 hour. If they work together, how long will it take them to pick 35 kg ?

11 Thinking about simultaneous

Simultaneously means 'at the same time'.

Toy cars

Alan and Billy are playing with their toy cars.
Alan has 5 more than Billy.
Here are all their cars put together.
How many belong to Alan and how many belong to Billy?

Buying flowers

Kevin buys a bunch of 10 roses and 5 carnations for his wife and they cost £2.75.
At the same stall, Marie buys a bunch of 8 roses and 10 carnations for her mother, and they cost £3.10.
Can you find out the cost of 1 rose, and 1 carnation?

Simultaneously eating and watching television

Synchronized swimming

equations

Simultaneous equations

An equation with 2 unknown letters, such as $3x + y = 11$, has many solutions.
Another equation, such as $2x - y = 4$, has many solutions.
But there is one solution which satisfies both equations.
Can you find the solution ?

Sheep and cows

Farmer Giles came home from market and said 'I bought some cows for £500 each and some sheep for £40 each, and that cost me £2320. I bought 12 animals altogether'.
Can you find out how many cows, and how many sheep, he bought ?

If he bought c cows and s sheep, then
$c + s = 12$, and
$500c + 40s = 2320$

These are simultaneous equations since we need a solution to satisfy both equations.
Using the 2nd equation, what is the value of $25c + 2s$?
Using the 1st equation, what is the value of $2c + 2s$?
So, what is the value of $23c$, and of c ?
Then, what is the value of s ?
How many cows, and sheep, did Farmer Giles buy altogether ?

11 Simultaneous equations

Examples

1 Solve the equations $5x + 2y = 53$
$$3x - 2y = 19$$

The first equation has an unlimited number of solutions such as $x = 0$, $y = 26\frac{1}{2}$ or $x = 10$, $y = 1\frac{1}{2}$, and the second equation also has an unlimited number of solutions, e.g. $x = 7$, $y = 1$ or $x = \frac{1}{3}$, $y = -9$.

To solve the equations **simultaneously** means that we have to find a solution which satisfies both equations.

If we add the left hand sides of both equations together, they will be balanced by the right hand sides added together.
The left hand sides added together are $5x + 2y + 3x - 2y$ which equals $8x$.
The right hand sides added together are $53 + 19$ which equals 72.
So $8x = 72$
$\qquad x = 9$
To find y, substitute the value $x = 9$ into either of the original equations.
$$5x + 2y = 53$$
$$5 \times 9 + 2y = 53$$
$$45 + 2y = 53$$
$$2y = 8$$
$$y = 4$$
The solution of the simultaneous equations is $x = 9$, $y = 4$.

You can check the solution in both equations.
In the first equation, when $x = 9$ and $y = 4$,
LHS $= 5 \times 9 + 2 \times 4 = 45 + 8 = 53$
RHS $= 53$, so the solution is correct.
In the second equation, when $x = 9$ and $y = 4$,
LHS $= 3 \times 9 - 2 \times 4 = 27 - 8 = 19$
RHS $= 19$, so the solution is correct.

Notice that:

If the equations are written down underneath each other with the x's in one column and the y's in another, it is easy to add them up.

$$5x + 2y = 53$$
$$3x - 2y = 19$$
Adding, $8x \qquad = 72$

By adding the equations together the terms involving y disappeared. Then we were able to find the value of x.

The terms involving y disappeared because they had the same numerical **coefficient**, both 2. Also one term was $+2y$ and the other $-2y$.
Often the coefficients are not the same so we have to make them the same before we add the equations.

(In the next example, to make it simpler to describe what we are doing, we label the equations (1) and (2).)

2   Solve the equations $3x + 2y = 5$ (1)
$5x - 6y = 27$ (2)

The coefficients of y are 2 and -6.
We can make $2y$ into $6y$ by multiplying by 3. We must multiply every term of (1) by 3.

Multiply (1) by 3, and write down (2) again.
$9x + 6y = 15$ (1a)
$5x - 6y = 27$ (2)

Add (1a) and (2)
$14x = 42$
$x = 3$
Substitute $x = 3$ in (1)
$3 \times 3 + 2y = 5$
$9 + 2y = 5$
$2y = -4$
$y = -2$
The solution is $x = 3$, $y = -2$.

To check the solution:

For (1), LHS $= 3x + 2y = 3 \times 3 + 2 \times (-2) = 9 - 4 = 5$, and RHS $= 5$
For (2), LHS $= 5x - 6y = 5 \times 3 - 6 \times (-2) = 15 + 12 = 27$ and RHS $= 27$
The solution is correct.

3   Solve the equations $3x - 5y = 15$ (1)
$2x + 3y = 29$ (2)

Make both coefficients of y into 15.
Multiply (1) by 3 and (2) by 5

$9x - 15y = 45$ (1a)
$10x + 15y = 145$ (2a)
Add (1a) and (2a)
$19x = 190$
$x = 10$
Substitute $x = 10$ in (2)
$2 \times 10 + 3y = 29$
$20 + 3y = 29$
$3y = 9$
$y = 3$
The solution is $x = 10$, $y = 3$.

You can check for yourself that this solution is correct.

Exercise 11.1

Solve these simultaneous equations.

1. $x + y = 8$
$x - y = 2$

2. $5x + y = 5$
$7x - y = 13$

3. $5x - 3y = 9$
$2x + 3y = 12$

4. $2x + 3y = 1$
$3x - y = 7$

5. $2x - 3y = 47$
$4x + y = 45$

6. $5x + 4y = 10$
$6x - y = -17$

7. $4x + 3y = 43$
$3x - 2y = 11$

8. $2x + 3y = 4$
$3x - 4y = 6$

9. $7x - 5x = -5$
$3x + 2y = 2$

10. $2x - 3y = 5$
$3x + 2y = 1$

Using subtraction

Examples

4 Solve the equations $3x + 2y = 10$ (1)
$$7x + 2y = 26 \quad (2)$$

Although the coefficients of the terms in y are the same, they are both $+2$.
To eliminate the terms in y, we must subtract.

Subtract (1) from (2)
$$4x = 16$$
$$x = 4$$

If, instead, you subtract (2) from (1) you get
$$-4x = -16$$
$$4x = 16$$
$$x = 4, \text{ as before.}$$

Substitute $x = 4$ in (1)
$$3 \times 4 + 2y = 10$$
$$12 + 2y = 10$$
$$2y = -2$$
$$y = -1$$
The solution is $x = 4$, $y = -1$.

To check the solution:
In (1), LHS $= 3x + 2y = 3 \times 4 + 2 \times (-1) = 12 - 2 = 10$, and RHS $= 10$
In (2), LHS $= 7x + 2y = 7 \times 4 + 2 \times (-1) = 28 - 2 = 26$, and RHS $= 26$
The solution is correct.

5 Solve the equations $5x - 3y = 29$ (1)
$$4x - 2y = 24 \quad (2)$$

Make both terms in y into $-6y$.
Multiply (1) by 2 and multiply (2) by 3
$$10x - 6y = 58 \quad (1a)$$
$$12x - 6y = 72 \quad (2a)$$
Subtract (1a) from (2a)
$$2x = 14$$
$$x = 7$$

(Notice that when subtracting, $(-6y)$ take away $(-6y)$
$$= (-6y) - (-6y)$$
$$= (-6y) + 6y$$
$$= 0 \quad)$$

Substitute $x = 7$ into (2)
$$28 - 2y = 24$$
$$28 = 24 + 2y$$
$$4 = 2y$$
$$y = 2$$
The solution is $x = 7$, $y = 2$.

You can check for yourself that this solution is correct.

Sometimes it may be easier to eliminate x rather than y.

6 Solve the equations $3x + 5y = 9$ (1)
$$x + 6y = -10 \quad (2)$$

Multiply (2) by 3. Write down (1) again, if you want to.
$$3x + 18y = -30 \quad (2a)$$
$$3x + 5y = 9 \quad (1)$$
Subtract (1) from (2a)
$$13y = -39$$
$$y = -3$$
Substitute $y = -3$ in (2)
$$x + 6 \times (-3) = -10$$
$$x - 18 = -10$$
$$x = 8$$
The solution is $x = 8$, $y = -3$.

To check the solution:
For (1), LHS $= 3x + 5y = 3 \times 8 + 5 \times (-3) = 24 - 15 = 9$, and RHS $= 9$
For (2), LHS $= x + 6y = 8 + 6 \times (-3) = 8 - 18 = -10$, and RHS $= -10$
The solution is correct.

Be very careful if subtracting numbers or terms with negative signs.
e.g. in a case like $3x - 6y = 6$ (1)
$$3x - 5y = 11 \quad (2)$$
When subtracting (2) from (1), $(-6y) - (-5y) = (-6y) + 5y = -y$
When subtracting (1) from (2), $(-5y) - (-6y) = (-5y) + 6y = y$

Exercise 11.2

Solve these simultaneous equations.

1. $2x + y = 7$
   $x + y = 4$

6. $3x - y = 26$
   $x - 5y = 4$

2. $x + 7y = 20$
   $x + 2y = 5$

7. $x + 5y = 18$
   $2x + 3y = 8$

3. $2x - 6y = 20$
   $2x - 5y = 18$

8. $3x + 2y = 5$
   $7x + 3y = 15$

4. $2x - y = 5$
   $3x - 2y = 7$

9. $2x - 3y = 1$
   $3x - 2y = 4$

5. $2x + 3y = 2$
   $x + 6y = 4$

10. $5x + 3y = 12$
    $7x + 5y = 16$

Solving by substitution

This method is useful when we have a term containing x (i.e. not $2x$, $3x$, etc.) or y.

Examples

7 Solve the equations $\quad x - 8y = 3 \quad$ (1)
$\qquad\qquad\qquad\qquad 3x - 10y = 2 \quad$ (2)

(1) can be written as $x = 3 + 8y \quad$ (1a)
Substitute this expression for x in (2)
$3(3 + 8y) - 10y = 2$
Remove the bracket and solve in the usual way.
$\qquad 9 + 24y - 10y = 2$
$\qquad\qquad 9 + 14y = 2$
$\qquad\qquad\qquad 14y = -7$
$\qquad\qquad\qquad\quad y = -\frac{1}{2}$

Use (1a) again, substituting $y = -\frac{1}{2}$
$x = 3 + 8 \times (-\frac{1}{2})$
$\quad = 3 - 4$
$\quad = -1$
The solution is $x = -1$, $y = -\frac{1}{2}$.

To check the solution $x = -1$, $y = -\frac{1}{2}$:
For (1), LHS $= x - 8y = (-1) - 8 \times (-\frac{1}{2}) = (-1) + 4 = 3$, and RHS $= 3$
For (2), LHS $= 3x - 10y = 3 \times (-1) - 10 \times (-\frac{1}{2}) = (-3) + 5 = 2$, and
RHS $= 2$.
The solution is correct.

8 Solve the equations $2x - 3y = 5$ (1)
$\qquad\qquad\qquad\qquad 3x + y = 2$ (2)

(2) can be written $y = 2 - 3x$ (2a)
Substitute this expression for y in (1)
$$2x - 3(2 - 3x) = 5$$
$$2x - 6 + 9x = 5$$
$$11x - 6 = 5$$
$$11x = 11$$
$$x = 1$$
Use (2a) again, substituting $x = 1$
$$y = 2 - 3 \times 1$$
$$= 2 - 3$$
$$= -1$$
The solution is $x = 1$, $y = -1$.

You can check for yourself that this solution is correct.

Exercise 11.3

Solve these equations by the method of substitution.

1. $x - 4y = 29$
$\quad\;\; 3x + 2y = 17$

2. $4x - 3y = 11$
$\quad\;\; 2x + y = 13$

3. $x - 2y = 27$
$\quad\; 7x + y = 9$

4. $x + 2y = 1$
$\quad 3x + 5y = 1$

Solve these equations using any suitable method.

5. $x - y = 5$
$\quad 3x - 4y = 16$

6. $x + 2y = -3$
$\quad\; x - y = 0$

7. $5x + 3y = 1$
$\quad 7x + y = 11$

8. $7x + 4y = 9$
$\quad 5x + 6y = 19$

9. $10x + 3y = 11$
$\quad\; 5x + 4y = 23$

10. $5x - 7y = 20$
$\quad\; 3x - 2y = 12$

Using simultaneous equations to solve problems

Example

9 3 lamps and 4 metres of wire cost £38, and 5 lamps and 14 metres of wire cost £67. What is the cost of a lamp, and how much does a metre of wire cost ?

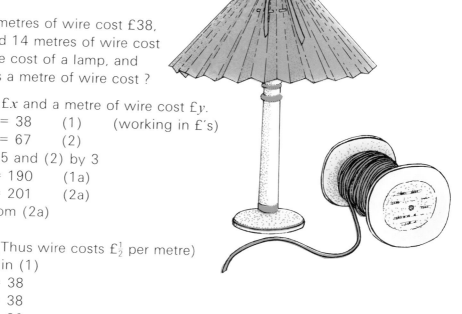

Let a lamp cost £x and a metre of wire cost £y.
Then $3x + 4y = 38$ (1)   (working in £'s)
    $5x + 14y = 67$ (2)
Multiply (1) by 5 and (2) by 3
    $15x + 20y = 190$ (1a)
    $15x + 42y = 201$ (2a)
Subtract (1a) from (2a)
    $22y = 11$
      $y = \frac{1}{2}$ (Thus wire costs £$\frac{1}{2}$ per metre)
Substitute $y = \frac{1}{2}$ in (1)
    $3x + 4 \times \frac{1}{2} = 38$
      $3x + 2 = 38$
        $3x = 36$
         $x = 12$ (Thus a lamp costs £12)

A lamp costs £12 and a metre of wire costs 50p.

You can check the solution using the details of the question.

Exercise 11.4   Applications and Activities

1. The sum of two numbers is 43 and their difference is 19. What are they ?
(Let the numbers be x and y.)

2. May buys 6 oranges and 5 grapefruit and they cost £2.12.
June buys 8 oranges and 3 grapefruit and they cost £1.80.
What is the cost of 1 orange, and of 1 grapefruit ?
(Let 1 orange cost x pence and 1 grapefruit cost y pence.)

3. Jamil has saved some 20-pence and some 50-pence coins. He has 23 of these coins altogether, and they are worth £7. How many coins of each value has he ? (Let him have x 20-pence coins and y 50-pence coins.)

4. Write down two equations satisfied by x and y in these triangles, and solve them to find the angles of both triangles.

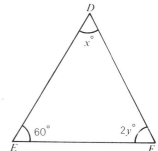

5. A pile of money consists of £10 and £20 notes and amounts to £660. If there were twice as many £20 notes and half as many £10 notes there would be £120 more. How many of each kind of note are there ? (Let there be $2x$ £10 notes and y £20 notes.)

6. In this triangle the perimeter is 84 cm and $AB = AC$.
Write down 2 equations involving x and y, simplify them and solve them.
Find the numerical values of the sides of the triangle.

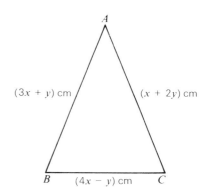

7. A stallholder sells two kinds of T-shirts, one kind priced at £4 each, the others at £6.50 each. On one morning she sold 52 T-shirts for £233.
How many of each kind did she sell ?

8. For casual workers, a firm pays adults £x per day and teenagers £y per day.
On one day they employed 12 adults and 8 teenagers and paid out wages of £460.
The next day they employed 4 less adults and 2 more teenagers and the wages that day were £60 less than the day before.
Write down two equations connecting x and y, and solve them, to find the daily wages paid to an adult and to a teenager.

9. To fill a water barrel, Dad used the big bucket and tipped in 7 bucketfuls of water, while Pip used his smaller bucket and tipped in 3 bucketfuls of water. The barrel holds 71 litres.

    The next time the barrel was empty, Dad tipped in 2 bucketfuls then he was called away, and Pip completed the job by bringing 11 bucketfuls, using the small bucket.

    How much water does the big bucket hold, and how much does Pip's bucket hold ?

10. **A number game to play in class**

    For this game, two friends sit together. They each choose a number. Here, let the friends be Anne and Barbara.

    Give them some instructions to work out.

    e.g. What is 3 times Anne's number plus 4 times Barbara's number ?

    They will work this out together and tell you the answer.

    Then give them another set of instructions.

    e.g. What is 4 times Anne's number minus 3 times Barbara's number ?

    They will tell you the answer.

    The rest of you can write down 2 equations and solve them to find the two numbers.

    In the example above, if the 1st answer was 33 and the 2nd answer was 19, then, letting Anne's number be a and Barbara's number be b, the equations are

    $3a + 4b = 33$
    $4a - 3b = 19$

    What were the two numbers chosen ?

    For the next turn, two other people should choose numbers, and the instructions you give them should be different ones.

    Very occasionally you might find that because of the instructions you gave them, it is not possible to solve the equations and find the numbers. If this happens, can you discover why ?

12 Thinking about circles and cylinders

Circles

With circles we want to find and use the relationships connecting radius, or diameter, and circumference and area.

Circumference and diameter

When a bicycle is wheeled through 1 revolution, what distance is travelled? How can we use this measurement to find the connection between the diameter and the circumference of the wheel?

Area of a circle

A circle was made with string.
When the string was cut, a triangular shape was made.

Base of triangle = circumference of circle
$$= 2\pi r$$
Height of triangle = radius of circle
$$= r$$
Area of circle = area of triangle
$$= \tfrac{1}{2}bh = \tfrac{1}{2} \times 2\pi r \times r = \pi r^2$$

Cylinders

With cylinders we want to find and use the relationships connecting volume or surface area with radius and height.

Make a list of objects which are cylindrical in shape.
Include some very large objects in your list.
Include some very small objects in your list.

12 Circles and Cylinders

There is an introduction to this chapter on page 100.

Circles

Circumference = π × diameter = 2π × radius

$C = \pi d$
$C = 2\pi r$

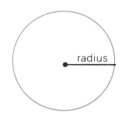

radius

Area = π × (radius)^2

$A = \pi r^2$

π is the Greek letter pi (pronounced pie).
π is a number which cannot be written as an exact fraction or decimal.
It is approximately 3.14159, but for normal calculations we use 3, 3.1, 3.14 or 3.142, depending on how accurate we need to be.
Most scientific calculators have a key for π and it is quicker and more accurate to press this than to enter 3.142.
Because π is not an exact decimal, you should normally give an answer correct to 3 significant figures. The answer might occasionally differ in the last figure, depending on which value you use for π.

Examples

1   Find the circumference of a circle with radius 8 cm.

$C = 2\pi r$
$= 2 \times \pi \times 8$ cm
$= 50.265\ldots$ cm, if using the π key on your calculator
(or 50.272 cm, if using $\pi = 3.142$)
$= 50.3$ cm, correct to 3 significant figures.

2   Find the circumference of a circle with diameter 7.5 cm.

$C = \pi d$
$\quad = \pi \times 7.5 \ \ \text{cm}$
$\quad = 23.561 \ldots \text{cm}$, if using the π key on your calculator
$\quad \quad$ (or 23.565 cm, if using $\pi = 3.142$)
$\quad = 23.6$ cm, correct to 3 significant figures.

3   Find the area of a circle with diameter 17.2 cm.

(If the diameter is 17.2 cm, the radius is 8.6 cm.)
$A = \pi r^2$
$\quad = \pi \times 8.6^2 \ \ \text{cm}^2$
$\quad = 232.35 \ldots \text{cm}^2$
$\quad = 232 \ \text{cm}^2$, correct to 3 significant figures.

Finding the radius or diameter

4   If the circumference of a circle is 1 m, what is its diameter ?

(Work in cm.   1 m = 100 cm)
$\quad \quad C = \pi d$
$\quad 100 = \pi \times d \quad \quad (d \text{ in cm})$

$$d = \frac{100}{\pi} \ \text{cm}$$

$\quad \quad = 31.830 \ldots \text{cm}$, if using the π key on your calculator
$\quad \quad \quad$ (or 31.826 $\ldots$ cm, if using $\pi = 3.142$)
$\quad \quad = 31.8$ cm, correct to 3 significant figures

5   If the circumference of a circle is 70 cm, what is its radius ?

$\quad \quad C = 2\pi r$
$\quad 70 = 2 \times \pi \times r \quad \quad (r \text{ in cm})$

$$r = \frac{70}{2 \times \pi} \ \text{cm}$$

$\quad \quad = 11.140 \ldots \text{cm}$
$\quad \quad = 11.1$ cm, correct to 3 significant figures.

6   If the area of a circle is 1 m^2, what is its radius ?

Working in m^2 and m,
$$A = \pi r^2$$
$$1 = \pi r^2 \qquad (r \text{ in m})$$

$$r^2 = \frac{1}{\pi}$$

$$r = \sqrt{\frac{1}{\pi}} \quad \text{m} \qquad\qquad \text{Press } 1 \ \boxed{\div} \ \boxed{\pi} \ \boxed{=} \ \boxed{\sqrt{}}$$

$$= 0.56418 \ldots \text{m}$$
$$= 56.4 \text{ cm, correct to 3 significant figures.}$$
(If you prefer to work in cm, $1 \text{ m}^2 = 10\,000 \text{ cm}^2$)

π **as a fraction**

π is not an exact fraction but a good approximation using small numbers is $3\frac{1}{7}$ or $\frac{22}{7}$.
Find $22 \div 7$ on your calculator to see how this approximation compares with the real value of π.
This fraction was often used, rather than using a decimal, in the days before calculators were available, and you might still find questions where you are told to take π as $\frac{22}{7}$.

7   Find the area of a circle of radius 21 cm, taking π as $\frac{22}{7}$.
$$A = \pi r^2$$
$$= \tfrac{22}{7} \times 21^2 \ \text{cm}^2 \qquad \text{(multiply 22 by } 21^2 \text{ before dividing by 7)}$$
$$= 1386 \text{ cm}^2$$
$$= 1390 \text{ cm}^2, \text{ correct to 3 significant figures.}$$

(Normally you will not use $\frac{22}{7}$ for π unless instructed to, as with a calculator it is as easy to use 3.142, which is a better approximation, or the π key which gives π accurate to several decimal places.)

Exercise 12.1

In this exercise, take π as 3.142 or use the π key on your calculator. Give answers corrected to 3 significant figures.

1.   Find the lengths of the circumferences of these circles.

1	Diameter = 12 cm	**4**	Diameter = 9.2 cm
2	Radius = 5 cm	**5**	Radius = 6.7 cm
3	Radius = 8.2 cm		

2.   Find the areas of the circles of question 1.

3.   **1**   If the circumference of a circle is 50.8 cm, find its diameter.
      2   If the circumference of a circle is 80 cm, find its radius.
      3   If the area of a circle is 60 cm^2, find its radius.
      4   If the circumference of a circle is 28.3 cm, find its radius, and hence
              find its area.

4.   The circle is inscribed in a square of
      side 8 cm.
      Find,
      1   the area of the square,
      2   the area of the circle,
      3   the total shaded area.

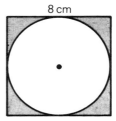

5.   This circle has radius 9 cm, and has a
      square inscribed in it.
      Find,
      1   the area of the circle,
      2   the area of the square (by considering
              it as 2 or 4 triangles),
      3   the total shaded area.

6.   This circle has radius 10 cm.
      1   Find its circumference.
      2   What fraction of the circumference is
              the arc *AB* if $\angle AOB = 45°$?
      3   What is the length of the arc *AB* ?

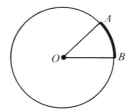

Cylinders

Volume

Since the cylinder is a solid figure of uniform
cross-section,
volume = area of cross-section × height
$$= \pi r^2 \times h$$
$$= \pi r^2 h$$

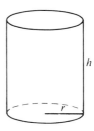

Surface area

If the curved surface is cut and opened out it
can form a rectangle.
The length of the rectangle is the distance
round the cylinder. This is the circumference of
the base.
The breadth of the rectangle is the height of the
cylinder.

Curved surface area = circumference × height

$$= 2\pi r \times h$$
$$= 2\pi rh$$

To find the total surface area if the cylinder has two circular ends, add on
2 × area of circle = $2\pi r^2$
Total surface area = $2\pi r^2 + 2\pi rh$
This can be written as $2\pi r(r + h)$, which is quicker to work out, finding $r + h$ first and
then multiplying by 2, π and r.
If the cylinder is an open one with only one end, the total surface area = $\pi r^2 + 2\pi rh$,
which is $\pi r(r + 2h)$

$V = \pi r^2 h$	V is the volume.
$S = 2\pi rh$	S is the curved surface area.
$T = 2\pi r(r + h)$	T is the total surface area, including two ends.

Height may sometimes be described as length or thickness.

length

thickness

Examples

8   Find the volume of a cylinder with base-radius 8 cm
    and height 6 cm.

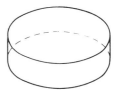

$$V = \pi r^2 h$$
$$= \pi \times 8^2 \times 6 \ \ cm^3$$
$$= 1206.37 \ldots cm^3, \text{ if using the } \pi \text{ key on your calculator,}$$
$$\text{or } 1206.528 \, cm^3 \text{ if using } \pi = 3.142$$
$$= 1210 \, cm^3, \text{ correct to 3 significant figures.}$$

9 Find the curved surface area and the total surface area of the cylinder of example **8**.

For the curved surface area:
$$S = 2\pi rh$$
$$= 2 \times \pi \times 8 \times 6 \text{ cm}^2$$
$$= 301.59 \ldots \text{ cm}^2$$
$$= 302 \text{ cm}^2, \text{ correct to 3 significant figures.}$$

For the total surface area:
$$T = 2\pi r(r + h)$$
$$= 2 \times \pi \times 8 \times (8 + 6) \text{ cm}^2$$
$$= 703.71 \ldots \text{ cm}^2$$
$$= 704 \text{ cm}^2, \text{ correct to 3 significant figures.}$$

10 A cylinder with curved surface area of 200 cm² has a base-radius of radius 5 cm. What is its height ?

$$S = 2\pi rh$$
$$200 = 2 \times \pi \times 5 \times h \qquad (h \text{ in cm})$$

$$h = \frac{200}{10 \times \pi} \text{ cm}$$

$$= 6.366 \ldots \text{ cm}$$
$$= 6.37 \text{ cm, correct to 3 significant figures.}$$
$$\text{or } 6.4 \text{ cm, correct to the nearest mm.}$$

11 A cylinder with volume 1000 cm³ has a height of 8 cm. What is the radius of its base ?

$$V = \pi r^2 h$$
$$1000 = \pi \times r^2 \times 8 \qquad (r \text{ in cm})$$

$$r^2 = \frac{1000}{8 \times \pi} \qquad (r \text{ in cm})$$

$$r = \sqrt{\frac{1000}{8 \times \pi}} \text{ cm}$$

$$= 6.3078 \ldots \text{ cm}$$
$$= 6.31 \text{ cm, correct to 3 significant figures,}$$
$$\text{or } 6.3 \text{ cm, correct to the nearest mm.}$$

Exercise 12.2

In this exercise, take π as 3.142 or use the π key on your calculator. Give answers corrected to 3 significant figures.

1.   Find the volumes of these solid figures.
      1   A cylinder with base-radius 11 cm and height 30 cm.
      2   A disc with radius 8 cm and thickness 2 cm.
      3   A long circular rod with radius 2 cm and length 2 m.
      4   A cylinder with diameter 12 cm and height 18 cm.
      5   A cylindrical drum of radius 15 cm and height 50 cm.

2.   Find the areas of the curved surfaces of the solid figures of question 1.

3.   **1**   A closed cylindrical tin has radius 4 cm and height 6 cm. Find its total surface area.
      2   An open cylindrical container has radius 7 cm and height 6.5 cm. Find the total area of its curved surface and its circular base.

4.   **1**   If the volume of a cylinder is 215 cm³ and its radius is 3.8 cm, find its height.
      2   If the volume of a cylinder is 142 cm³ and its height is 7.5 cm, find its radius.
      3   If the curved surface area of a cylinder is 400 cm² and the height is 14.9 cm, find its radius.

Exercise 12.3   Applications and Activities

1.   A rectangular pond, 24 m long and 20 m wide, was lengthened by a semicircular addition at one end. What is the new area of the pond ?

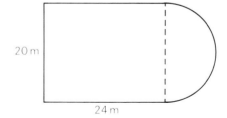

2.   A car wheel has a diameter of 52 cm. How far has the wheel travelled along the ground when it has made 1 revolution ?
      If the car is travelling at 60 km/hour, how many revolutions does the wheel make in one minute ?

3.   A running track is in the
      shape of a rectangle with
      semicircles at the ends.
      If the distance round the
      track is 400 m, with each
      semicircular and each straight
      part being 100 m, what is the
      width across the track, to the
      nearest 0.1 m ?

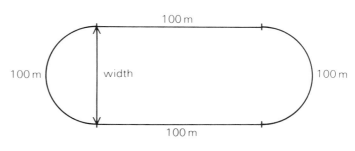

4.   A pipe with circular section and internal
      radius 30 cm, is full of water flowing at
      1.5 metres per second.
      What is the flow in litres per minute ?

5.   Rain falls on 30 m^2 of a flat roof to a depth of 1.5 cm. It runs into a cylindrical
      tank of diameter 1.2 m. Find the depth of water in the tank, to the nearest cm.

6.   The cross-section of a tunnel, 100 m long,
      is semicircular, with diameter 3 m.
      1   What is the volume of soil which
             had to be dug out, to make the tunnel
             (in m^3, to the nearest 10 m^3) ?
      2   The curved walls of the inside of the
             tunnel have to be painted. What is
             the area to be painted ?

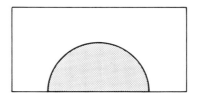

7.   Find the volume, and the weight in kg, of a solid brass cylinder, diameter 30 cm,
      height 50 cm, if brass weighs 8 g per cm^3.

8.   A circular pond of diameter 44 m is surrounded by a path of width 3 m and
      outside that there is a solid wooden fence 1.5 m high. The fence is to be painted
      on both sides. Find the area to be painted, and find how much paint is needed
      for 2 coats of paint on each side, if 1 litre of paint covers 18 m^2.

9.   A caterer has a large cylindrical container full of fruit juice. Its diameter is 40 cm
      and its height is 50 cm. The fruit juice is to be poured into glasses, also of
      cylindrical shape, with diameter 7 cm, to a depth of 10 cm. How many glasses
      can be filled from the juice in the container ?

10.   A children's circular paddling pool is 2.5 m in diameter and 45 cm deep.
       How many litres of water will it hold ?

11.   **Enclosing an area**

       A farmer wants to make an enclosure
       to keep sheep in, and he has enough
       fencing for a perimeter of 160 m.
       If he makes a square enclosure,
       what will its area be ?
       If he makes the enclosure circular,
       how much extra area will there be
       in it ?

12.   **Pythagoras' theorem again**

       Draw a right-angled triangle and
       construct semicircles on the 3 sides.
       Is there any relationship connecting the
       areas of these semicircles ?

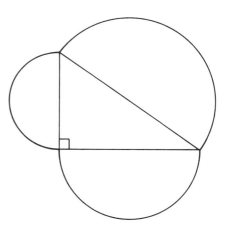

13. A cylindrical tin is to be produced to
     hold 1 litre of a soft drink.
     The manufacturers want the area of
     metal needed to be as small as
     possible.
     Should it be a small can with a large
     radius or a taller can with a smaller
     radius ?

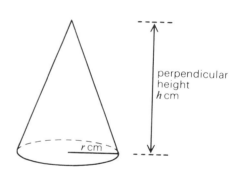

     Investigate this problem by trial, starting
     by assuming radii of 1 cm, 2 cm, 3 cm, . . .
     and finding the height, and then the total surface area in each case.
     Give the measurements of the can which uses the least area of tin, in cm, to the
     nearest mm. (Ignore any extra tin needed at the edges and for the overlap.)

14. **The volume of a cone**

     You can make a rough model of the
     curved part of a cone (without a base),
     from a sector of a circle, and measure the
     radius of the base of the cone, r cm, and
     the perpendicular height, h cm.
     Then make a cylinder which has the same
     radius and height. This needs a base but
     does not need a lid.
     What is the formula for the volume of the
     cylinder ?

     Now, fill the cylinder with sand or something similar, and by transferring this to
     the cone, see if you can discover the connection between the volumes, and so
     find the formula for the volume of a cone.

PUZZLE

26. Seven women, who are all friends, are having a celebration lunch, because they are all in
     town on the same day. In how many days time will they next be able to lunch together if:
     Anthea is in town every day,
     Beryl is in town every other day,
     Charlene visits town every 3rd day,
     Davina visits town every 4th day,
     Ethel visits town every 5th day,
     Freda visits town every 6th day,
     Greta visits town every 7th day?

Miscellaneous Section B

Aural Practice

These aural exercises, B1 and B2, should be read to you, probably by your teacher or a friend, and you should write down the answers only, doing any working out in your head. You should do the 15 questions within 10 minutes.

Exercise B1

1. 33% of the members of a society are female. What percentage are male ?

2. A train leaves London at 3.35 pm. It arrives in Bournemouth at 5.15 pm. How long does the journey take ?

3. There are some red and blue beads in a bag. Roger decides that if he picks one bead out at random, the probability of getting a red one is 0.4. If there are 100 beads in the bag, how many, approximately, should be red ones ?

4. If the instructions in a flow diagram say 'Square x and add 1', what number is obtained if $x = 8$?

5. What is the perimeter of a rectangular field 120 metres long by 80 metres wide ?

6. Emma describes a number. It is between 20 and 30, it is prime, and when it is divided by 4 there is a remainder 1. What is the number ?

7. Luke wants 2 litres of squash but he can only buy $\frac{1}{2}$-litre bottles. How many bottles does he need to buy ?

8. A cuboid has measurements 5 cm by 4 cm by 3 cm. What is its volume ?

9. If the sides next to the right angle in a right-angled triangle are 3 cm and 4 cm, how long is the hypotenuse ?

10. If $3x$ is less than 21, what can you say about x ?

11. How many edges does a triangular prism have ?

12. I thought of two numbers.
When I added the two numbers I got 14, when I multiplied the two numbers I got 33.
What two numbers did I think of ?

13.   What is the name for a quadrilateral with all sides equal and all angles right angles ?

14.   What is the value of 0.9 ÷ 0.3 ?

15.   The numbers of packets of crisps sold on 4 days were 40, 25, 15 and 20. What was the average number sold per day ?

Exercise B2

1.   What is the value of $6^2 - 4^2$?

2.   Fiona is paid time and a half for overtime. If the basic rate is £2.40 an hour, how much should she be paid for 1 hour overtime ?

3.   2 angles of a triangle are 40° and 65°. What is the size of the 3rd angle ?

4.   What is the value of 3.6 ÷ 100 ?

5.   If you stretch out a continuous loop of rope to make a right-angled triangle, and one side of the triangle is 4 m long and the side opposite the right angle is 5 m long, how long is the third side ?

6.   Simplify the expression $3b^3 \times 2b^2$.

7.   3645 people attended an open-air concert. Write this number correct to 2 significant figures.

8.   Jack and Jill each think of a number. The sum of the numbers is 30, and Jack's number is 2 more than Jill's number. What is Jack's number ?

9.   What is the mean of the numbers 0.2, 0.3 and 0.7 ?

10.   If you toss a fair coin 3 times and get heads twice and tails once, what is the probability that the next time you toss it, you will get a tail ?

11.   Write down the next 2 numbers in the sequence 81, 64, 49, 36, . . .

12.   A motorist travels at an average speed of 42 miles per hour for 3 hours. How far does he travel in this time ?

13.   If $5x + 2$ is greater than 22, what can you say about x ?

14.   A sheet of cardboard 32 cm long and 20 cm wide is cut into squares of side 4 cm. How many squares can be made ?

15.   A piece of wood, 45 cm long, is cut into 2 pieces such that one piece is twice as long as the other. What is the length of the longer piece ?

Exercise B3   Revision

1.   A clock loses 20 seconds each hour. If it is set right at 9 am, what time will it show at 9 am the next morning ?

2.   Simplify these expressions, leaving the answers in index form.
     1 $2^7 \times 2^2$ **2** $5^4 \div 5$ **3** $(3^4)^2$

3.   A rectangle has sides 0.05 m and 0.03 m.
     1   What is the length of its perimeter, in metres ?
     2   What is its area, in m^2 ?

4.   What are the possible values of x, if x is a whole number, also
     $2x + 3 > 17$ and $15 - x > 5$?

5.   **1**   Find the area of $\triangle ABC$.
     2   Find the length of AC.
     3   Use **1** and **2** to calculate the length of BX, giving the answer to the nearest mm.

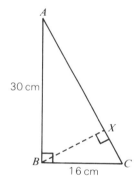

6.   The average age of 5 boys is 10 years 11 months.
     1   What is the total of their ages ?

     A sixth boy of age 11 years 5 months joins the group.
     2   What is the total of the 6 ages ?
     3   What is the average age of the whole group ?

7.   Simplify these expressions.
     1 $3a + 4b + 2(a - 2b)$
     2 $3(c + 2d) - 2(c - 3d)$
     3 $6e + 4 - (e - 5)$

8.   I handed a bundle of £5 and £20 notes into a bank. There were 18 notes and their value was £150.
     Let the number of £5 notes be x and the number of £20 notes be y. Write down 2 equations for x and y and solve them.
     How many of each kind of note did I have ?

9.   Find the sizes of the angles
     a, b and c.

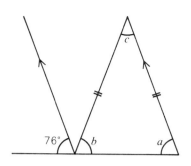

10. The diagram shows the cross-section of a
     bar which is 3.5 m long.
     Find

     1   the area of the cross-section, in cm^2,
     2   the volume of the bar, in cm^3,
     3   the weight of the bar, if it is made of
           metal weighing 8 g/cm^3.

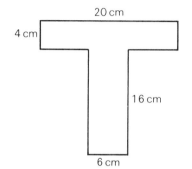

11. Simon made a wooden die, and he tested it to see if it was a fair one.
     In 500 throws, here are the results.

Number	1	2	3	4	5	6
Frequency	80	120	64	27	99	110

     Based on these experimental results,
     1   what is the probability of scoring a 1 or 2,
     2   what is the probability of scoring an even number ?
     3   If Simon threw the die another 200 times, how many times approximately
           could he expect to get the number 6 ?

12. 12 cm lengths of wire are bent to make a variety of plane shapes.
     1   What 2 possible shapes can be made with all sides 3 cm long ?
     2   What shape is made with all sides 4 cm long ?
     3   If a triangle is made, with one side 3 cm long and another side 4 cm long,
           how long is the third side, and what sort of triangle is it ?
     4   If a regular pentagon is made, how long is each side ?

13.   The number of tomatoes on each truss on tomato plants in a greenhouse were counted. Here are the results:

9	8	4	7	7	5	3	5	3	6	5	1	5	6	5
5	4	1	8	6	3	9	5	2	7	4	1	4	7	4
6	3	4	6	4	2	3	4	4	5	2	8	6	4	4
6	6	2	5	7										

Make a frequency table of these results.
1   What is the mode number of tomatoes per truss ?
2   What is the median number ?
3   What is the mean number ?

14.   The circle is inscribed in a square of side 12 cm.
Find,
1   the perimeter of the square,
2   the circumference of the circle, to the nearest mm.
3   How much greater is the perimeter of the square than the circumference of the circle ?

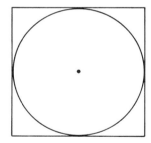

15.   Find the 1st 4 terms of these sequences whose nth terms are given here.

1 $7n + 4$
2 $10 - 3n$
3 5^n
4 $\dfrac{2n - 1}{2n + 1}$
5 $n^3 - 1$

16. **1**   If $a = 10$ cm and $b = 5$ cm, calculate c, correct to the nearest mm.
    2   If $a = 11$ cm and $c = 13$ cm, calculate b, correct to the nearest mm.

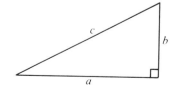

17.   For a school outing, 27 children paid 65p each. The total expenses of the outing were £15.
      1   How much money was left to be refunded to the children ?
      2   This money was divided equally among the children, and the few pence left over were put into the charity collection.
              How much did each child receive, and how much was left over ?

18.   Draw a rectangle *ABCD* with *AB* = 12 cm and *BC* = 8 cm.
      Construct the locus of points inside the rectangle which are
      1   3 cm from the side *AB*.
      2   6 cm from mid-point of the side *CD*.
      Find two points *P* and *Q* which are 3 cm from *AB* and 6cm from the mid-point of *CD*.
      Measure the distance *PQ*.

19.   30 kg of fertilizer costing £1.60 per kg is mixed with 70 kg of plant food costing £1.30 per kg.
      1   What is the total cost of the mixture ?
      2   What is the cost per kg of the mixture ?

20.   A closed cylindrical tin has radius 3 cm and height 7 cm.
      Find
      1   its total surface area,
      2   its volume.
      Give the answers correct to 3 significant figures.

Exercise B4   Activities

1.   **Planning a cycling or walking holiday**

     This is a good way for older teenagers to explore different parts of Britain.
     You can plan such a holiday, and you may be able to carry out your plans, with friends, when you are older.
     Your holiday may simply be a chance to see and enjoy the countryside or to visit places of historical interest. Or you may have a more definite challenge such as to walk along the Pennine Way, or to do some voluntary conservation work.

First, decide on the main points, e.g. which region of Britain you want to visit, who will go with you, whether you will cycle or walk and how long the trip will last.
Then make more detailed plans, with the help of a good map.
Perhaps you may start your journey by train, to give you more time to explore the chosen region. You will need somewhere to stay. Perhaps you can use Youth Hostels, or bed-and-breakfast accommodation, or perhaps you will take lightweight tents with you.

Write about your plans. Include details of your route, showing how far you will travel each day, and the approximate costs, and a list of the clothing and equipment that you will take with you.

2. **Making a Maths Magazine**

This is a project for the whole class.

A Maths magazine could have articles about things you have learnt recently, or you could use library books to find out about other things, such as about great Mathematicians and their discoveries. It could also include pictures, cartoons, puzzles and competitions. There should be an attractive title page.

Decide on the size of the page. If you are going to photocopy the magazine then A4 size, or A5 size, so that you can fit 2 pages on an A4 sheet, will be best. Ask for all contributions to be printed or written neatly using one side of the paper only, and on the right size of paper. Ask everyone to submit an entry for the magazine. Decide on a date by which these should be given in. Choose an editor and a committee to sort out the entries and decide on a varied selection to be included.

In making-up the magazine, the original entries can be cut up and arranged to fit the pages. Drawings, if too big, can be reduced by using the photocopier. Some articles may need correcting or altering, and some may be easier to read if they are typed. Can you find a volunteer to do the typing ?
You will have to work out how much it will cost for the paper and the use of the photocopier. Decide how many copies you are going to print, and how much you will charge for them. If you can think of a different way of raising money to cover the cost you could give everyone in the class a free copy.

3.   **Spirograph patterns**

This amazing toy was first produced about 30 years ago, and an improved version is still on sale.

Different-sized circles have cogs so that one circle can move around another without slipping. There are holes in the circles so that you can draw the path of the hole, with a biro, as a circle moves around a fixed circle.

You can also move circles round or inside other shapes. You can make many patterns. There are some examples below.

If you have a spirograph set, or can borrow one to use, investigate the effects of different-sized circles and different holes.

Display your patterns on a poster.

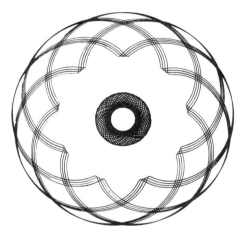 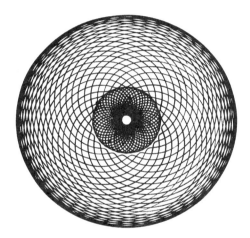

4.   **Painted cubes**

Several cubes of edge 1 cm are stacked together to form a larger cube. This larger cube is then painted on the outside. Thus the small cubes may have some of their faces painted. Make a table of results for the small cubes.

Edge of large cube	Number of small cubes	Number with these faces painted			
		0 faces	1 face	2 faces	3 faces
2 cm	8	0	0	0	8
3 cm	27				
4 cm					
5 cm					
...					

Do you notice any patterns ? What would be the results for a large cube of edge 10 cm ?

What would be the results for a cube of edge n cm ?

5. **Tangrams**

This is an old puzzle. You can make a set of 7 pieces for yourself. It is best to use thick cardboard, plywood or something similar. The pieces can be used either side up.
Begin with 2 squares. In cardboard, squares of side 8 cm would be suitable. Divide them as shown.

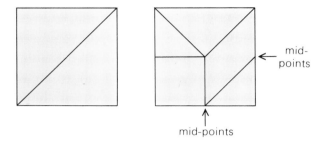

Since all the triangles are right-angled triangles, you can calculate the lengths of all the edges using Pythagoras' theorem. This knowledge may help you to fit equal edges together.

Since the 2 squares are equal, they fit on 2 sides of an isosceles right-angled triangle, and they are equal in area to the square on the hypotenuse.
It is possible to rearrange the 7 pieces to make this square, so do this.

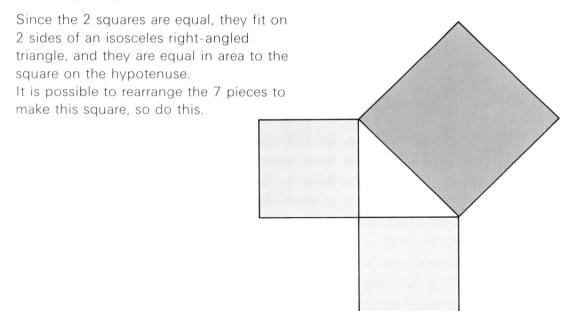

The same pieces can make many more shapes, using all 7 pieces each time. Make a parallelogram, an isosceles trapezium, a rectangle, an isosceles right-angled triangle, a trapezium with 2 adjacent right angles and a hexagon. Keep a record of how the pieces fit together.

Here are some other shapes to make, and there are more on page 297. You can invent others.

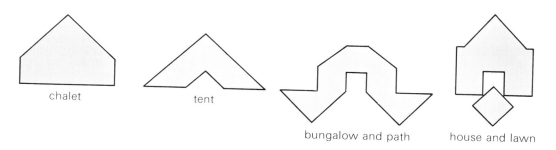

chalet   tent   bungalow and path   house and lawn

6. **Circumference of a circle**

Archimedes, about 2000 years ago, found a way to investigate the relationship between the diameter and circumference of a circle.

π is the ratio $\dfrac{\text{circumference}}{\text{diameter}}$.

Archimedes 287–212 BC

Archimedes investigated the value of π by considering regular polygons and calculating their perimeters, using mathematical methods.

We will consider a regular hexagon
inside a circle of radius 5 cm.
What is the diameter of the circle ?
6 triangles are formed.
What kind of triangles are they ?
What is the length of *AB* ?
What is the perimeter of the hexagon ?

What is the value of $\dfrac{\text{perimeter of hexagon}}{\text{diameter of circle}}$?

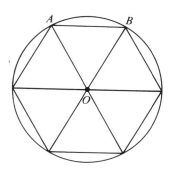

Now the circumference of the circle is a bit bigger than the perimeter of the hexagon, since it takes a curved path instead of cutting across in straight lines, so the value of π will be slightly bigger than the value you have just worked out.

We will now consider a regular hexagon drawn outside the circle.

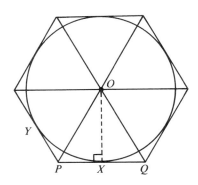

6 equilateral triangles are formed.
$OX = 5$ cm (radius)
Let $PX = x$ cm, then $OP = PQ = 2x$ cm
Using Pythagoras' theorem in the right-angled triangle OPX,
$OP^2 = PX^2 + OX^2$
$4x^2 = x^2 + 25$
Solve this equation to find the value of x.
What is the perimeter of the hexagon ?

What is the value of $\dfrac{\text{perimeter of hexagon}}{\text{diameter of circle}}$?

Now the circumference of the circle is a bit smaller than the perimeter of the hexagon, since it takes a curved path, e.g. going from Y to X instead of going from Y to P then P to X. So the value of π will be slightly smaller than the value you have just worked out.
Now you have found a range of values between which π lies.

Archimedes continued, using polygons with 12 sides, then with 24, 48 and 96 sides. These give closer and closer ranges for π.

You cannot go further until you learn some trigonometry, so we have given you some results which you may work out using your calculator.
sin 15° (pronounced sine 15°) can be found from your scientific calculator by pressing 15 [sin], and tan 15° is found by pressing 15 [tan]. (Make sure your calculator is set to work in degrees.)

Using 12 sides, π lies between 12 × sin 15° and 12 × tan 15°,
using 24 sides, π lies between 24 × sin 7.5° and 24 × tan 7.5°,
using 48 sides, π lies between 48 × sin 3.75° and 48 × tan 3.75°,
using 96 sides, π lies between 96 × sin 1.875° and 96 × tan 1.875°.

You now have a very good idea of the value of π.

7.   **The converse of Pythagoras' theorem**
   Pythagoras' theorem is about a right-angled triangle.
   If we have a right-angled triangle, then $a^2 = b^2 + c^2$, where a is the hypotenuse.

   The opposite way round for this statement is:
   If, in a triangle with sides of length a, b and c, $a^2 = b^2 + c^2$, then the angle
   opposite to side a is a right angle.

   This result is also true and it is called the **converse** of Pythagoras' theorem.

   Example

   $\triangle ABC$ has $AB = 12$ cm, $BC = 35$ cm and
   $AC = 37$ cm.
   Is $\angle B = 90°$?

   The side opposite $\angle B$ is AC.
   $AC^2 = 37^2 = 1369$
   The other two sides are AB and BC.
   $AB^2 + BC^2 = 12^2 + 35^2$
   $\qquad\qquad\quad = 144 + 1225$
   $\qquad\qquad\quad = 1369$
   So $AC^2 = AB^2 + BC^2$

   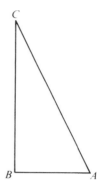

   And $\angle B = 90°$ (using the converse of Pythagoras' theorem)

   Use the converse of Pythagoras' theorem to find whether these triangles are right-
   angled.

   1

   2

   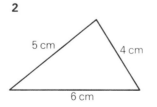

   3

   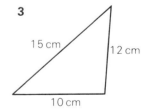

   4

   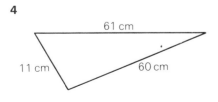

   5

   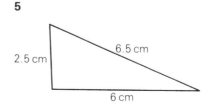

8. **The regular solid figures (2)** (continued from page 102)

These two regular solid figures were discovered
by Poinsot (1777–1859). They can be made
from their nets, but here are alternative methods,
which you may find easier to use.

The great dodecahedron

Draw this pattern on tracing paper. The
dotted lines are 6.5 cm long and all the
other lines are 4 cm long.
If you alter the measurements, keep them
in the same proportion. The short lines are
0.618 × the longer lines.
Transfer the pattern to cardboard. You need
10 pieces altogether.
Score all the short lines including the
edges with a tab on, and then turn the
cardboard over and score along the 5 long
lines. (Prick through the points to find
them on the other side.)
Cut out the pieces. Crease all scored lines,
bending them away from the side they
were scored on.
Glue the tabs onto the opposite faces, e.g.
AB to *AC*, *DE* to *DF*. Glue the tabs onto
the side with the drawing on, making 2
raised pyramids. These will become the
inside of the model.

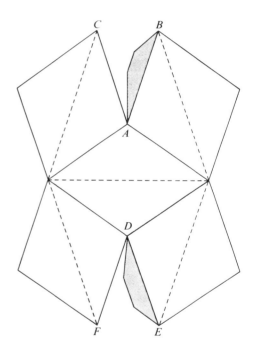

Using the other, clean side of the pieces as the outside, overlap and glue 2 pieces
along one ridge, overlapping 2 triangular pieces.
Glue a 3rd piece along a ridge to the 1st piece, and along another ridge to the
2nd piece, forming a raised 5-pointed star and an extra bit.
Continue overlapping triangles in suitable ways to make further 5-pointed stars
until you have used all the pieces and you have a complete, closed model.
Notice the 12 interlocking pentagons.
Paint the model to match the others.

The great icosahedron

This has a rather complicated pattern. Draw it on tracing paper.
The long lines are 6.5 cm long. (Actually, the long dotted lines should be 6.6 cm long but 1 mm is not going to make much difference.) The next lines are 4 cm long and the short lines are 2.5 cm long. If you alter the measurements, keep them in the same proportions.

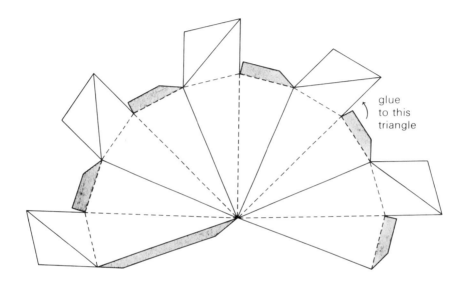

glue
to this
triangle

Transfer the pattern to cardboard. You need 12 pieces altogether.
Score along all the lines. The dotted lines should be scored on the other side.
Cut out the pieces. Crease all scored lines, bending them away from the side they were scored on.
Glue the long tab to the opposite face to make a star point, with the clean side of the cardboard on the outside. Then glue the 5 small tabs to the opposite small triangles.
Overlap and glue 2 pieces along one small ridge, overlapping 2 small triangular pieces.
Glue a 3rd piece in a similar way to the first 2 pieces.
Continue glueing on other pieces until you have a complete, closed model.
Notice the 20 interlocking equilateral triangles.
Paint the model to match the others.

When you have made all four of these solid figures take a photograph of them, as a record.
Well done!

9. **Square root search**

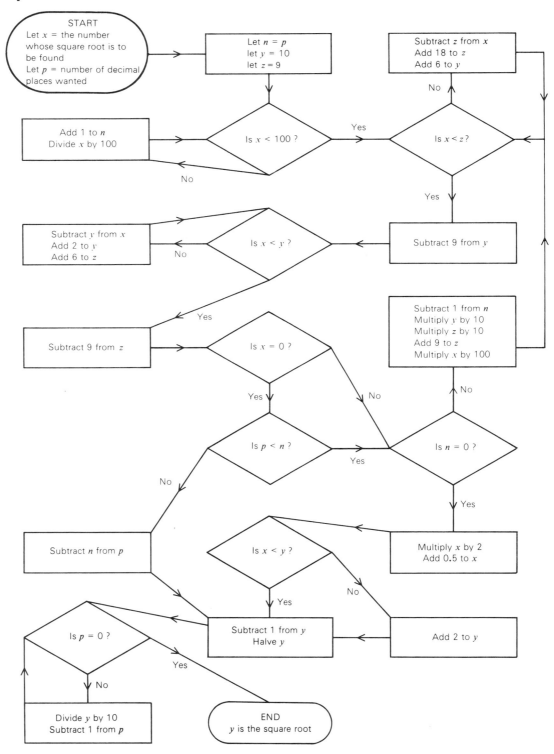

Here is a flow diagram which will find the square root of any number.
It takes longer than using your calculator but it is interesting to try using it, and
good practice in following instructions and doing straightforward arithmetic.
You and your friends can make a race game of this. You all begin with the same
number and see who is first to reach the end, with the correct answer.

For working through the flow diagram, write down x, y, z, n and p in columns.

As an example, here are the numbers you would write down if you began with
169, and asked for the answer correct to 1 decimal place.
(The answer is 13 so the 1st decimal place was not needed.)

x	y	z	n	p
169	10	9	1	1
1.69			2	
	1			
0.69	3	15		
		6		
	30	60	1	
69		69		
0	36	87		
	27			
		78		
	26			0
	13			

Practise working through the diagram by finding the square roots of these
numbers:
4, to the nearest whole number,
64, to the nearest whole number,
800, to the nearest whole number,
31, correct to 1 decimal place,
0.05, correct to 2 decimal places.

You can choose other numbers yourself, and you can use your calculator to check
your answers.

10. **Classifying quadrilaterals**

Here is a flow diagram that can be used to classify quadrilaterals.
Identify which of the words parallelogram, rectangle, rhombus, square, trapezium, should go in each of the boxes labelled A, B, C, D, E.

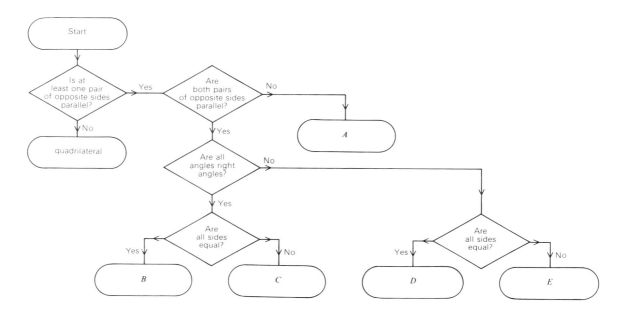

11. **Ages of cars**

A survey of cars, made in Mid-Wales in the last week of July, 1989, gave the following results:

Age of car in years	0 to under 2	2 to under 4	4 to under 6	6 to under 8	8 to under 10	10 to under 12	Total
Number of cars	60	51	34	27	20	8	200

1   What is the modal class of ages ?
2   What is the centre of interval of the class 0 to 2 ?
3   Make a frequency table with x as the centres of intervals and find an estimate for the mean age.
4   Draw a histogram of the distribution and comment on its shape.

Here is a similar survey, made in NW England in the last week of July, 1991, showing the car registration year letters.
List the results in a similar table, find the averages and draw a histogram.

(The ages are 0 to under 2 years, letters H and G,
              2 to under 4 years, letters F and E,
and similarly for letters D and C, B and A, Y and X, W and V, T and S.)

E	D	Y	Y	A	E	E	A	Y	W	B	A	W	W	W
T	E	E	C	H	G	G	E	A	F	B	B	G	A	D
D	D	A	C	G	G	B	X	A	A	V	A	C	G	V
C	A	E	W	V	C	A	V	G	D	B	G	F	C	G
G	E	A	B	G	B	B	Y	F	D	G	H	C	D	Y
T	F	A	B	X	G	V	F	V	D	C	D	A	F	E
A	Y	D	A	F	E	B	F	Y	H	W	B	H	Y	C
E	E	E	X	X	C	B	B	G	C	E	C	C	C	H
X	B	V	C	H	C	C	A	E	G	V	V	G	A	H
V	Y	S	A	C	B	X	D	Y	F	E	V	A	E	Y
C	Y	G	D	V	A	C	E	E	F	Y	G	E	A	H
B	A	Y	E	S	C	W	D	Y	A	B	E	G	X	D
B	D	V	E	B	F	Y	G	C	F	H	W	Y	H	H
C	C	T	V	B										

On one graph, draw frequency polygons of both distributions. Compare the surveys. Comment on any similarities or differences.

Perhaps you can do a similar survey yourself.
If you are not doing it in July, you will have to adjust the ages according to the month, to work out the averages, and you should not draw a histogram or frequency polygon as the range of time in the first class will not be equal to the others.

12.   **Using a computer**

Here are more suggestions for ways in
which computer programs can help you in
your work.

You can use computer simulations to find
experimental results of probability
investigations and then compare them with
the theoretical probabilities, e.g. of
throwing a die, or more than one, to find
the probabilities of various outcomes; or of
tossing coins; or of using random
numbers. (A basic program was listed in
Level 5, page 228.)

A flow diagram is a useful way to plan a computer program. You can rewrite
some of the flow diagrams of Chapter 8 as programs to be run on a computer.

The calculations of Pythagoras' theorem can be done by a short computer
program. Input the lengths of two sides of a right-angled triangle and it will
calculate the length of the third side.
A program can be used with the converse theorem to check whether a triangle is
right-angled.
The number patterns which give whole numbers for the sides of a right-angled
triangle can be found by using these formulae for the 3 sides, $2mn$, $n^2 - m^2$,
$n^2 + m^2$. The computer can give a list of possible lengths, by substituting whole
numbers for m and n with $m < n$.

Means of sets of numbers, or of frequency distributions, can be found by
entering the data into a suitable spreadsheet program. The program may also
draw a histogram or a frequency polygon of a frequency distribution.

Simultaneous equations can be solved by using a computer program, but since
you are trying to learn the methods of solution for yourself you are not likely to
want to use this at present.

You can find areas and volumes of circles or cylinders with a suitable program,
and you can investigate what happens to the volume or surface area of a
cylinder when small changes are made in the measurements. You can find, by
trial, the best measurements for a tin which will hold a certain volume of liquid,
and yet have the least possible surface area.

PUZZLES

27.   In this sum, each figure is represented by a
      different letter.
      Given that H = 0, E = 4, M = 5, find which
      figure each other letter represents.

```
  M A T H S
        A T
  L E V E L
+ S E V E N
  ─────────
  L E A R N T
```

28.   The circle has centre *O* and radius 10 cm.
      The angle shown at *O* is a right angle, and
      OABC is a rectangle.
      What is the length of the line *AC* ?

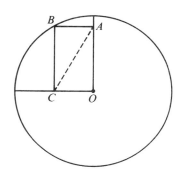

29.   On cardboard, or paper, make 4 copies of this
      pentagon. (Find the top point using
      compasses.) Also make a square of side 6 cm.
      Cut out the 5 pieces and fit them together to
      form

      1   a square,
      2   an octagon.

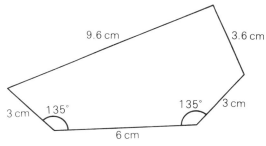

      (The lengths 3.6 cm and 9.6 cm have been given correct to the nearest mm. Perhaps you
      can work out what their exact measurements ought to be.)

30.   In this sentence, each letter of the alphabet has been substituted by another letter chosen
      at random (the same one each time that letter occurs). Can you decode the sentence,
      and say whether it is a true mathematical statement ?

      **KWLY   OWL   AOLBG   QXL   QXXQYPLN   AY   IXNLX
      ID   GAEL,   OWL   BLNAQY   AG   OWL   MQRJL   ID
      OWL   BANNRL   AOLB,   IX   OWL   MQRJL   WQRDKQS
      ULOKLLY   OWL   BANNRL   OKI   AD   OWLXL   AG   QY
      LMLY   YJBULX   ID   AOLBG.**

31.   Two brothers were playing with their toy cars.
      The younger one said, 'Lend me one of your cars, and then I'll have as many as you
      have'.
      The elder one said, 'No, give me one of yours, then I'll have twice as many as you have'.
      How many toy cars do they each have ?

13 Thinking about coordinates and

Using graphs

Here is an example of how a graph can be useful:

A business firm wishes to order some reams of paper.

From one supplier the paper costs £3.80 per ream, and there is a delivery charge of £4.50. From a local supplier the paper costs £4.20 per ream, and there is no delivery charge.

From which supplier should the firm buy their paper ?

The solution

If they buy x reams, the cost £y from the first supplier is given by the function $y = 3.8x + 4.5$

If they buy from the local supplier the function is $y = 4.2x$

Here are sketch graphs of the two functions (scales are not shown).

The local supplier is cheaper if they are not buying much paper, but its graph crosses the graph of the other function when $x = 11.25$. So for up to 11 reams the local supplier is cheaper, but for 12 reams and over, the first supplier is cheaper.

You can draw these graphs accurately and check the solution.

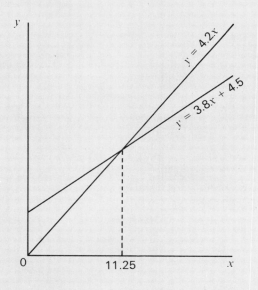

graphs

Coordinates in 3-dimensions

Instead of knowing our position on land, sometimes height or depth is important as well, and coordinates in 3-dimensions are needed to describe the position.

A deep-sea diver at work

A submarine

A plane in flight

A block of flats

13 Coordinates and Graphs

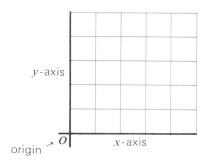

Examples

1 Point A has x-value 1 and y-value 2. This can be written as the point $(1, 2)$.

A is $(1, 2)$
B is $(-2, 1)$
C is $(0, -3)$
D is $(-3, -2)$
E is $(3, -3)$

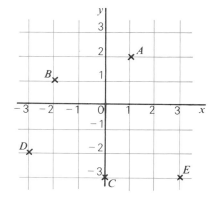

Functions and straight-line graphs

2 For this question, use graph paper with x from -1 to 3 and y from -3 to 9. Use a scale of 2 cm to 1 unit on the x-axis and 1 cm to 1 unit on the y-axis.

This is a table of numbers connecting x and y for a particular function.

x	-1	0	1	2	3
y	-1	0	1	2	3

To represent these values on the graph paper, plot the points $(-1, -1)$, $(0, 0)$, $(1, 1)$, $(2, 2)$, $(3, 3)$.
These points lie on a straight line. Draw it, using a ruler.
The connection in the table between y and x is $y = x$.
So the function is $y = x$.
The equation of the line is $y = x$. Label the line with its equation.

Here is another table of numbers.

x	-1	0	1	2	3
y	-2	0	2	4	6

To represent this, plot the points $(-1, -2)$, $(0, 0)$, $(1, 2)$, $(2, 4)$, $(3, 6)$ on the same graph as before, and draw the straight line through these points.
The function is $y = 2x$, and the equation of the line is $y = 2x$. Label this line with its equation.

Make tables for the functions $y = 3x$, and $y = \frac{1}{2}x$, and draw these lines on your graph.

Gradient of a line

The line $y = x$ has gradient 1.
This means that for every 1 unit x increases,
y also increases 1 unit.
(These will not look equal when different
scales are used on the x and y axes.)

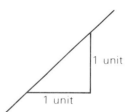

The line $y = 2x$ has gradient 2.
This means that for every 1 unit x increases,
y increases 2 units.

What is the gradient of the line $y = 3x$?
What is the gradient of the line $y = \frac{1}{2}x$?

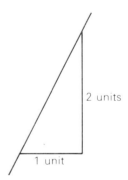

Here is a table of numbers for the function $y = -x$.

x	-1	0	1	2	3
y	1	0	-1	-2	-3

Draw this line on your graph.
This line has gradient -1.
This means for every 1 unit x increases,
y decreases by 1 unit.

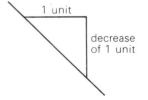

Can you say what the gradient is for a line $y = mx$, where m is any number ?

3 For this question, use graph paper with x from -1 to 3 and y from -5 to 9. Use a scale of 2 cm to 1 unit on the x-axis and 1 cm to 1 unit on the y-axis.

Plot the points given in this table, and draw the line.

x	-1	0	1	2	3
y	1	3	5	7	9

The equation of the line is $y = 2x + 3$

Draw the line $y = 2x$ on the same graph.
What do you notice about these two lines ?

Make a table for the line $y = 2x - 3$, and plot this line on the same graph.

Functions of the form $y = mx + c$, where m and c are numbers, are straight-line graphs.

Other types of functions, e.g. $y = x^2$, $y = x^3$, $y = \dfrac{1}{x}$, will produce graphs which are curves.

If you know that a function has a graph which is a straight line, then you do not need to calculate and plot a great number of points. Two points are sufficient to fix the line, so work out the y-values corresponding to values of x near each end of the line, which will depend on the range of values you are using for x. Plot these two points.
Then work out the coordinates of another point, and plot it.
If the 3 points lie on a straight line then you have (probably) found the correct line and you can draw it, using a ruler.
If the 3 points do not lie on a straight line, then at least one of the points is wrong. If you cannot find your mistake, you should work out the coordinates of another point, and plot it. This may help you to discover which of the original points was wrong.

Exercise 13.1

1. Draw axes with x from -4 to 4 and y from -5 to 5, taking equal scales on both axes. Draw the lines representing these functions, for x from -4 to 4.

    1 $y = 1 - x$
    2 $y = \frac{1}{2}x - 1$
    3 $y = \frac{1}{2}x + 2$
    4 $y = -x - 1$

    What sort of quadrilateral is enclosed by these 4 lines ?

2. Draw the x-axis from 0 to 8 and the y-axis from 0 to 9, taking a scale of 2 cm to represent 1 unit on both axes.

1 Plot the points $(2, 0)$, $(3, 1\frac{1}{2})$, $(7, 7)$, $(8, 9)$.

Three of these points lie on a straight line. Draw the line.
Write down the coordinates of two more points which lie on the line.

2 Complete the pattern of points $(0, 7)$, $(1, 6)$, $(2, 5)$, . . . , $(7, . . .)$.

Plot these points and join them with a straight line.

3 What are the coordinates of the point where the two lines drawn in **1** and **2** cross each other ?

3. On graph paper, draw axes for x from -3 to 4, using a scale of 2 cm to represent 1 unit, and y from -6 to 9, using a scale of 1 cm to represent 1 unit.
For each table of numbers given, plot the points on the graph and join them with a straight line.
If you can discover the function for y in terms of x for each line, label the lines with their equations.

1

x	y
-3	-4
0	-1
2	1
4	3

2

x	y
-3	3
0	0
2	-2
4	-4

3

x	y
-3	-5
0	1
2	5
4	9

4

x	y
-3	$-1\frac{1}{2}$
0	0
2	1
4	2

5

x	y
-3	8
0	2
2	-2
4	-6

4. Draw axes with x and y from -6 to 6, taking equal scales on both axes.
Draw the lines representing these functions.

1 $y = 3x - 6$, for x from 0 to 4
2 $y = -2x - 6$, for x from -6 to 0
3 $y = 4 - \frac{1}{3}x$, for x from -6 to 6

What sort of triangle is enclosed by these 3 lines ?

5.   For the function $y = 3x - 2$, copy this table and fill in the values for y.

x	-1	0	4
y			

On graph paper, draw axes for x from -1 to 4, and for y from -6 to 10, using a scale of 2 cm to 1 unit on the x-axis and 1 cm to 1 unit on the y-axis.
Plot the points and draw the graph of the function.

Make a similar table for the function $y = 2 - 2x$, and draw its graph, using the same axes.

What are the coordinates of the point where the two lines cross ? (Give the answer correct to 1 decimal place.)

Simultaneous equations

In chapter 11 you solved simultaneous equations by calculation.
You can also find the solutions graphically.

In question 5 of the last exercise, you found the point where the two lines $y = 3x - 2$ and $y = 2 - 2x$ crossed.
The coordinates of this point (0.8, 0.4) give the solution of the simultaneous equations
$y = 3x - 2$
$y = 2 - 2x$ and the solution is $x = 0.8$, $y = 0.4$.

Example

4   Use a graphical method to solve the simultaneous equations $x + y = 6$, $4x - y = 2$.

For $y = 6 - x$

x	-2	0	3
y	8	6	3

For $y = 4x - 2$

x	-2	0	3
y	-10	-2	10

Draw the x-axis from -2 to 3 and the y-axis
from -10 to 10.
Use a scale of 2 cm to 1 unit on the x-axis
and 1 cm to 1 unit on the y-axis.
Plot the points for each line and draw the
lines on the graph. Label each one with its
equation.

The equations are satisfied simultaneously at
the point which lies on both lines.
Draw dotted lines from this point to both
axes, to read off the coordinates. The point
is (1.6, 4.4).
The solution of the equations is
$x = 1.6,\quad y = 4.4$.

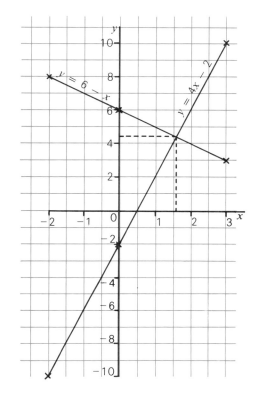

(Sketch diagram)

Exercise 13.2

1.   Solve the equations $3x + y = 13$, $5x - 2y = 18$, graphically.

   1   Rearrange $3x + y = 13$ in the form $y = \ldots$
        Make a table of values for $x = 0$, $x = 3$, $x = 6$.

   2   Show that $5x - 2y = 18$ can be rearranged as $y = 2\frac{1}{2}x - 9$.
        Make a table of values for $x = 0, 2, 6$.

   3   Draw axes, for x from 0 to 6 and y from -9 to 13. Use a scale of
        2 cm to 1 unit on the x-axis and 1 cm to 2 units on the y-axis.
        Draw the straight lines for the equations in **1** and **2**.

   4   Give the solution of the equations.

2. Draw axes with x from -4 to 4 and y from -10 to 26. Use a scale of
    2 cm to 1 unit on the x-axis and 1 cm to 2 units on the y-axis.
    Draw the graph of $y = 3x + 4$, by finding values of y when $x = -4$, 0 and 4 and
    plotting the three points.
    Also draw the graph of $y = 18 - 2x$ in a similar way.
    Using your graphs, solve the simultaneous equations $y = 3x + 4$ and $y = 18 - 2x$.

3. Draw x and y axes from 0 to 8.

    1 To draw the graph of $2x + 3y = 6$.

    If $x = 0$, what is the value of y ? Mark the point corresponding to these values
    on the graph.
    If $y = 0$, what is the value of x ? Mark the point corresponding to these values
    on the graph.
    Join these two points.

    In a similar way, draw the graphs of
    2 $3x + 4y = 12$,
    3 $8x + 5y = 40$,
    4 $6x + 7y = 42$.
    From your graphs, find the solution of the simultaneous equations $6x + 7y = 42$,
    $8x + 5y = 40$.

Coordinates in 3-dimensions

Coordinates are used to indicate position.
By introducing another axis (the z-axis) we can
represent positions in 3-dimensions.
If the x and y axes are in a horizontal plane
(such as on a level table), the z-axis goes
vertically upwards.
The origin is the point $(0, 0, 0)$. The axes are all
at right angles to each other.

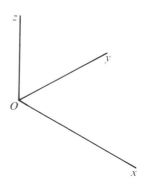

To find the point (4, 3, 2) first find the point
(4, 3) as usual, using the axes Ox, Oy.
Then move upwards (i.e. in the direction of the
z-axis) for 2 units.

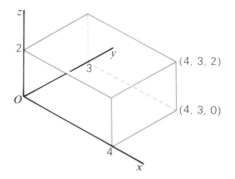

Example

5   A cuboid has one vertex at the origin and three of its edges on the x, y and z axes.
     One vertex is at the point (3, 1, 2).
     What are the coordinates of the other vertices ?

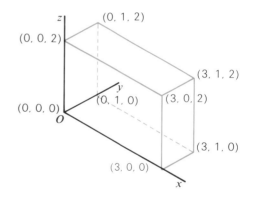

These are shown on the diagram.
Notice that all the points on the base of the
cuboid have z-coordinate 0, the others have
z-coordinate 2.
Notice which vertices have x-coordinate 0,
and which have x-coordinate 3.
Notice which vertices have y-coordinate 0,
and which have y-coordinate 1.

Exercise 13.3

1. $ABCDEFGH$ is a cuboid.
     A is the point (1, 1, 0).
     B is the point (6, 1, 0).
     D is the point (1, 4, 0).
     E is the point (1, 1, 5).
     Find the coordinates of the points
     C, F, G and H.

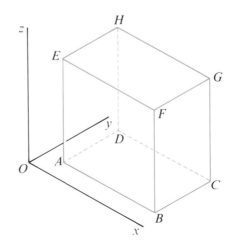

2. *ABCDEFGH* is a cuboid.
    A is the point (3, 2, 4).
    AB has length 5 units and is parallel
    to the *x*-axis.
    AD has length 1 unit and is parallel
    to the *y*-axis.
    AE has length 2 units and is parallel
    to the *z*-axis.
    Find the coordinates of the points
    B, C, D, E, F, G and *H*.

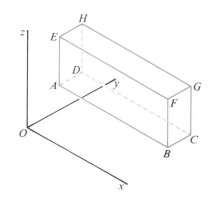

3. *ABCDEFGH* is a cuboid.
    G is the point (7, 8, 5).
    HG has length 10 units and is parallel
    to the *x*-axis.
    FG has length 9 units and is parallel
    to the *y*-axis.
    CG has length 7 units and is parallel
    to the *z*-axis.
    Find the coordinates of the points
    A, B, C, D, E, F and *H*.

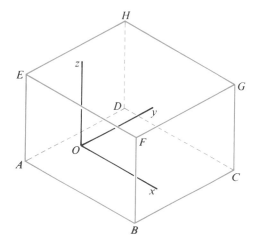

Exercise 13.4   Applications and Activities

1. A service engineer who visits offices to mend equipment charges a call-out fee of
    £40 plus an amount for the time the job takes, at the rate of £30 per hour.

    Copy and fill in a table showing the total charges for various times.

Time, *x* hours	0	1	2	3	4
Total cost, £*y*	40				

    Plot the points given by the values of *x* and *y* on a graph.
    Draw the *x*-axis from 0 to 4 using a scale of 2 cm to 1 unit, and the *y*-axis from
    0 to 160, using a scale of 1 cm to 10 units.
    Join the points with a straight line.
    Write down the equation of the line, with *y* in terms of *x*.

2. Gareth and Robin carried out an experiment to find the length of a spring when various weights were hanging on the end. Here are some of the results.

weight, x kg	0.1	0.2	0.3	0.4	0.5	0.6
length, y cm	30.7	35.3	39.9	44.5	49.1	53.7

Plot these results on a graph. Put weight on the horizontal axis, labelling it from 0 to 0.6, and length on the vertical axis, labelling it from 0 to 60.
The connection between weight and length obeys a straight-line law.
Draw the line.

Using the line, estimate,
1   the length of the unstretched spring (i.e. when there was no weight hanging on it),
2   the length of the spring if a weight of 0.55 kg is hanging on it,
3   the weight needed to stretch the spring to a length of 43 cm.

3. For prizes for a children's party, Mrs Gill decides to buy some bars of chocolate at 24p each, and some packets of sweets at 12p each.
She needs 25 prizes altogether. If she buys x bars of chocolate and y packets of sweets, write down an equation involving x and y.
On graph paper draw x and y axes from 0 to 40. Draw the graph of the equation.
Mrs Gill decides to spend £4.80 on the prizes. Write down another equation using this fact. (Work in pence.)
Simplify this equation by dividing each term by 12. Draw its line on your graph.
Use your graph to find how many bars of chocolate and how many packets of sweets she buys.

4. *ABCDEFGH* is a cuboid.
A is the point (1, 5, 3).
B is the point (5, 5, 3).
D is the point (1, 8, 3).
E is the point (1, 5, 15).
Find the coordinates of the points
C, *F*, *G* and *H*.

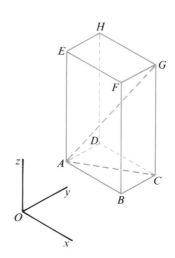

State the lengths of *AB* and *BC* and use Pythagoras' theorem to find the length of *AC*.
State the length of *CG*.
What is the size of $\angle ACG$?
Find the length of *AG*.

14 Thinking about enlargement

Enlargement

When things are enlarged, lengths are increased in the same proportion.
When things are reduced, lengths are decreased in the same proportion.

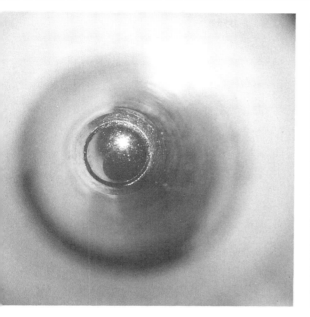

he tip of a ball-point pen

A knot in wood

fossil

Driftwood

14 Enlargement

Similar figures have the same shape.
All corresponding angles are equal.
All corresponding lengths are in proportion, i.e. they are in the same ratio as all other lengths.

Similar triangles

Similar cylinders

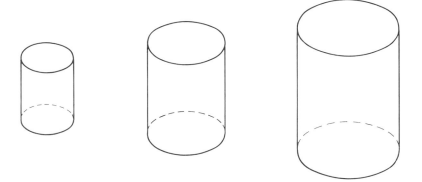

Enlargements

A figure and its enlargement are similar figures.
The **scale factor** of the enlargement is the number of times the original has been enlarged.
e.g. If the scale factor is 2, all lines on the enlargement are twice as long as corresponding lines on the original.
If the scale factor is 3, all lines on the enlargement are three times as long as corresponding lines on the original.

Examples

1 Enlargement with scale factor 2

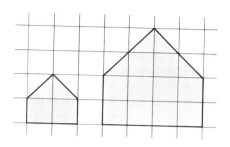

2 Enlargement with scale factor 3

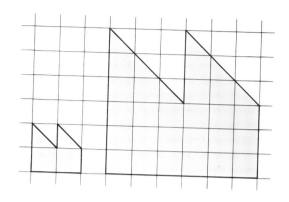

Length of line on enlargement = scale factor × length of line on original

$$\text{Scale factor} = \frac{\text{length of line on the enlargement}}{\text{length of line on the original}}$$

The scale factor need not be a whole number.

e.g. If the scale factor is $1\frac{1}{2}$, all lines on the enlargement are $1\frac{1}{2}$ times as long as the corresponding lines on the original.
Since $1\frac{1}{2} = \frac{3}{2}$, this is equivalent to the ratio 3 : 2.
The length on the enlargement : length on original = 3 : 2.

This triangle has been enlarged with scale factor $1\frac{1}{2}$.

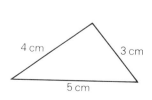

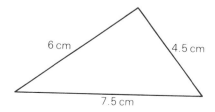

Example

Trapezium *PQRS* is an enlargement of trapezium *ABCD*.
Find the scale factor of the enlargement, and the lengths of *QR*, *RS* and *SP*.

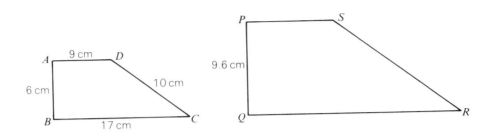

$$\text{scale factor} = \frac{\text{length of } PQ}{\text{length of } AB} = \frac{9.6 \text{ cm}}{6 \text{ cm}} = 1.6 \text{ (or } 1\tfrac{3}{5})$$

length of *QR* = scale factor × length of *BC*
$\qquad\qquad = 1.6 \times 17 \ \text{cm}$
$\qquad\qquad = 27.2 \text{ cm}$
length of *RS* $= 1.6 \times 10 \ \text{cm}$
$\qquad\qquad = 16 \text{ cm}$
length of *SP* $= 1.6 \times 9 \ \text{cm}$
$\qquad\qquad = 14.4 \text{ cm}$

Reduction

If you 'enlarge' a shape by a scale factor less than 1, then you are actually making a reduction of the figure.

e.g. Enlargement by a scale factor $\tfrac{3}{4}$.

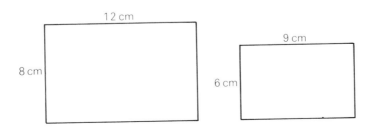

Exercise 14.1

1. Copy each of these figures on squared paper and for each one draw an enlargement with scale factor $1\frac{1}{2}$.

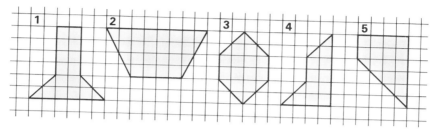

2. What is the scale factor of the enlargement which transforms figure A into figure B ?

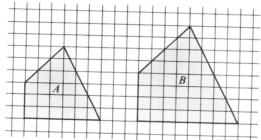

3. This rectangle is enlarged with a scale factor $2\frac{1}{3}$.
   What are the measurements of the enlarged rectangle ?

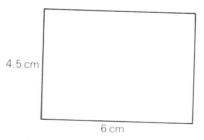

4.5 cm

6 cm

4. The cylinders are similar.

   1 What is the scale factor of the enlargement to turn the small cylinder into the large one ?

   2 The radius of the small cylinder is 1.6 cm. What is the radius of the large one ?

4 cm

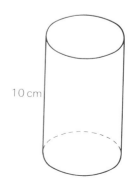

10 cm

5.   △*DEF* is an enlargement of △*ABC*.

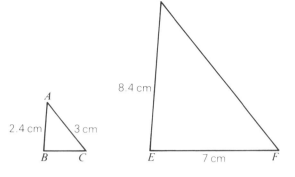

   1   What is the scale factor of the
         enlargement ?
   2   What is the length of *DF* ?
   3   What is the length of *BC* ?

6.   Each figure consists of a semicircle above
      a rectangle.
      B is a reduction of *A*.

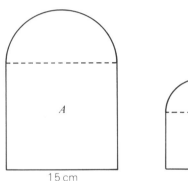
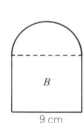

   1   By what scale factor must the lengths
         of *A* be multiplied to give the
         corresponding lengths of *B* ?
   2   If the perimeter of *A* is 70 cm, what is
         the perimeter of *B* ?

Exercise 14.2   Applications and Activities

1.   Copy this drawing of a box, on squared
      paper, and then draw an enlarged box
      using a scale factor of $1\frac{1}{2}$.

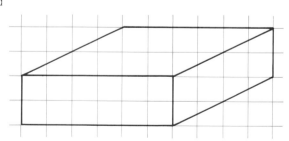

2.   On graph paper draw the x-axis from -12 to 15 and the y-axis from 0 to 10,
      using the same scale on both axes.
      Plot these points and join them in order to make the letter W, $(-12, 4)$, $(-10, 0)$,
      $(-9, 2)$, $(-8, 0)$, $(-6, 4)$.
      Enlarge this letter, starting with the top left-hand point at $(0, 10)$, and using a
      scale factor of $2\frac{1}{2}$.

3. An upright pole of length 1 m casts a shadow of length 1.4 m. At the same time, the shadow of a tree is 6.3 m long. How tall is the tree ?

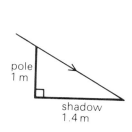

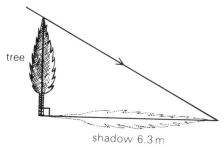

(The triangles shown are similar, since the sun is so far away that its rays form parallel lines.)

4. **Finding heights**

Here is a method that you can use for estimating the heights of trees and tall buildings.

You need a metre rule and a length of rope which is 20 m long.

Measure out 20 m from the tree and lie down there.

Your friend should use the rule to measure 2 m towards the tree and hold the rule upright there.

With your eye as close to the ground as possible, look towards the top of the tree. Your friend should slide his hand up and down the rule until you can see the top of his hand in line with the top of the tree. Note how far this measurement is from the ground.

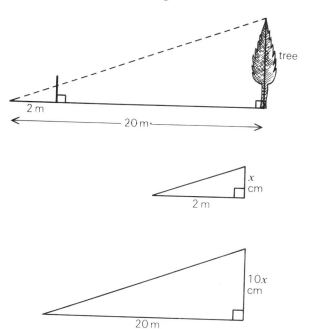

If this is x cm, then the tree is $10x$ cm tall. You can tell this is so because you have used similar triangles.

You can change places with your friend and get a second measurement, and then take the average of the two heights as your estimate.

If the object is over 10 m tall then you will have to measure 40 m back before lying down. You can work out for yourself how you can calculate the height then.

5.   On a photograph a building is 6 cm high and 7.2 cm wide. On an enlargement of the photograph, the building is 10 cm high. What is its width ?
      If the actual building is 30 m wide, how tall is it ?

6.   **The width of a river**

      Here is one way to estimate this.
      Choose a landmark, such as a tree, on the other side of the river and stand opposite to it. Walk along the bank for (say) 50 paces and mark the spot with an upright stick. Walk for another 25 paces. Then turn to walk directly away from the river until the stick and the tree appear in a straight line. Measure how far (x m) you have walked from the river.

      Here is a sketch of your walk.

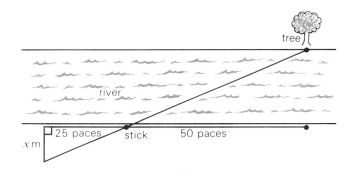

      Here is a diagram to work out the width.

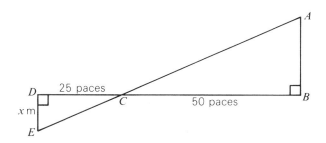

      Notice that triangles ABC, EDC are similar, although not the same way up.
      What is the scale factor to enlarge $\triangle EDC$ into $\triangle ABC$?
      What is the distance AB ?

      You can vary the number of paces if 50 and 25 are not suitable lengths to walk. In fact, you could make several different estimates, walking different distances, and then take the average of all the results.

7.   **A rag doll**

Here is a pattern for a simple doll, which you can make to give to a young child.
Copy the pattern on centimetre-squared paper, by noticing where the drawing
meets the lines of the grid.
(The drawing is 32 cm long and 12 cm wide, so you need a large sheet of paper,
or several sheets stuck together.)
To make the doll, you need some soft material such as towelling. You need
2 pieces size 32 cm by 24 cm.
Fold the material because the pattern only shows half of a piece.
Cut out 2 pieces for the front and back.
When you have cut out the pieces, turn them inside out and sew together, leaving
a gap on the inside of the legs so that you can turn them right-side out again.
Then fill the doll with stuffing and sew up the gap.
Embroider on features such as nostrils and lips. You can make eyes by
embroidering or by sewing on felt circles.
You can make hair using loops of brown or yellow wool.
You can also make some simple clothes for your doll.

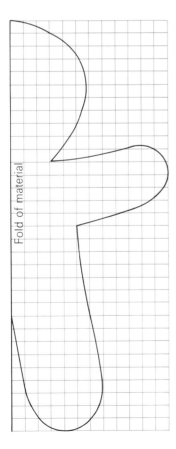

Fold of material

15 Thinking about lines of best fit

A scatter graph

Here is a (fictitious) graph
showing the daily rainfall and the
sales of umbrellas.
We can see a general relationship.
The wetter it is, the more umbrellas
are sold.
We can show this relationship by a
line of best fit on the graph.

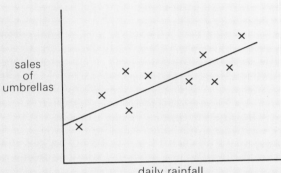

Inverse correlation

Mrs Andrews heats her living room with a gas fire.
The colder it is outside, the more gas she uses to heat her room.

Here is a (fictitious) graph showing the
daily temperature outside and the
number of units used.

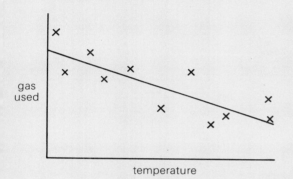

Apparent correlation

Sometimes there may appear to be a
relationship but the two variables are
not related to each other at all.

Both these sales are related to temperature.
There is no direct connection between them.

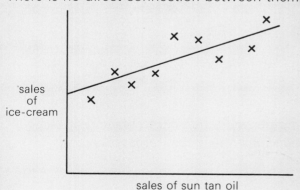

15 Line of best fit

You are probably familiar with drawing scatter diagrams and using them to see if there is any correlation between two sets of data.

Here is a scatter diagram of examination marks in two papers, for a class of 10 pupils.

There is positive correlation, i.e. high marks in Paper 1 match high marks in Paper 2, lower marks in Paper 1 match lower marks in Paper 2.

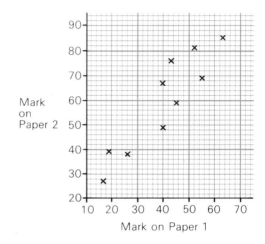

We can draw a line along the graph, representing an 'average' relationship between the marks.
This is called a line of best fit.

If we consider a mark of 20 on Paper 1, reading from the line we see that an estimate of the mark on Paper 2 is 35. A mark of 50 on Paper 1 would correspond to a mark of 71 on Paper 2.

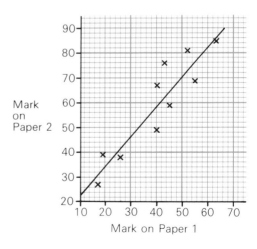

The line gives us a clearer idea of the relationship between the marks obtained on the two papers. It is not an exact line. The actual marks may be greater or less than this average relationship.

The line we have drawn is, as its name suggests, a line which best shows the trend of the data.

If there is perfect correlation between two variables then the points will all lie on a line and this is automatically the line of best fit.

If the correlation is not so exact then we try to draw a line which matches the slope shown by the points on the graph. It should have some of the points on either side of it, so that it is an average line.

Diagrams showing lines of best fit

(Scales are not shown.)

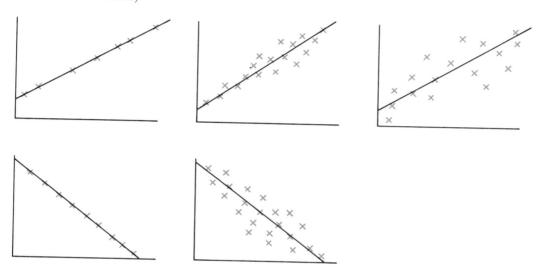

To draw a line of best fit

Example

1 Draw a scatter diagram to show the relationship between the examination marks, as on page 236.

The marks for the 10 pupils are:

Mark in Paper 1	17	19	26	40	40	43	45	52	55	63
Mark in Paper 2	27	39	38	49	67	76	59	81	69	85

Use the horizontal axis for the marks on Paper 1. The marks range from 17 to 63 so you can label from 10 to 70 using 2 cm to represent 10 marks.

Use the vertical axis for the marks on Paper 2. The marks range from 27 to 85 so you can label from 20 to 90, using the same scale.

Notice that labelling on scatter diagrams need not start at 0. It is not essential to use the same scale on both axes but it is suitable in this question.

Plot the 10 points to represent the data.

Method 1   By inspection.

You just draw the best line you can, deciding by putting your ruler (or your set-square may be better) on the graph and trying it in various positions, until you have a slope which matches the general slope of the points, and an average position where the points are balanced with some on both sides of the line.

If you are using this method, draw the line on your graph.

Method 2   Going through the average point.

Find the mean of the x-values, called $\bar{x}$.
The x-values are the values using the horizontal axis, in this example they are the marks gained in Paper 1, and $\bar{x}$ is the average mark gained in Paper 1.
Find the mean of the y-values, called $\bar{y}$. In this example, $\bar{y}$ is the average mark gained in Paper 2.
Plot the point on the graph corresponding to $(\bar{x}, \bar{y})$.
Do not mark this in the same way as the data as it is not one of the pairs. If you mark the data with crosses, one way in which you can mark this point is by a dot with a ring round it ⊙

The mean of the x-values

$$\bar{x} = \frac{\Sigma x}{n} = \frac{400}{10} = 40$$

The mean of the y-values

$$\bar{y} = \frac{\Sigma y}{n} = \frac{590}{10} = 59$$

Plot the point $(\bar{x}, \bar{y})$, i.e. (40, 59), marking it ⊙

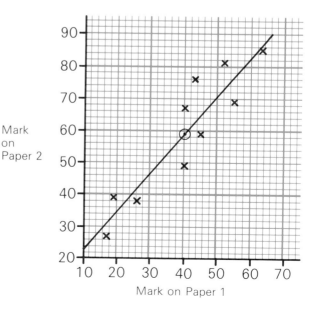

Mark on Paper 2

Mark on Paper 1

(not drawn full-size)

Now you are going to draw the line of best fit passing through this point. (We are drawing an average line so it is logical to draw it through the average point !)
You have now to decide on the best slope for the line which passes through the average point, and whose slope matches the general slope of the points, with points balanced on either side of the line.

Your teacher will decide which method you should use.

A statistician might use either of these methods for making a rough estimate, but has a different method for more advanced work.

Using the line of best fit

If a pupil had taken Paper 1 and gained 33 marks, but was absent for Paper 2, we can look on the graph and find from the line of best fit that the mark for Paper 2 corresponding to a mark of 33 on Paper 1 is 50. We could use this as an estimate of the mark the pupil would have got had he not missed Paper 2. In a similar way, a pupil who missed Paper 1, but got 69 on Paper 2, could have an estimated mark for Paper 1 of 48.

These estimated marks could be used in comparing these pupils' progress with the rest of the class.

Use your line of best fit to find your estimated marks.

For a mark of 33 on Paper 1, draw a dotted line up from 33 on the horizontal axis to meet your line and then a dotted line sideways from this point, to read off the value on the vertical axis. Your line may not be the same as the one we have drawn so you may get a different answer. Our answer is 50.

For a mark of 69 on Paper 2, draw a dotted line sideways from 69 on the vertical axis to meet your line of best fit, and then a dotted line downwards from this point, to read off the value on the horizontal axis. Our answer is 48.

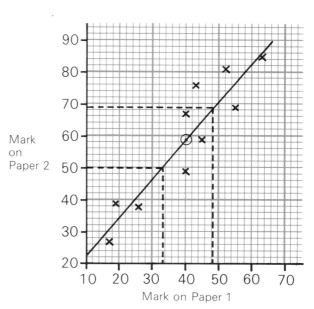

Scientific data

Two sets of data may be related by a mathematical equation such that points representing corresponding values, when plotted on a graph, would lie on a straight line. In this case, values obtained by experiment may not lie exactly on a line, due to errors in measurement or other experimental errors. In this case, a line of best fit can be drawn and used as an estimate of the true line.

Exercise 15.1

Draw scatter diagrams to represent the data of these questions.
Put the first quantity given on the horizontal axis.
Draw a line of best fit.
(The data for these questions was given in *Level 6*. If you have already drawn any of these graphs and have them available, just complete them by drawing the lines of best fit.)

1. The heights of 10 boys and their fathers are given in this table.

Height of father (in cm)	167	168	169	171	172	172	174	175	176	182
Height of son (in cm)	164	166	166	168	169	170	170	171	173	177

2. The marks of 10 students in 2 Maths exams were as follows:

1st year	70	68	60	55	49	46	43	40	36	30
2nd year	65	63	55	55	50	45	46	44	39	40

3. The heights and weights of 8 young men are given in this table.

Height (in cm)	167	169	172	178	182	183	184	186
Weight (in kg)	68	70	70	74	75	76	78	79

4. Here are the lengths and widths of 11 leaves from a bush.

Length (in cm)	7.5	6.7	7.3	6.8	6.6	5.6	5.1	4.7	5.5	6.2	6.4
Width (in cm)	3.9	2.8	3.4	3.7	3.1	2.1	2.3	1.5	2.2	2.6	2.6

5. Here are the figures for the number of vehicles on the road, and the deliveries of motor spirit, in Great Britain, for 8 years.
   ('Motor spirit' means petrol and other fuels for vehicles.)

Year	67	68	69	70	71	72	73	74
Vehicles (millions)	14.1	14.4	14.8	15.0	15.5	16.1	17.0	17.3
Motor spirit (Million tons)	12.3	13.0	13.4	14.2	15.0	15.9	16.9	16.5

6. The figures show the numbers of tractors and horses used on farms in Great Britain, over a period when farming was becoming mechanized. (The figures are in 10 000's, to the nearest 10 000.)

	1930	1940	1950	1960	1970
Tractors	2	10	33	47	50
Farm horses	80	62	35	6	1

7. 8 plots were treated with different amounts of fertilizer and the crop yield recorded.

Amount of fertilizer (units/m^2)	1	2	3	4	5	6	7	8
Yield (in kg)	36	41	58	60	70	76	75	92

Exercise 15.2   Applications and Activities

For questions 1 to 5, draw scatter diagrams to represent the data. Put the first quantity given on the horizontal axis.
Draw a line of best fit.
Use the line of best fit to answer the questions.

1. Water was flowing from the tap at the bottom of a tank. The depth of water left in the tank at various times was as follows:

time, t (sec)	0	5	10	15	20	25	30	35	40
depth, d (cm)	118	104	96	84	68	62	50	35	26

Estimate how long it took for the depth to decrease to 80 cm.

See the general instructions on the previous page.

2.   A firm wished to see how, over the last few years, the more money spent on
      advertising had led to increased sales.
      Here are the figures:

Year	1	2	3	4	5	6	7	8	9	10
Advertising, in £1000's	22	34	40	40	56	58	66	86	94	100
Sales, in £million	1.3	2.1	1.9	2.2	2.5	2.4	2.9	3.1	3.0	3.8

This year the firm decided to spend £80 000 on advertising.
What sales could they expect ?

3.   The cost per week, £c, of operating a machine over 6 working weeks was shown
      by the following table, where h is the number of hours the machine was used
      each week.

h	30	51	45	39	57	42
c	148	182	172	164	196	166

What would be the estimated cost of using the machine for 48 hours ?

4.   A new lifting-jack was tested and gave these results.

Weight lifted (in kg)	100	150	200	250	300	400
Effort applied (in kg)	8	10	12.5	14.2	17	22

      1   Find the effort needed to lift a weight of 350 kg.
      2   Find the weight which could be lifted by applying an effort of 20 kg.

5.   An experiment was carried out to find the expansion of a 10-metre metal bar
      when it was heated. Here are the experimental results:

Temperature in °C	60	80	100	120	140	160	180
Length over 10 m, in mm	5.0	8.0	10.9	13.8	16.8	19.0	22.6

      1   Find the length of the bar when the temperature was 70°C.
      2   What would the temperature be when the total length of the bar was
              10 m and 20 mm ?

6. Carry out an investigation with data with which you expect to find some kind of paired relationship.

Collect the data and represent it on a scatter diagram.

If there is a good relationship between the data, draw a line of best fit. Use your line of best fit to make other estimations.

Do not be too disappointed if your scatter diagrams do not show good correlation. Statistical data rarely matches perfectly as the figures are often affected by other factors as well as those you are measuring.

Here are some suggestions for investigations. You can probably think of others.

Heights and weights of children of the same age.
Heights and arm-spans.
Exam marks in similar subjects such as Maths and Science, French and German, Art and Craft.
Distances of pupils' homes from school and the times taken to walk to school (with separate graphs for those who cycle, travel by bus, etc.).
The lengths of an elastic band when various weights are hung from it.
Heights of children of the same age and the distances they can throw a cricket ball.
A tennis ball let fall from different heights, and the heights it rises to after bouncing once.

PUZZLE

32. Three married couples entered for a golf tournament, and one of the wives won it. Can you sort out who is married to whom, and which lady won the tournament ?

Lionel did better than Selina's husband.
Marcus is not Ruth's husband.
The man who had the worst score is not married to the woman who won.
Ruth's husband scored better than Lionel.
Tania scored better than Norman's wife.

16 Thinking about quadratic and

A quadratic equation

I think of a number, multiply it by itself and multiply the answer by 3, add 11 times the number I thought of, and the final answer is 342.
What number did I think of ?

You will probably find the answer by trial.
If you let x be the number thought of, you can write down an equation which involves x^2, so it is a **quadratic** equation.

Area

Here are 4 figures. The total area is 360 cm².
What is the value of x ?

2x cm		2cm		11 cm		x cm

x cm   9 cm   x cm   x cm

A paddock

A paddock was 3 times as long as it was wide.
Then its length was increased by 5 m and its width by 2 m, and the new area was 352 m².
What are the separate areas of the 4 parts of the paddock ?
What is an expression for the total area ?
Write down an equation and solve it to find the original measurements of the paddock.

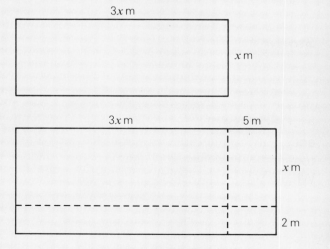

cubic equations

A cubic equation

I think of a number, multiply it by itself, then multiply the answer by a number 4 bigger than the number I thought of.
The final answer is 360.
What number did I think of ?

Again, you will probably find the answer by trial.
If you let x be the number thought of, you can write down an equation. This equation will include brackets, and if you remove the brackets you will have an equation which involves x^3, so it is a **cubic** equation.

Building with cubes

With her 400 1 cm cubes, Heidi builds a cube, and she starts to build another cube of the same size, but she only builds the first 4 layers, and then has 40 cubes left. How many small cubes are there along each edge of the large one ?

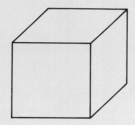 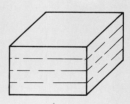

Storage

4 of these cubical storage tanks and 2 of these cuboid tanks together hold 1440 m³ of liquid. What is the value of x ?

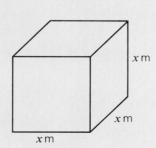 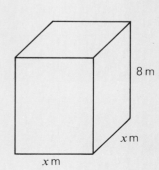

16 Quadratic and Cubic Equations

An equation such as $5x - 8 = 22$ is called a **linear** equation.
Equations can include powers of x, such as x^2, x^3 or higher powers.
An equation such as $x^2 - 5x + 3 = 0$, with highest power x^2, is called a **quadratic** equation.
An equation such as $x^3 - 5x^2 + 3x + 7 = 0$, with highest power x^3, is called a **cubic** equation.

Simple equations

Examples

1   Solve the equation $3x^2 = 51$

Divide both sides by 3
$$x^2 = 17$$
$$x = \sqrt{17}$$
$$= 4.12, \text{ correct to 2 decimal places.}$$

There is also a negative solution, $x = -4.12$, since $(-4.12)^2 = 17$ (approximately), but we will not consider negative solutions at present.

2   Solve the equation $\frac{1}{4}x^3 = 25$

Multiply both sides by 4
$$x^3 = 100$$
$$x = \sqrt[3]{100}$$
$$= 4.64, \text{ correct to 2 decimal places.}$$

There is no negative solution.

You can find cube roots on your scientific calculator using the cube root key $\boxed{\sqrt[3]{}}$ or, if there is not such a key, use $\boxed{\sqrt[x]{y}}$ or $\boxed{\sqrt[y]{x}}$ by pressing $\boxed{\text{number}}$ $\boxed{\sqrt[x]{y}}$ 3 $\boxed{=}$

Equations whose solutions are whole numbers

3   Solve the equation $2x^2 - 7x = 30$

We will rearrange this equation to put all terms on one side of the equation, with 0 on the other side.
Collect terms on the side which makes the coefficient of the highest power of x positive.
(This is not absolutely necessary but it will fit in with other methods you may learn later.)

The equation becomes $2x^2 - 7x - 30 = 0$

Make a table of values of $2x^2 - 7x - 30$ for different values of x. You can set these down in rows or columns.
We are going to set them down in rows, putting a few values of x along the top row and adding more if necessary.

x	0	1	2	3	4	5	6	7	8
x^2	0	1	4	9	16	25	36	49	64
$2x^2$ $-7x$ -30	0 0 -30	2 -7 -30	8 -14 -30	18 -21 -30	32 -28 -30	50 -35 -30	72 -42 -30	98 -49 -30	128 -56 -30
$2x^2 - 7x - 30$	-30	-35	-36	-33	-26	-15	0	19	42

The x^2 row is an extra row to help to work out $2x^2$.
The final row is found by adding the last 3 rows.

You can see from the table that a solution is $x = 6$, because when $x = 6$, the value of $2x^2 - 7x - 30$ equals 0. By noticing that $2x^2$ is getting much bigger, it seems unlikely that there will be another solution with x positive. (There is also a negative solution, which we are not trying to find.)

A quadratic equation can have 0, 1 or 2 solutions.

4   Solve the equation $x^3 - 3x = 52$

Write this as $x^3 - 3x - 52 = 0$
Make a table of values.

x	0	1	2	3	4	5	6
x^3 $-3x$ -52	0 0 -52	1 -3 -52	8 -6 -52	27 -9 -52	64 -12 -52	125 -15 -52	216 -18 -52
$x^3 - 3x - 52$	-52	-54	-50	-34	0	58	146

The solution is $x = 4$.

From looking at the table it seems unlikely that there will be another solution with x positive.

A cubic equation can have 1, 2 or 3 solutions.

5 Solve the equation $(x + 1)(x + 3)(x - 4) = 48$

Rewrite this as $(x + 1)(x + 3)(x - 4) - 48 = 0$
Make a table of values.

x	0	1	2	3	4	5	6
$x + 1$	1	2	3	4	5	6	7
$x + 3$	3	4	5	6	7	8	9
$x - 4$	-4	-3	-2	-1	0	1	2
$(x + 1)(x + 3)(x - 4)$ -48	-12 -48	-24 -48	-30 -48	-24 -48	0 -48	48 -48	126 -48
LHS	-60	-72	-78	-72	-48	0	78

The 5th row is found by multiplying the 3 rows above.
The last row is $(x + 1)(x + 3)(x - 4) - 48$, and is found by adding the last 2 rows.
The solution is $x = 5$.

Exercise 16.1

1. Solve these equations, finding positive solutions only and giving the answers, if not exact, correct to 2 decimal places.

1 $3x^2 = 75$
2 $2x^3 = 432$
3 $\frac{1}{2}x^2 = 40$
4 $12x^3 = 39$
5 $9x^3 = 100$

2. Solve these quadratic equations by trial, finding solutions which are positive whole numbers.

1 $x^2 - x = 2$
2 $x^2 + 4x = 45$
3 $x^2 + x = 20$
4 $x^2 - 2x = 24$
5 $2x^2 - 3x + 1 = 0$
6 $x^2 - 7x + 10 = 0$ (2 solutions)
7 $x^2 = 8x - 7$ (2 solutions)
8 $3x^2 + 10 = 17x$
9 $(x + 3)(x - 2) = 50$
10 $(2x + 1)(x - 4) = 26$

3. Solve these cubic equations by trial, finding solutions which are positive whole numbers.

1 $x^3 - x^2 - x = 2$ **4** $x^3 + x^2 = 14x + 24$
2 $x^3 = 10x + 24$ **5** $(x + 1)(x + 2)(x - 1) = 90$
3 $x^3 = x^2 + 5x + 3$

Equations whose solutions are not whole numbers

6 Solve the equation $2x^2 = 5x + 10$, correct to 1 decimal place.

Rewrite the equation as $2x^2 - 5x - 10 = 0$
Make a table of values

x	0	1	2	3	4	5
x^2	0	1	4	9	16	25
$2x^2$ $-5x$ -10	0 0 -10	2 -5 -10	8 -10 -10	18 -15 -10	32 -20 -10	50 -25 -10
$2x^2 - 5x - 10$	-10	-13	-12	-7	2	15

When $x = 3$, $2x^2 - 5x - 10 = -7$ (negative)
When $x = 4$, $2x^2 - 5x - 10 = 2$ (positive)
So the value of $2x^2 - 5x - 10$ will be 0 somewhere between 3 and 4 (and probably nearer to 4 than to 3).
We now use trial and improvement methods to find the solution correct to 1 decimal place.
Find the value of the function when $x = 3.7$, using your calculator. (We chose 3.7 because we think the solution is greater than 3.5)
We can set the working down in the table of values, but it is probably just as easy to work it out in one stage.
Press 2 ☒ 3.7 $\boxed{x^2}$ ☐ 5 ☒ 3.7 ☐ 10 ☐ and you will get -1.12, which is negative.
Now we know that the solution is between $x = 3.7$ and $x = 4$.
Try $x = 3.8$ next.
Using your calculator, you will get -0.12, still negative.
Now we know that the solution is between $x = 3.8$ and $x = 4$, and seems quite near to $x = 3.8$.
Trying $x = 3.9$ gives the value 0.92, which is positive.
So now we know that the solution is between $x = 3.8$ and $x = 3.9$.
Since we want the answer correct to 1 decimal place, we want to know whether it is nearer to 3.8 or to 3.9. So we find the value of the function for x halfway between 3.8 and 3.9, i.e. for $x = 3.85$.

The value is found to be 0.395, which is positive.
So the solution is between $x = 3.8$ and $x = 3.85$, and correct to 1 decimal place it
is $x = 3.8$.

If you wanted the solution correct to 2 decimal places you would have to continue
using this method, trying (say) 3.82 next. To 2 decimal places the solution is
$x = 3.81$.

Note. **Quadratic** equations can be solved by other methods. If the solutions are
whole numbers or exact fractions, the solutions can be found by a method using
algebraic factors, and any solutions can be found by using a general formula. You will
learn these methods later, and you may prefer to find out about them now, rather than
using trial and improvement methods. If so, your teacher can help you. You will still
need to use trial and improvement methods to solve cubic equations.

7   Solve the equation $x^3 + 3x - 20 = 0$, correct to 1 decimal place.

Make a table of values.

x	0	1	2	3	4	5
x^3	0	1	8	27	64	125
$3x$	0	3	6	9	12	15
-20	-20	-20	-20	-20	-20	-20
$x^3 + 3x - 20$	-20	-16	-6	16	56	120

The table shows that there will be a value 0 somewhere between $x = 2$ and $x = 3$,
and probably nearer to 2 than to 3.
Find the value of the function when $x = 2.3$

Press 2.3 $\boxed{y^x}$ 3 $\boxed{+}$ 3 $\boxed{\times}$ 2.3 $\boxed{-}$ 20 $\boxed{=}$ and you will get -0.933, which is negative.
Try $x = 2.4$ and you will get 1.024, which is positive.
So the solution is between $x = 2.3$ and $x = 2.4$.
Since we want the answer correct to 1 decimal place, we find the value of the
function when $x = 2.35$. This is 0.028, which is positive.
So the solution lies between $x = 2.3$ and $x = 2.35$, and correct to 1 decimal place it
is $x = 2.3$.

Exercise 16.2

Solve these equations by trial and improvement, finding solutions which are positive numbers, correct to 1 decimal place.

1. $x^2 - 2x = 1$
2. $2x^2 + x = 25$
3. $x^2 - 4x = 9$
4. $x^3 - x^2 = 90$
5. $x^3 + x = 20$

6. $x^3 - x - 15 = 0$
7. $x^3 = 2x + 30$
8. $2x^2 = x + 60$
9. $x^3 + 8x = 270$
10. $x^2 - 40 = 8x$

Exercise 16.3 Applications and Activities

1. $ABCD$ is a rectangular field with $AB = x$ metres. BC is 8 m longer than AB. The area of the field is $105 \, \text{m}^2$.

   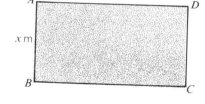

   1 Write down an expression for the length of BC.
   2 Write down an expression (in terms of x) for the area of the field, and hence write down an equation involving x.
   3 Solve the equation, and find the lengths of the sides AB and BC.

2. A solid pyramid has a square base of side x cm. The distance from the vertex to the mid-point of each edge of the base is 10 cm.

   1 Show that the total surface area of the pyramid, $S \, \text{cm}^2$, is given by the formula $S = x^2 + 20x$.
   2 Find the value of S when $x = 7$.
   3 Use a trial method to find the length of a side of the square base, correct to 0.1 cm, when the total surface area is $200 \, \text{cm}^2$.

   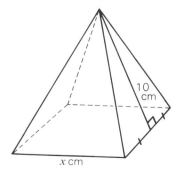

3. I think of a number between 1 and 10, cube it and add 9 times the original number. The result is 170.
   What is the original number ?

4. This carton has a square base of edge
   x cm and height $3x$ cm.
   1   Find an expression for its volume.
   2   If the carton holds $\frac{1}{2}$ litre of a soft
           drink, how many cm^3 is this ?
   3   Write down an equation and solve it
           to find the value of x, correct to
           1 decimal place.

3x cm

x cm

5. Liquid from a storage tank is being pumped out at such a rate that the volume
   V m^3 of liquid remaining in the tank t minutes after the start is given by the
   formula $V = 2t^2 - 24t + 72$.
   1   How much liquid is in the tank at the start (when $t = 0$) ?
   2   How much liquid is in the tank after 2 minutes ?
   3   How long does it take to empty the tank ?

6. An object is slid down a slope so that its
   distance s metres from the top of the slope
   after t seconds is given by the equation
   $s = 5 + 3t + t^2$.
   1   How far is the object from the top of
           the slope at the starting-time ?
   2   How far is the object from the top
           after 1 second ?
   3   The slope is 25 m long. To the nearest
           0.1 second, how long will it take the
           object to reach the bottom of the
           slope ?

PUZZLES

33.   **Pentominoes** are arrangements of 5 equal squares which join together with edges of adjacent squares fitting exactly together, such as

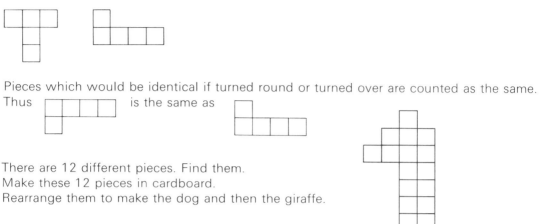

Pieces which would be identical if turned round or turned over are counted as the same. Thus ▢▢▢▢ is the same as ▢▢▢▢

There are 12 different pieces. Find them.
Make these 12 pieces in cardboard.
Rearrange them to make the dog and then the giraffe.

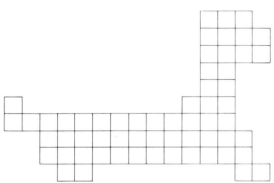

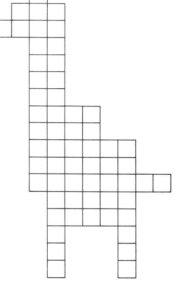

Can you also rearrange the pieces to form a rectangle with sides 10 units by 6 units, or one with sides 20 units by 3 units ? You can also try to make an 8 by 8 square with a square 2 by 2 hole in the centre.

34.   Tessa was proud of her record collection. She was asked if she had got 100 records. 'No, not yet, but if I had three times as many LP's or twice as many singles I would have 100 then.'

How many of each kind did she have ?

35.   Mr Jones made a circular pond in his garden. The concrete for the bottom of the pond cost him £15. For the safety of small children, he put a fence 40 cm high around the pond, and that cost him £30.
Mr King decided that he would also have a circular pond, but he wanted his to have twice the diameter of Mr Jones's pond. He also wanted to put a fence, 40 cm high, round it.
What would it cost Mr King for the fence, and for the concrete ?

17 Thinking about the probability of

Combined events

There are many times when one of two or more events can happen.
If we know the separate probabilities of these events, we can use the OR rule to find the probability of a combined event.

Mutually exclusive events

At a certain set of traffic lights on a main road,
the probability of the lights being red is 0.3,
the probability of the lights being red and amber is 0.03,
the probability of the lights being green is 0.6,
the probability of the lights being amber is 0.06,
the probability of the lights not working is 0.01.

Since only one of these five situations can happen at any one time, these are called **mutually exclusive events**.
Since it is certain that one of these situations must happen, what is the sum of these separate parts ?

Mr Shah passes through this junction each day.
Unless the lights are showing green, he has to stop.
What is the probability that he has to stop ?

Mrs Turner crosses the road at this set of traffic lights every day.
She can cross safely when the lights are showing red.
Unless the lights are showing red, she has to wait.
What is the probability that she has to wait ?

ombined events

Adding probabilities

At a local children's annual party the entertainment is chosen by the organiser, and depending on her preference, the cost and the particular entertainer she can hire, the entertainment is either a magician, a puppet show, cartoon films or an adventure film.

Sally and Tom decide that the probabilities of it being each one are as follows:

an adventure film 0.1

a magician 0.3

cartoon films 0.4

a puppet show 0.2

These are mutually exclusive events because only one of the four can happen.
What is the sum of the probabilities ?
Sally wants to watch a puppet show or a magician. What is the probability of getting her choice ?
Tom hopes that there will be a magician or an adventure film.
What is the probability of getting his choice ?

17 Probability of combined events

The formula for probability

Probability of a successful outcome $= \dfrac{s}{n}$

where n is the total number of equally likely outcomes
and s is the number of successful outcomes.

The probability scale goes from 0 to 1.

0		$\frac{1}{2}$		1
No chance of success	Success is less likely to happen than not	Success will happen in $\frac{1}{2}$ of the outcomes	Success is more likely to happen than not	Certain chance of success

Mutually exclusive events

When there are two or more outcomes of an event and at each time only one of the outcomes can happen (because if one outcome happens, this prevents any of the other outcomes happening), then the outcomes are called mutually exclusive events.

Examples

1   There are 11 discs in a bag. 5 are red, 4 blue and 2 green. One is taken out without looking.
What is the probability that it is red, blue, green ?

The probability that it is red $= \frac{5}{11}$
The probability that it is blue $= \frac{4}{11}$
The probability that it is green $= \frac{2}{11}$

These are mutually exclusive events because if the one taken out is red then it cannot be blue or green.
These are the only possible events.
The sum of their probabilities is $\frac{5}{11} + \frac{4}{11} + \frac{2}{11} = \frac{11}{11} = 1$.

The sum of the probabilities of all possible events is 1 because it is certain that one of them will occur.
The probability of the disc being red **or** blue is $\frac{9}{11}$, since there are 9 discs which are red or blue.
So P(red or blue) = P(red) + P(blue)
(P(red or blue) means 'the probability of being red or blue'.)

This rule is true for all mutually exclusive events.

The OR rule

If there are two mutually exclusive events A or B, then the probability of A or B occurring = the probability of A occurring + the probability of B occurring.
i.e.

$$P(A \text{ or } B) = P(A) + P(B)$$

If there are 3 events, A or B or C, then

$$P(A \text{ or } B \text{ or } C) = P(A) + P(B) + P(C)$$

The rule is similar if there are more than 3 events.

2 In the last year in a certain school, pupils must study one of the subjects Music, or Art, or Latin.
25% of the pupils study music and 60% of the pupils study art.
If a pupil from that year is chosen at random, what is the probability that the pupil studies music, art, music or art, Latin ?

$P(\text{music}) = \frac{25}{100} = \frac{1}{4}$, $P(\text{art}) = \frac{60}{100} = \frac{3}{5}$

$P(\text{music or art}) = \frac{25}{100} + \frac{60}{100} = \frac{85}{100} = \frac{17}{20}$

$P(\text{Latin}) + P(\text{music or art}) = 1$

so $P(\text{Latin}) = 1 - \frac{17}{20} = \frac{3}{20}$

Exercise 17.1

1. Lucy plays a game where she can either win, draw or lose.
    The probability of her winning is $\frac{1}{2}$, the probability of her drawing is $\frac{1}{3}$.
    1 What is the probability of her winning or drawing ?
    2 What is the probability of her losing ?

2. In a tombola game, the probability of winning a star prize is $\frac{3}{100}$, and the probability of winning one of the other prizes is $\frac{1}{5}$.
    If you draw one counter out of the drum,
    1 what is the probability of winning a prize,
    2 what is the probability of not winning a prize ?

3.   When 5 coins are tossed, the probability of getting 5 heads is $\frac{1}{32}$, the probability of getting 4 heads and 1 tail is $\frac{5}{32}$, and the probability of getting 3 heads and 2 tails is $\frac{10}{32}$.

If you toss 5 coins once, what is the probability of getting
1   at least 3 heads,
2   at least 4 heads,
3   at least 1 tail ?

4.   When 2 dice are thrown, the probability of both dice showing a six is $\frac{1}{36}$, and the probability of getting five on one die and six on the other is $\frac{1}{18}$.

What is the probability of a total score of
1   11 or 12,
2   10 or less ?

5.   5 men, 4 women, 3 boys and 1 girl enter for a contest.
If they each have an equal chance of winning, what is the probability that the winner is
1   a woman,
2   an adult,
3   female ?

6.   A carton contains packets of crisps. There are 12 packets of ready salted crisps, 6 packets of salt and vinegar crisps, 3 packets of smoky bacon flavour, 2 packets of cheese and onion flavour and 1 packet of prawn flavour. If you choose a packet without looking, what is the probability that it will be
1   either salt and vinegar or smoky bacon flavour,
2   not salt and vinegar nor smoky bacon flavour ?

7.   Explain why these outcomes are not mutually exclusive and work out the correct probabilities. (Do not use the mutually exclusive rule.)

1   A pack of 52 cards is shuffled and cut. What is the probability that the top card is either a heart or an ace ?

2   Numbers 1 to 24 are written on slips of paper and these are put into a bag. A slip is drawn out at random. What is the probability that the number on it is divisible by 3 or by 4 ?

3   A fair coin is tossed 3 times in succession and the results, head or tail, are recorded. What is the probability that at least one of the three results is a head ?

Exercise 17.2 Applications and Activities

1. In a Football league it is estimated that the probability of a home team winning is 0.5, and the probability of an away team winning is 0.2.
   1 What is the probability of a match being drawn ?
   2 What is the probability of the home team either winning or drawing ?

2. Hanif leaves home at the same time each morning, to walk to school. He allows extra time for waiting to cross the busy roads, and calculates that the probability of arriving at school on time is 0.45, and the probability of arriving early is 0.5.
   1 What is the probability of him arriving early or on time ?
   2 What is the probability of him being late ?

3. In a box of blue, red, yellow and green ribbons, there are twice as many blue ribbons as red ones, three times as many yellow ribbons as red ones, and four times as many green ones as red ones.
   What is the probability that if a ribbon is pulled out at random,
   1 it is green,
   2 it is yellow,
   3 it is green or yellow,
   4 it is blue or red ?

4. The probability of Alice winning the prize in a raffle is 0.08, the probability of Beryl winning it is 0.05 and the probability of Charlotte winning it is 0.12.
   What is the probability that
   1 the prize will be won by either Alice or Beryl,
   2 the prize will be won by either Alice, Beryl or Charlotte,
   3 none of the three girls will win the prize ?

5. The weather forecaster says that there is a 70% chance of fine weather this weekend, and a 20% chance of light showers. Otherwise it will be very wet.
   What is the probability that
   1 it will be very wet,
   2 there will be some rain this weekend ?

6.   Edward is playing on a games machine at a local club. On any turn he estimates
      that the probability of winning 10p is 0.16, the probability of winning 20p is 0.1,
      and the probability of winning more than 20p is 0.04.
      What is the probability of
      1   winning either 10p or 20p,
      2   winning more than 10p,
      3   winning some money,
      4   not winning any money ?

7.   You may prefer to work in groups to do this activity.

      Use 5 dice and throw them together.
      Record on a tally chart the number of sixes obtained on each throw.
      Repeat this 100 times altogether.

Number of sixes	Tally	f
0		
1		
2		
3		
4		
5		
		100

      Use your results to estimate the probabilities that, when 5 dice are thrown, there
      will be
      1   0 sixes shown,
      2   at least 1 six shown,
      3   2 or more sixes shown,
      4   less than 2 sixes shown.

      If the dice are fair ones, the theoretical probabilities of each number of sixes can
      be calculated and they are shown here.

Number of sixes	0	1	2	3	4	5
Probability	0.402	0.402	0.161	0.032	0.003	0*

      * the probability of 5 sixes is about 0.00013.

      What are the theoretical probabilities for questions **1** to **4** above, given as decimals
      to 2 decimal places ?

      Compare your experimental results with the theoretical ones and make a comment
      about them. (Do not expect them to match exactly.)

8. **A multi-choice test**
    This is an example of a multi-choice question where you have to answer
    A, B or C.

    If two coins are tossed, what is the probability that both will show heads ?

    A $\frac{1}{4}$ B $\frac{1}{3}$ C $\frac{1}{2}$

    What is the correct answer ?

    If you do not know, or are not sure, you will probably make a random guess.
    Was your answer correct ?

    Here is an activity where the whole class should take part.
    This is an imaginary test, and as you are going to answer the questions by
    random guessing we do not need to actually ask you the questions.
    On a slip of paper, number from 1 to 20 for the 20 questions, and then write
    down the answers, choosing at random from A, B or C.
    Ask everyone in the class to do the same. If you can collect more results by
    asking other classes as well, then do so.
    Collect in the slips. Decide on the correct answers.
    One way to do this is to throw a die for each question. If the number thrown is
    1 or 2, A is the answer, if the number is 3 or 4, B is the answer, and if the
    number is 5 or 6, C is the answer.
    Mark each person's answers and count up how many are correct.
    Write the results on a tally chart or frequency table.
    Use your results to estimate the probabilities of a pupil who uses random
    guessing in a multi-choice test, with 3 possible answers A, B or C,
    1   getting 8 or more answers correct, out of 20,
    2   getting 10 or more answers correct.

    A multi-choice test is no use if people can pass simply by random guessing.
    Statisticians work out the probability of this happening. Here are the theoretical
    results for your test.
    The probability of getting a score of 8 or more = 0.34,
    the probability of getting a score of 10 or more = 0.09.
    What is the probability of getting a score of 7 or less ?
    What is the probability of scoring 8 or 9 ?

    How do your estimated probabilities match these theoretical results ? (If only
    about 30 pupils took part, this is not enough to give reliable results, so do not
    worry if there is a big difference.)

18 Thinking about travel graphs and

The race between Achilles and the tortoise

This is an ancient problem.
Achilles could run 10 times as fast as the tortoise so he gave him 100 m start.
But he never caught him up, and so the tortoise won, because:

When Achilles had run the 100 m he was behind, the tortoise had travelled another 10 m,
When Achilles had run the 10 m, the tortoise had travelled another 1 m,
When Achilles had run the 1 m, the tortoise had travelled another 0.1 m, and so on.
So Achilles never caught up !
Or so you may believe.

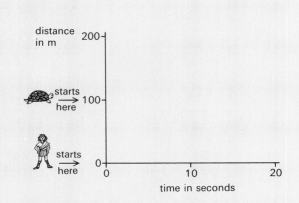

Now draw an accurate travel graph.
Assume that the tortoise travels at 1 m/s and Achilles travels at 10 m/s.
When and where does Achilles overtake the tortoise ?

Cars

The earliest cars travelled at about 10 mph (16 km/h).
In Britain, nowadays, there is a maximum speed limit of 70 mph. But Richard Noble, with Thrust 2, a 34 000 horse power jetcar, set a land speed record of 633.5 mph (1019.4 km/h) in 1983.

other graphs

Other graphs

Here is an unusual graph showing the costs of postage for letters.

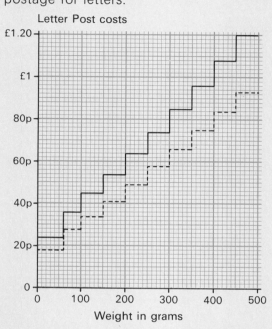

Letter Post costs

Cost

— 1st class
--- 2nd class

(Rates as in September 1991)

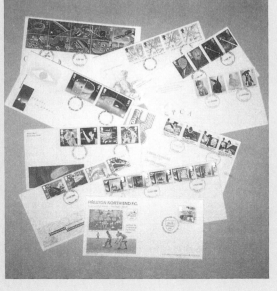

18 Travel graphs and other graphs

Distance-time graphs

Examples

1 Here is a graph of the journey of a cyclist. He leaves his home at 8 am, going towards a town 50 km away. During the first hour he cycles at a steady speed of 20 km/hour.
At 9 am he rests for $\frac{1}{2}$ hour, and then continues cycling at a steady speed of 15 km/hour. When he reaches the town he stops there until 12 noon, then he cycles home at a steady speed of 16 km/hour.
At what time does he reach the town ?
At what time does he arrive home ?

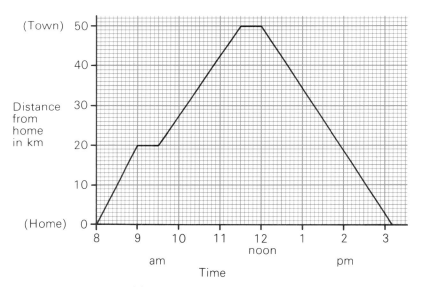

He reaches the town at 11.30 am.
He arrives home at 3.10 pm (approximately).

The graph is a straight line when the speed is steady. If the speed is not steady, the graph will not be a straight line.

2 Here are 3 travel graphs drawn on the same axes.
For graph (1), what is the time taken from O to A ?
What is the distance travelled ?

Find the speed, using the formula speed $= \dfrac{\text{distance}}{\text{time}}$

Repeat for graph (2) from O to B, and for graph (3) from O to C.

Name the 3 graphs in order ot the speeds, slowest first,

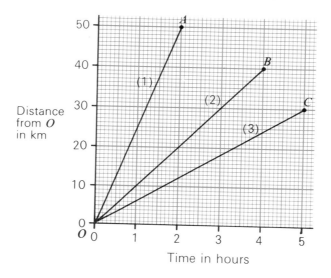

For (1), time = 2 hours, distance = 50 km, speed = 25 km/h.
For (2), time = 4 hours, distance = 40 km, speed = 10 km/h.
For (3), time = 5 hours, distance = 30 km, speed = 6 km/h.
In order, (3), (2), (1).

The speed of the object is given by the gradient (slope) of the line.
The greater the speed, the greater the slope of the line.

Exercise 18.1

1. Draw axes as shown and draw travel
    graphs to represent the following journeys,
    all starting at A and travelling towards B.
    Assume all people travel at steady speeds.

    1 Mr Gibson sets off at 9 am and travels
       48 km by car in $1\frac{1}{2}$ hours.
    2 Pauline sets off at 9.30 am, walks 6 km
       in $1\frac{1}{2}$ hours and then catches a bus
       which takes her another 44 km in 2 hours.

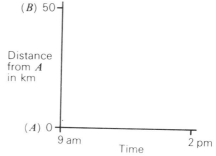

    3 Rajesh cycles, setting off at 11 am and he goes 40 km in $2\frac{1}{2}$ hours.
    4 At what times do they each pass over a bridge which is 30 km from A ?

2.   Henry left his home at 3 pm to watch a football match. After the match he
      returned home.
      The travel graph shows his journeys to and from the match.

      1   How far is the football field from his home ?
      2   How long did he spend at the football field ?
      3   What was his speed going to the match ?
      4   What was his speed on the journey home ?

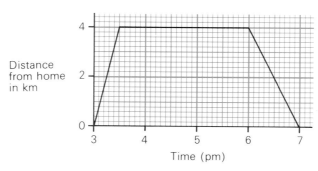

3.   This graph represents Mrs Moran's journey from a village *A* to a town *B*.

      She left at 2 pm and walked for 30 minutes to the railway station.
      1   At what speed did she walk ?

      She travelled the rest of the journey to *B* by train.
      2   How long did the train journey take ?
      3   How far was the train journey ?
      4   What was the speed of the train ?

      The next part of the graph shows
      the time she spent in town.
      5   How long did she stay in
             town ?

      The final part of the graph shows
      the journey home by car.
      6   How long did the car
             journey take ?
      7   How far was the journey
             home ?
      8   What was the speed of the
             car ?

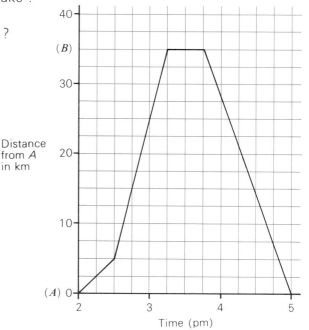

4. The diagram represents the journeys of 4 trains travelling from town *A* to town *B*,
    60 km away.

    1 Which two trains travel at the same speed ?
    2 Which train has the slowest speed ? What is its speed ?
    3 At what speed does train (3) travel ?

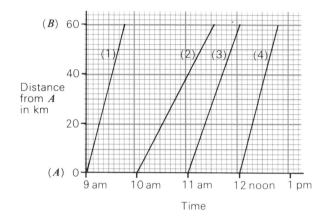

5. Fiona walks from home to a bus stop and catches a bus to the town. She then
    walks the remaining distance to school.
    The graph shows her journey.

    1 What is the total distance
        that Fiona walks ?
    2 How long does she have to
        wait for the bus ?
    3 What is the speed of the
        bus ?
    4 A friend lives $2\frac{1}{2}$ km from
        Fiona's home, on the bus
        route. At what time does
        the bus pass her house ?
    5 At what speed does Fiona
        walk after she has got off
        the bus ?

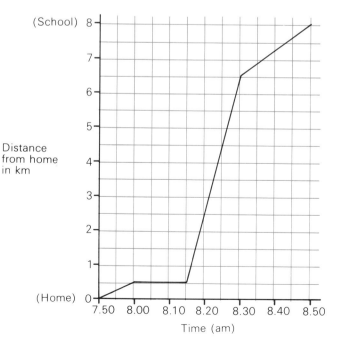

Other graphs

Example

3 A Gas Company makes a standing charge of £10 a quarter plus a cost of 55p for every therm used.
What would be the total bill if 800 therms were used ?
What would be the total bill if 400 therms were used ?
If no gas was used, there would still be the £10 standing charge to pay.

Draw an accurate graph, with the number of therms on the horizontal axis, from 0 to 800, using a scale of 2 cm to 100 therms, and with cost in £'s on the vertical axis, from 0 to 450, using a scale of 2 cm to 50.
Plot the 3 points corresponding to 0 therms, 400 therms and 800 therms used, and join them with a straight line.

Use your graph to find the amount of the bill when 270 therms were used. Also find the number of therms used if a gas bill was for £300.

(The sketch graph shows how your accurate graph will look and how it can be used.)

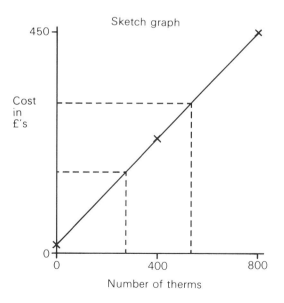

800 therms cost £450,
400 therms cost £230.
270 therms cost £160 (approximately),
£300 is the cost for 530 therms (approximately).

Exercise 18.2

1. Here is a list of prices charged by a firm for printing leaflets.

Number of copies	100	500	1000	5000	10 000
Price in £'s	11	17	25	85	150

Using your graph paper sideways, if necessary, draw a graph with number of copies on the horizontal axis, from 0 to 10 000, using a scale of 2 cm to 1000, and price in £'s on the vertical axis, from 0 to 150, using a scale of 2 cm to 20. Plot the points representing the prices given.
Join the points with a series of straight lines, as the price increases steadily between 100 and 500, between 500 and 1000, between 1000 and 5000, and between 5000 and 10 000.

Use your graph to find
1   the price paid for 800 leaflets,
2   the price paid for 8000 leaflets.
3   Mrs Hill paid £70 for some leaflets. Approximately how many copies had she ordered ?

2. Miss Taylor estimates that the cost of running her car consists of two parts, firstly the fixed charges such as licence and insurance and the loss in value of the car. She works these out as costing £1200 per year. Secondly there are the running costs, such as for petrol, oil and repairs, which she thinks cost 12p per mile.

1   What will it cost if she uses the car for 5000 miles per year ?
2   What will it cost if she uses the car for 10 000 miles per year ?

Draw a graph showing the total cost for mileages up to 10 000 miles. Put the distance in miles on the horizontal axis, from 0 to 10 000, and the cost in £'s on the vertical axis, from 0 to 2500.

3   Miss Taylor estimates that she travels about 75 miles per week. What will be the estimated cost of running her car for the year (52 weeks) ?

3. An Electricity Company charges a fixed quarterly charge of £9 per quarter and
    6.5p for each unit of electricity used.
    Draw a graph to show the total cost of up to 8000 units.
    Put units on the horizontal axis, from 0 to 8000, and cost in £'s on the vertical
    axis, from 0 to 600.

    Use your graph to find
    1   the amount to be paid when 5000 units were used,
    2   how many units were used if a bill was for £120.

Exercise 18.3   Applications and Activities

1. A ship leaves harbour A for harbour B at 1 pm and maintains a steady speed of
    20 km/hour.
    At 2 pm another ship leaves B for A maintaining a steady speed of 18 km/hour.
    The distance between A and B is 90 km.

    Draw the travel graphs for these 2 ships using the same axes.
    Draw the time axis with times from
    1 pm to 7 pm and the distance axis with
    distances from A from 0 to 90 km, with
    A at 0 and B at 90.
    Use the graph to find at what time the
    ships pass each other and how far they
    are from A at that time.

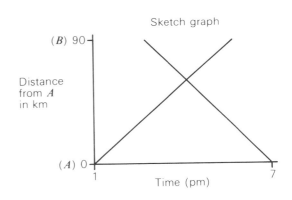

2. A single railway line runs between Ayrton and Bryton, which are 60 km apart.
    A goods train leaves Ayrton at noon, travelling at an average speed of 30 km/h,
    and it waits for 10 minutes in a siding 25 km from Ayrton to let a passenger train,
    travelling from Bryton to Ayrton, pass. This passenger train left Bryton at
    12.20 pm, and travels at a speed of 60 km/h.

    Draw graphs to show these journeys.

    Find
    1   the time at which the passenger train passes the siding,
    2   the distance apart of the trains at 1.10 pm.

3. **The snail**

    This is an old problem.

    A snail climbs up a wall 10 m high. Each day it climbs up 3 m and each night it slips down 2 m. How long does it take the snail to reach the top of the wall ?

    Draw a graph showing the snail's travel.
    Assume that it climbs at a steady speed, and that it slips down at a steady speed, and that the day and night are both 12-hour periods.
    How long **does** it take the snail to reach the top of the wall ?

4. **Income tax**

    Draw a graph to show the income tax payable for various amounts of income from £0 to £40 000.

    On the horizontal axis, put income in £'s, from 0 to 40 000, using a scale of 2 cm to 5000 (so that each small square will represent £500).
    On the vertical axis, put tax in £'s, from 0 to 12 000, using a scale of 2 cm to 2000 (so that each small square will represent £200).

    Here is the data from the 1991 Budget. The details may change slightly in later years and if you have more up-to-date figures you may prefer to use them.
    (1)   There is a personal allowance of £3295 so the tax is £0 for incomes from £0 to £3295. Draw a line to represent this.
    (2)   The basic rate of tax is 25% so for incomes from £3295 to £23 700 the tax is 25% of the amount above £3295. So for an income of £23 700 the tax payable is £5100, approximately. Join (3295, 0) to (23 700, 5100) with a straight line.
    (3)   Higher rate tax on income above £23 700 is at 40%. So for an income of £40 000 the tax payable on the first £23 700 is £5100 and the tax on the rest is £6520 making a total of £11 620. Join (23 700, 5100) to (40 000, 11 620) with a straight line.
    1   Find the tax to be paid by Miss Marie Smith who has an income of £10 000, and by Miss Jane Smith who has an income of £30 000.
    2   Mr Jones said he paid income tax of £10 000 last year. What was his income ? Keith Jones paid tax of £1000. What was his income ?

    Note   There are additional allowances, such as married couple's allowance, which we have not considered here. In addition there are certain ways of legally avoiding paying tax on all your income, for instance, investing money in TESSA's, PEP's, or by paying money into a pension fund. Maybe you could find out more about these.

5. **Track records**

Find the up-to-date record times for
athletics in the men's events in the 100 m,
200 m, 400 m and 800 m races.
Draw on the same axes travel graphs to
show these, putting time on the horizontal
axis, labelling it from 0 to 120 seconds,
and distance on the vertical axis, from
0 to 800 m.
(Assume that the speeds are steady.)
Up to 1989, here are the World Record times,
for men.
100 m, 9.92 s;   200 m, 19.72 s;
400 m, 43.29 s;   800 m, 1 min 41.73 s.

You can also show the women's record times
on the same graph.
You can draw similar graphs showing times
for other distances, or for other sports such as
swimming or cycling.

USA sprinter Carl Lewis
winning a 100-metre race.

6. In the manufacture of a certain article there is a fixed initial cost of £700, and in
addition it costs £80 to make each 100 articles.
Draw a graph showing the total cost of manufacturing any number of articles up
to 3000. On the horizontal axis label for number of articles from 0 to 3000 taking
2 cm to 500. On the vertical axis label for cost, in £'s, from 0 to 3500 taking 2 cm
to 500.

By using a new process the initial cost would be raised to £1100 but the cost of
manufacturing each hundred articles would be reduced to £40.
On the same diagram draw a second graph to show the costs using this process.

Find from the graphs
1   the number of articles for which the total cost would be the same using
    both methods,
2   the amount saved using the new process if 1500 articles are made,
3   how many extra articles can be made using the new process for a total cost
    of £2000.

PUZZLES

36. **Optical illusions**
    1 Label x and y axes from 0 to 4 taking 2 cm to represent 1 unit.
    Draw these lines.
    Join (1, 2) to (1, 4), (2, 1) and (3, 2).
    Join (1, 4) to (3, 4) and (2, 3).
    Join (4, 3) to (2, 3), (3, 4) and (4, 1).
    Join (4, 1) to (2, 1) and (3, 2).
    Join (3, 2) to (3, 4).
    Join (2, 3) to (2, 1).

    Ask your friends to say which is the front of the cube.

    2 Label x and y axes from 0 to 6 taking 2 cm to represent 1 unit.
    Draw these lines.
    Join (2, 2) to (1, 3), (2, 5) and (3, 3).
    Join (2, 5) to (1, 4) and (3, 4).
    Join (5, 2) to (4, 1), (6, 1) and (5, 5).
    Join (5, 5) to (4, 6) and (6, 5).

    Ask your friends to say which of the upright lines is longer.

37. Draw 7 regular hexagons of the same size on cardboard and cut them out.
    Join the 3 pairs of opposite points on each hexagon to divide the hexagon into 6 equal triangles.
    Colour these triangles as shown.
    Red (R), orange (O), yellow (Y), green (G), blue (B), purple (P).

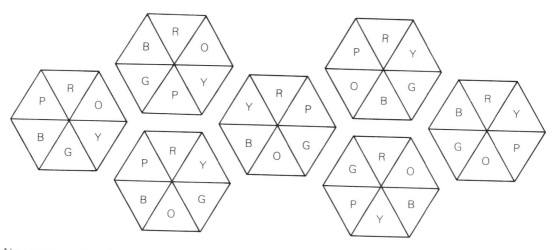

Now arrange the hexagons with one in the centre and the other six around it, so that all hexagons meet each other edge to edge. Where two edges meet, their triangles should have the same colour.

Miscellaneous Section C

Aural Practice

These aural exercises, C1 and C2, should be read to you, probably by your teacher or a friend, and you should write down the answers only, doing any working out in your head. You should do the 15 questions within 10 minutes.

Exercise C1

1. Ian drives 60 miles at an average speed of 40 miles per hour. How long does the journey take ?

2. If a triangle is enlarged by scale factor 4, what is the new length of a side of the triangle which originally was 7.5 cm long ?

3. A piece of rope is 10 m long. It is divided in the ratio 2 : 3. What is the length of the shorter piece ?

4. Write down the next 2 numbers in a sequence, after the number 10, if the rule is 'Double the last number and add 5'.

5. The probability of Lilian winning her next game of chess is $\frac{1}{7}$, and the probability of a draw is $\frac{2}{7}$. What is the probability that she will either win or draw ?

6. What is the equation of the line which passes through the points with coordinates (0, 0), (1, 2), (2, 4) and (3, 6) ?

7. What is the value of 0.65×10 ?

8. 3 angles of a triangle have sizes $x°$, $3x°$ and $5x°$. What is the value of x ?

9. Mrs Moore bought 2 kg of sugar and used 500 grams of it. How many grams of sugar did she have left ?

10. Simplify the expression $c^3 \div c^2$.

11. Mr Driver had a breakfast consisting of egg and bacon, costing £2.40, and a cup of coffee costing 60 pence.
He had a £5 note to pay for the breakfast. How much change should he receive ?

12. If a boat sails 3 km due North and then 4 km due West, how far is it in a direct line from its starting point ?

13. By trial, find a whole number solution for x in the equation $x^3 + x = 30$.

14.   When Kathryn cycles to school she decides that the probability of the traffic lights at the crossroads showing green in her direction is $\frac{1}{3}$. What is the probability of them not showing green ?

15.   Scott measures a line three times and gets 4.0 m, 4.1 m and 4.5 m. He decides to take the average of the three measurements. What is that ?

Exercise C2

1.   Bus fares are increased by 10%. If the old fare was 60 pence, what is the new fare ?

2.   A rectangular sports ground measures 70 m by 90 m. What is its area ?

3.   How many lines of symmetry has a square ?

4.   Find a positive whole number solution for x, for the equation $4x^2 = 36$.

5.   Thomas arrived at the station at 9.40 am. He was told that the next train was due in 40 minutes. At what time should it arrive ?

6.   How many packets of seed, each holding 250 grams, can be filled from a box containing 1 kg ?

7.   If the capital letters **M A H** are reflected in a mirror, what word is shown ?

8.   On the line with equation $y = 3x - 2$, what is the value of y when $x = 4$?

9.   The adult bus fare for a certain journey is 40 pence and children are charged half price. How much will it cost a family of 2 adults and 2 children ?

10.   If a line which was 4.2 cm long is enlarged to 12.6 cm, what is the scale factor of the enlargement ?

11.   The average pocket money for 3 children was £4 per child. Two of them got £3 each. How much did the third child get ?

12.   If the instructions on a flow diagram say 'Does B divide exactly by 9?', is the answer 'Yes' or 'No', if $B = 108$?

13.   If a train goes 60 km in 1 hour at a steady speed, how far will it go in 1 minute ?

14.   In the equation $x^2 = 6^2 + 8^2$, what is the positive value of x ?

15.   There are coloured beads in a bag. If one bead is picked out at random the probability that it is red is 0.4 and the probability that it is green is 0.3. What is the probability that it is red or green ?

Exercise C3   Revision

1. For the set of numbers 8, 7, 10, 13, 9, 8, 15,
    1 what is the mode,
    2 what is the median,
    3 what is the mean,
    4 what is the range ?

2. $\triangle ABC$ is an enlargement of $\triangle ADE$.
    What is the scale factor of the
    enlargement ?
    If $DE = 2.7$ cm, what is the length of BC ?

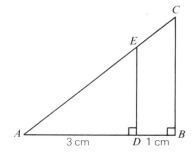

3. A factory machinist is tested on 2 pieces of work. She spends x minutes on the
    1st piece and y minutes on the 2nd piece.
    Write down algebraic statements expressing these conditions for x and y in order
    for her to pass the test.

    1 She must spend at least 2 minutes on the 1st piece but complete it within
         6 minutes.
    2 She must take between 3 and 8 minutes on the 2nd piece.
    3 She must not take longer than 10 minutes to complete both pieces.

4. A roll of cloth contains 20 m. To make an overall takes 1.7 m of the cloth.
    How many overalls can be made, and how much cloth is left over ?

5. An experiment was carried out to find the quantity of a chemical salt which can
    be dissolved in a given volume of water at different temperatures.
    Here are the results.

temperature °C	10	20	30	40	50	60
weight in grams	120	150	162	186	216	238

    Plot these results on a graph. The points do not lie on a straight line because of
    experimental errors. Draw a line of best fit and use it to answer these questions.

    1 Find the temperature at which 170 g of the salt will dissolve in the given
         volume of water.
    2 Find what amount of the salt will dissolve in the given volume of water at
         25°C.

6. A cylinder has a radius of 15 cm.
   1 Calculate the area of one end, correct to $0.1\,\text{cm}^2$.
   2 If its volume is $2000\,\text{cm}^3$, find the height, correct to the nearest mm.

7. *ABCDEFGH* is a cuboid.
   A is the point (2, 2, 0).
   AB has length 8 units and is parallel to the *x*-axis.
   AD has length 4 units and is parallel to the *y*-axis.
   AE has length 6 units and is parallel to the *z*-axis.
   Find the coordinates of the points
   B, C, D, E, F, G, H.

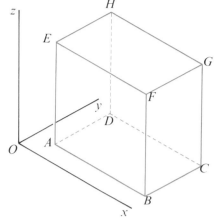

8. Simplify these expressions.

   1 $x^2 \times x^3$ **4** $(x^2)^4$
   2 $x^8 \div x^2$ **5** $x^5 \div x^5$
   3 $\sqrt{x^6}$

9. On a stretch of straight coastline there is a coastguard station at *A*. Their rescue boats patrol a region within 10 km of the coast, and there is a lookout at the station who can see a distance of 15 km through a telescope.
   Using a scale of 1 cm to 2 km, copy the diagram and mark in
   1 the boundary of the patrolled region,
   2 the boundary of the region at sea that the lookout can see.
   Shade the region of the sea which is not patrolled, but which is visible to the lookout.

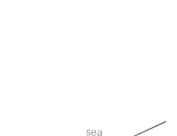

10. The diagram shows a plot of ground.
    1 Use Pythagoras' theorem to find the length of *AD*.
    2 Find the length of fencing needed to enclose the plot.

11. A firm employs skilled workers and trainee workers. The skilled workers are paid £40 per day and the trainees are paid £20 per day.
     If altogether there are 25 workers, of whom x are skilled and y are trainees, write down an equation involving x and y.
     On graph paper, draw axes with x from 0 to 30 and y from 0 to 50, and draw the line of the equation on the graph.
     If the daily wage bill is £900 write down a second equation, simplify it, and draw its line on the graph.
     Use the graph to solve the equations simultaneously, and say how many workers there are in each category.

12. A surveyor made measurements of a small field, as shown on the sketch.

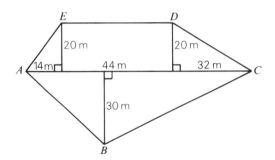

     1 What is the length of AC ?
     2 What is the area of $\triangle ABC$?
     3 What shape is $ACDE$?
     4 What is the area of $ACDE$?
     5 What is the total area of the field, in m^2 ?

13. Tara thinks of a number. She multiplied it by 5 and added 7.
     The result is the same if she multiplied the number by 3 and subtracted 3.
     What number did she think of ?

14. A frequency distribution is shown in this histogram.
     1 Write down the frequencies in a table.
     2 What is the mode of the distribution ?
     3 What is the median ?
     4 What is the mean ?

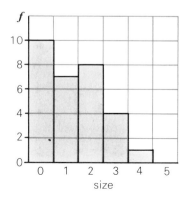

15. Find the number x if
$20 < x < 40$, also
x is a prime number,
$x - 8$ is a prime number, and
$2x + 1$ is divisible by 5.

16. In the diagram, $CA = CB = CD$.
$b = 68°$.
Find the sizes of angles a, c, d.
What is the size of $\angle DAB$?

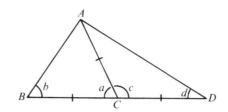

17. Draw axes as shown and show the journeys of a boy on his bicycle and his father in the car.

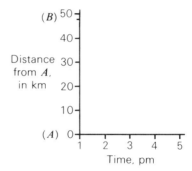

The boy starts from A at 1 pm and cycles at a steady speed of 16 km/hour for $1\frac{1}{2}$ hours. He then rests for $\frac{1}{2}$ hour and continues cycling to B, which is 48 km from A, arriving at 5 pm.

His father starts from A at 3 pm and arrives at B at 4.30 pm travelling at a steady speed.

1 What was the boy's speed on the second part of his journey ?
2 What was his father's speed ?
3 At what time did the father overtake his son ?
4 When the father overtook his son, how far were they both from B ?

18. Solve the simultaneous equations

1 $4x - 3y = 14$ **2** $3x + 2y = 4$
      $2x + y = 12$ $7x + 3y = 11$

19. 100 cartons of eggs were checked to find out how many cracked eggs there were in each carton.
70 cartons had no cracked eggs, 17 cartons had 1 cracked egg, 8 cartons had 2 cracked eggs, 3 cartons had 3 cracked eggs and 2 cartons had 4 cracked eggs. If a carton is chosen at random from these 100 cartons, what is the probability that it contains

1 no cracked eggs,
2 at least 1 cracked egg,
3 more than 1 cracked egg ?

20. The number of diagonals of a polygon with n sides is $\frac{1}{2}n(n-3)$.
     If a polygon has 90 diagonals, write down an equation involving n and show
     that it can be rearranged to $n^2 - 3n - 180 = 0$.
     Solve this equation by trial, to find how many sides the polygon has.

Exercise C4   Revision

1. Use your calculator to work out $\dfrac{10.32 \times 0.751}{22.6 - 15.9}$, giving the answer correct to
    3 significant figures.

2. A car travels 900 metres in 1 minute. What is its speed, in km/h ?

3. The diagram shows a circular path 2 m
    wide round a circular pond of diameter
    16 m.

    Find, giving answers to 0.1 m^2,
    1   the surface area of the pond,
    2   the total area covered by the pond
          and path,
    3   the area of the path.

4. A number in prime factors is $2^2 \times 3^4 \times 5^2$.
    Find the square root of the number in index form, and then work out its value.

5. This table shows the distribution of weights of 50 potatoes.

Weight, in grams	Number of potatoes
0–under 50	5
50–under 100	18
100–under 150	10
150–under 200	7
200–under 250	6
250–under 300	3
300–under 350	1
	50

    1   What is the modal class of weights ?
    2   What is the centre of interval of the class 0–50 ?
    3   Find the mean weight of the distribution.

6. 30 people went together to an exhibition. There were x adults, for whom the entrance fee was £5 each and the rest were children who were charged £3 each.

 1 In terms of x, how many children were there ?
 2 Write down an expression for the total cost, and simplify it.
 3 If the total cost was £126, write down an equation and solve it to find x.
 4 How many adults were there, and how many children ?

7. Here is a flow diagram to work out the amount of VAT to be paid on a bill.

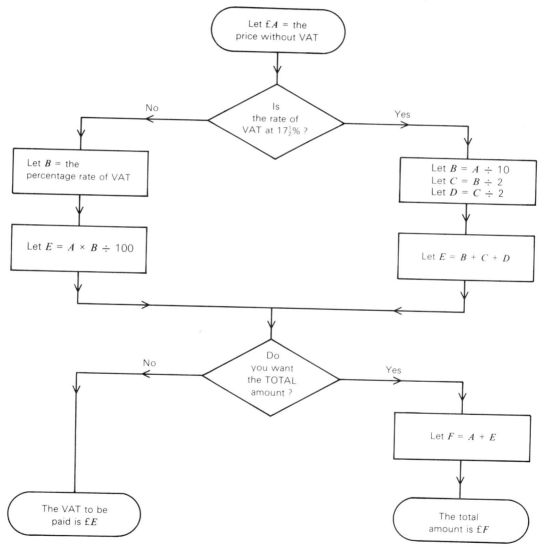

Use the flow diagram to find
1 the VAT on a price of £840,
2 the total price if the price without VAT is £4.40.

8.   An area of $2\frac{1}{2}$ hectares is divided into 60
     building plots.
     There were x larger plots of area $500\,m^2$, and
     y smaller plots of area $300\,m^2$.
     (1 hectare $= 10\,000\,m^2$)
     Write down 2 equations connecting x and y,
     simplify where possible, and solve them
     simultaneously.
     How many of each kind of plot were there ?

9.   A bag contains discs which are coloured red or blue.
     If 4 discs are pulled out without looking, it is calculated that these are the
     probabilities of the results that can occur.

	4 reds	3 reds 1 blue	2 reds 2 blues	1 red 3 blues	4 blues
probability	0.07	0.35	0.43	0.14	0.01

1   Which result is most likely to occur ?
2   Which result is least likely to occur ?
3   What is the probability of getting at least 2 blue discs ?
4   What is the probability of getting less than 2 blue discs ?

10. How many cubes of edge 3 cm can be packed into a rectangular box with inside
     measurements 33 cm by 24 cm by 15 cm ?

11. Here are the figures for current television licences, and admissions to cinemas,
     over a period of 11 years.

Year	67	68	69	70	71	72	73	74	75	76	77
TV licences (millions)	14	15	16	16	17	18	20	23	25	26	30
Cinema admissions (Ten millions)	27	24	22	19	18	16	13	14	12	10	10

     Draw a scatter diagram to represent this data, putting TV licences on the
     horizontal axis.
     Draw a line of best fit.

12. Simplify these expressions and give the numerical values.
     1 $2^5 \times 5^3 \div (2^3 \times 5)$
     2 $7^4 \div 7^4$
     3 $3^4 \div 3^6$

13. Three workmen charge for doing a job as follows:
     Mr *A* charges £250 for the 1st 20 hours and £5 an hour for any hours over 20.
     Mr *B* charges a flat-rate of £10 per hour.
     Mr *C* charges £350 for the job, regardless of how long it will take.

     Draw a graph with time on the horizontal axis, from 0 to 50 hours, and cost on
     the vertical axis from £0 to £500.
     Draw the straight line representing the costs for using Mr *C*.
     For Mr *B*, work out how much he would charge if the job took 0 hours,
     20 hours and 50 hours. Plot points representing these charges, and join them
     with a straight line.
     For Mr *A*, draw the straight line representing his charges if the job takes up to
     20 hours, and then find another line to represent his charges if the job takes
     longer.
     Label the graphs for Mr *A*, Mr *B* and Mr *C*.
     From your graphs find
     1   which man charges least if the job takes 25 hours,
     2   which man charges least if the job takes 35 hours,
     3   which man charges least if the job takes 45 hours.

14. **1**   Find, in terms of x, an expression for
            the area of this L-shaped figure.
     2   If the area is 116 cm², write down an
            equation and solve it by trial, to find
            the value of x.

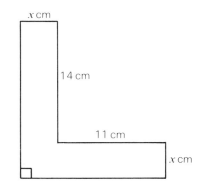

15. Draw a triangle *ABC* with *BC* = 9 cm, *AB* = 7.5 cm and *AC* = 6 cm.
     Construct the locus of points which are
     1   equidistant from *A* and *B*,
     2   equidistant from *A* and *C*.
     Mark a point *P* which is equidistant from *A*, *B* and *C*.
     Shade the region inside the triangle of points which are nearer to *B* than to *A*
     and nearer to *C* than to *A*.

16. A cylinder has radius 24 cm and height 40 cm. A similar cylinder has to be made
     with height 50 cm.
     What is the scale factor of the enlargement ?
     What is the radius of the enlarged cylinder ?

17.   A man planned to save 5% of his wages and thus save £625 a year, for his
       holiday fund. But he only managed to save £500. What percentage of his annual
       salary was this ?

18.   A wire is to be stretched between the
       tops of 2 posts AB and CD.
       Use Pythagoras' theorem to find the
       length of wire needed.

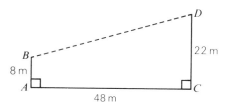

19.   Two rolls of carpet are together worth £1200. The first roll contains x metres
       costing £20 per metre, and the second contains y metres costing £15 per metre.
       Write down an equation connecting x and y. Simplify it by dividing all terms
       by 5.
       In this equation, if $x = 0$, what is the value of y ?
       If $y = 0$, what is the value of x ?
       Draw a graph, with x-axis from 0 to 60 and y-axis from 0 to 80. Draw the line
       representing your equation on the graph.
       If the second roll of carpet is 10 m longer than the first, write down another
       equation connecting x and y. Draw its line on the graph.
       Solve the equations simultaneously to find how much carpet there is in each
       roll.

20.   The cross-section of a railway cutting is
       in the shape of a trapezium with the
       measurements shown.
       If the cutting is 400 m long, what is the
       volume of earth which will have to be
       removed to construct the cutting ?

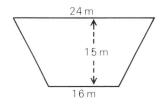

Exercise C5   Activities

1.   **Where to shop ?**

      When buying the weekly groceries for the family, which shop is cheapest ?
      Is there much difference between the prices in different supermarkets, or in a
      supermarket and a small shop ? You can do a survey to investigate this.
      First of all, you must decide what items to buy, and the quantities of each. Plan
      for a family, perhaps for your own family, or perhaps for an 'average' family with
      two adults and two children, and make a shopping list for a week's groceries.

Next, you should find out the cost of the
groceries in the different shops.
You can list the prices and the totals for the
different shops. You can illustrate your
answer with statistical diagrams, such as
bar charts. Perhaps you can plot some
prices from two shops on a scatter diagram,
and if there is some correlation, draw a line
of best fit.

Comment on the results of your survey.
(If you find that prices are much cheaper in
a particular shop, it is not necessarily the best place in which to do the shopping.
Shoppers take other facts into consideration, such as quality of fresh food,
opening hours, distance from home, and so on.)

2. **A picture graph**

Draw the x-axis from 0 to 40, and the y-axis from 0 to 25, using equal scales on
both axes.
Work out these functions for the values of x given, and draw the straight-line
graphs for the range of x or y given. Complete the picture by adding pegs,
background and other details, and colouring it.

1 $y = \frac{1}{3}(5x + 20)$ from $x = 2$ to $x = 11$

2 $y = 26.1 - 0.1x$ from $x = 11$ to $x = 31$

3 $y = 85 - 2x$ from $x = 31$ to $x = 40$

4 $y = 47 - 2x$ from $x = 11$ to $x = 22$

5 $y = \frac{1}{9}(x + 100)$ from $x = 17$ to $x = 35$

6 $x = 5$ from $y = 9$ to $y = 15$

7 $x = 11$ from $y = 7$ to $y = 25$

8 $x = 17$ from $y = 5$ to $y = 13$

9 $x = 35$ from $y = 8$ to $y = 15$

10 $y = \frac{1}{3}(32 - x)$ from $x = 5$ to $x = 8$ and
                                    from $x = 11$ to $x = 17$

11 $y = \frac{1}{3}(17x - 112)$ from $x = 8$ to $x = 11$

12 $y = \frac{1}{6}(x + 13)$ from $x = 17$ to $x = 35$

13 $y = 60 - 2x$ from $x = 23$ to $x = 28$

14 $y = 73 - 2x$ from $x = 29$ to $x = 34$

Now, invent a simple picture yourself, made with straight lines whose equations
you know or can easily work out.
Give the instructions to your friends, for them to draw your picture.

3.   **Powers of 2** (continued from page 16)

Folding a piece of paper

Did you manage to fold it in half, . . . , 9 times altogether ?
If not, why not ?

It can be done, just about, if you start with a big enough piece of thin paper,
such as tissue paper.
How many layers are there after each time you fold it ?

Number of folds	0	1	2	3	...	9
Number of layers	1	2	4	...		

Copy the table and complete it.

Folding it 50 times

How many layers will there be, expressed as a power of 2, if you could fold it 50 times ?
It has been said that the thickness of the number of layers needed would be high
enough to reach the moon! You may like to check this statement. The average distance
of the moon from us is about 376 000 km.

The blacksmith and the highwayman

It is easier to keep the counting in farthings.
The total number of farthings is $1 + 2 + 4 + 8 + \ldots + 2^{31}$.
To add up this sequence, investigate the pattern every time you add an extra number
on.

	Total
1	$2 - 1$
1 + 2	$4 - 1$
1 + 2 + 4	$8 - 1$
1 + 2 + 4 + 8	$16 - 1$

(i.e. $2^4 - 1$)

So what does this pattern give us for the sum of farthings ?

The highwayman should have been content to pay £320, because this new amount
comes to nearly £4 474 000.

The chessboard problem

The counting goes in a similar way to the last problem, but this time the total number of grains of wheat wanted is $2^{64} - 1$.

There are too many figures to be shown on your calculator. It may show 1.8446744   19 which means 1.8446744×10^{19}.

The exact answer is 18 446 744 073 709 551 615 grains.

The reward could not be given as there was not so much wheat in the whole world.

(A grain of corn is an ancient measure of weight, using 7000 grains to 1 lb, so you can find out the weight of wheat which would be needed.)

The tower of Hanoi puzzle

If you have only 1 disc, then only 1 move is needed.

If you have 2 discs, then 3 moves are needed.

If you have 3 discs, then 7 moves are needed.

We have mentioned this sequence before, so you should recognise it.

For 8 discs, there are 255 moves.

If you put the pegs in a triangular position, instead of in a line, then you will notice that the smallest disc moves in every alternate move, and it always goes in the same direction (clockwise or anticlockwise).

For 64 discs, the number of moves is $2^{64} - 1$, the same number as in the chessboard problem, so the time taken will be $(2^{64} - 1)$ seconds.

You can work out how many years the task would take. It is a long, long time.

You will notice from these problems that the doubling sequence grows to enormous numbers.

You may find other applications which you can think about.

There are more practical applications, for instance, bacteria in a culture whose numbers double every day.

You may like to investigate other sequences which multiply at a constant rate, e.g. the sequence 3, 9, 27, . . . or 4, 16, 64, . . . , which grow even faster than the doubling sequence.

The sequence 10, 100, 1000, . . . is used as the basis for our number system. (Notice how your calculator used 10^{19} in representing a very big number.)

4. **π**

π is a never-ending number.

Write π to as many decimal places as are shown on your calculator.

Here is π given to 35 decimal places:

3.14159265358979323846264338327950288

People have invented phrases or rhymes to help them to remember the first few decimal places of π. One pupil, Alison, thought of 'How I hate a Maths education-al lesson where the class struggles'. The number of letters in each word gives 3.14159265359. Can you invent a phrase or rhyme ?

Although you learnt about π as the value of $\dfrac{\text{circumference}}{\text{diameter}}$ in a circle, π is

involved in many aspects of mathematics, not always connected with circles. There are various infinite (never ending) series which give π, such as

$$\pi \ = \ 4 - \tfrac{4}{3} + \tfrac{4}{5} - \tfrac{4}{7} + \tfrac{4}{9} - \ldots$$

Use your calculator to work out several terms of this.

A man called Shanks, in 1873, worked out 707 decimal places of π. This was an incredible task, in the days when there were no computers.

More recently, using modern computers, π has been calculated to over a thousand million decimal places, by two American brothers at Columbia University.

Here is a method which you can use to find the value of π experimentally. It only uses probability and random numbers.

If you choose 2 numbers at random they can either have a common factor, e.g. 40 and 75 have a common factor 5, or they can be prime to each other, i.e. have no factor in common except 1, e.g. 40 and 63 have no common factor although they both have factors.

The probability that 2 numbers are prime to each other is $\dfrac{6}{\pi^{2}}$.

Ask each person in the class to get 30 pairs of random numbers. You can get these from random number tables, a computer, or using numbers from a telephone directory. Numbers should in theory be any size but in practice numbers up to 100 will do.

Write your numbers in a list.
First cross out any pair which are both even (they
both divide by 2).
Then of the remaining pairs, cross out those numbers
which both divide by 3. (What is the quick way to tell
if a number divides by 3 ?)
Then cross out pairs which both divide by 5.
Of the pairs of numbers which are left, you should be
able to identify some which quite clearly have no
common factor. Write P (for prime) by these.
Then look at the remaining pairs, crossing them out
if they have a common factor such as 7, 11, 13, . . .
and writing P if you decide that they have no factor
in common.
(If 1 appears, let it be prime to any other number except another 1.)

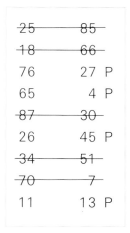

Now find p, the number of pairs prime to each other, and n, the total number of pairs
you have used, using everyone's results.

Put $\dfrac{p}{n} = \dfrac{6}{\pi^2}$. This rearranged gives $\pi = \sqrt{\dfrac{6n}{p}}$.

What is your experimental value for π ?
Is it close to the true value ?

5.   **An interesting locus**

A and B are two fixed points on a sheet of
paper, 10 cm apart.
P is a point which moves on the paper so
that the distances $PA + PB = 16$ cm.
What is the locus of P ?
You can make a guess first.

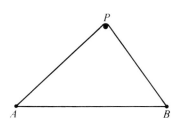

Then you can draw the locus in this way:
Get a piece of string 16 cm long.
Ask someone to hold the ends down on the paper at A and B.
Hold the string tight with a pencil point (as at point P in the diagram). Then,
since the string is 16 cm long, if it is tight, $PA + PB = 16$ cm.
Move the pencil, keeping the string tight. As it moves, it draws the locus. After
drawing the part on one side of AB, reposition the pencil to draw the other part.
Can you find out the name of the shape you have drawn ?

You can repeat this, taking different lengths for AB, and for $PA + PB$.

6. **Sequences based on quadratic functions**

It is not easy to recognise the nth term of a sequence if it involves n^2. You might like to try using this method, although it is not a method that you need to learn specially.

You probably remember how to continue a sequence using the difference method.

e.g. the sequence 2, 5, 10, 17, 26, . . .

2   5   10   17   26 ⟶ 37 ⟶ 50 ⟶ 65 ⟶ 82

    3   5   7   9 ⟶ 11 ⟶ 13 ⟶ 15 ⟶ 17

       2   2   2   2   2   2   2

If the 3rd row is a row consisting of the same number each time, the sequence is based on a quadratic function and the nth term is of the form $an^2 + bn + c$, where a, b and c are numbers.

You can find the values of a, b and c as shown in this example.

e.g. For the sequence 9, 7, 11, 21, 37, . . .

Find the next 2 rows as if using the difference method and check that the numbers in the 3rd row are all the same.

Then find the numbers which would come in front of the sequence on the 3 rows, if following the same rule. Do this by working backwards from the 3rd row.

17 ⟵ 9   7   11   21   37

   −8 ⟵ −2   4   10   16

     6 ⟵ 6   6   6

Then, a is half the number in the 3rd row, in this example, $a = 3$.

c is the 1st number in the 1st row of the new pattern, here, $c = 17$.

The 1st (new) number in the 2nd row is $a + b$, so, here, $a + b = -8$, $b = -11$.

The nth term of the sequence is $3n^2 - 11n + 17$.

You can check this.

Putting $n = 1$, $3n^2 - 11n + 17 = 3 - 11 + 17 = 9$.

Putting $n = 2$, $3n^2 - 11n + 17 = 3 \times 2^2 - 11 \times 2 + 17 = 12 - 22 + 17 = 7$, and so on.

Working backwards for the sequence 2, 5, 10, 17, 26, . . .

1 ← 2   5   10   17   26

1 ← 3   5   7   9

2 ← 2   2   2

a is half the number in the 3rd row, so $a = 1$.
c is the 1st number in the new pattern, so $c = 1$.
The 1st number in the 2nd row is $a + b$, so $a + b = 1$, $b = 0$.

The nth term is $n^2 + 1$.

You can check this by putting $n = 1$, $n = 2$, $n = 3$, . . . in turn.
You can use this formula to find any term of the sequence.
Putting $n = 10$ gives the 10th term, which is 101.

Here are some sequences based on quadratic functions.
Use this method to find their nth terms. Then, by putting $n = 10$, find the 10th
term of each.

1   9, 19, 33, 51, 73, . . .
2   3, 14, 33, 60, 95, . . .
3   6, 14, 24, 36, 50, . . .
4   11, 20, 35, 56, 83, . . .
5   3, 20, 47, 84, 131, . . .
6   Here is the sequence of triangular numbers, 1, 3, 6, 10, 15, . . .
        Find the nth term.
        What is the 100th triangular number ?

7.   **Clock Patience**

To play this game of patience, you need a pack of 52 cards.
Shuffle them well and deal out 12 of
them, face downwards, to represent the
positions 1 to 12 shown on a clock
face. Put the 13th card face downwards
in the centre of the circle. Go round the
circle and the centre three times more,
putting cards on top of each other, so
having 4 cards in each pile and all 52
cards used.

The starting position

Begin the game by turning up the top card of the centre pile. If this is (say) 7, put it on the outside of the circle in place 7. Now turn up the top card of that (7's) pile, and if this is (say) 3, put it in place 3. Continue in a similar way. Use Jacks for 11 and Queens for 12. The next similar card turned up goes on top of the first one.

If a King is turned up it goes in the centre and you turn up another card from the centre pile.

A game in progress

If you use all the cards with the last King turning up last of all then you win, i.e. the patience has 'worked out' and you have completed the clock.

More often the last King turns up sooner, and since there are no cards left in the centre the patience has not worked out. In this case, count how many cards are left not turned up.

Play the game many times. Your friends can also play. Keep a record of the number of cards not turned up in each game.

Using your experimental results, estimate the probabilities for each number of cards left and write them down in a table like this.

Use your table to estimate
1   the probability of winning,
2   the probability of having only 1, 2 or 3 cards left to be turned up,
3   the probability of having 4, 5, 6 or 7 cards left to be turned up,
4   the probability of having more than 7 cards left to be turned up.

Number of cards left	Frequency (Number of times)	Estimated probability of this result
0		
1		
2		
3		
4		
5		
6		
7		
8		
9		
10 or more		
Total		

8. **Networks**

Any system of lines which connect a set of points on a surface is called a **network**.

Examples

(a) (b) (c) (d)

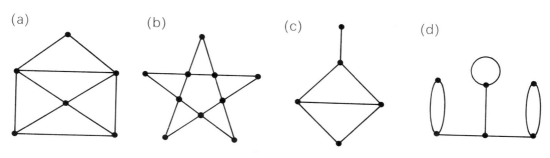

The points ● are called vertices.
Any join of 2 vertices will be called an arc, even if it is a straight line.
The arcs divide the surface into regions. These include the outside region.
A vertex with an odd number of arcs leaving it will be called an odd vertex.
A vertex with an even number of arcs leaving it will be called an even vertex.
If you can draw the complete network without taking your pencil off the paper and without going along any arc more than once the network is said to be **traversable**, and if you can get back to the starting point it is said to be **unicursal**.

You can fill in details of each network in a table.

Network	Vertices V	Regions R	Arcs A	$V + R - A$	Odd vertices	Even vertices	Traversable	Unicursal
a	6	6	10	2	2	4	Yes	No
b	10	7	15				Yes	Yes
c	5	3					No	No
d	6	4	8		4	2	No	No
.								
.								

Copy this table, including space for more entries.
Fill in the missing numbers.

Investigate the networks **1** to **16** shown below, together with any other networks you wish to include, and add the results to the table.
Can you make any conclusions from the table ?

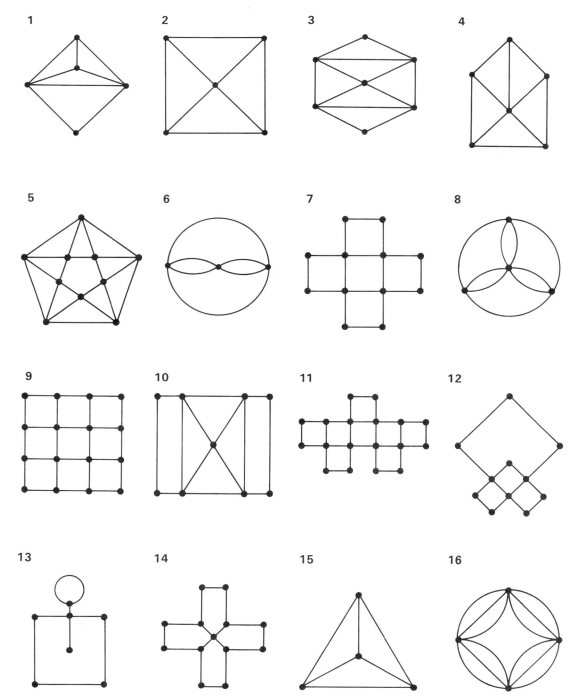

9. **Curves of Pursuit**

Imagine a dog chasing a hare. At every leap the dog will change direction according to the position the hare has reached.

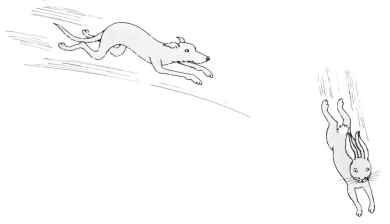

Example

The hare is moving along the line AB in the direction from A to B.
The dog is at D when the hare starts at A. We have made AD = 10 cm. Assume the dog and the hare move at equal speeds.

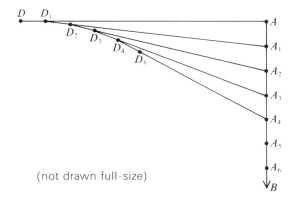

(not drawn full-size)

Mark off A_1, A_2, A_3, ... , all 1 cm steps in the path of the hare.
Join the line DA.
Using steps of 1 cm, assume the hare reaches A_1 when the dog reaches D_1.
Now the dog notices that the hare is at A_1 and it changes track, aiming along D_1A_1.
Join D_1A_1 and mark off 1 cm along it to get to point D_2.
Now join D_2A_2 and mark 1 cm along it to get to point D_3.
Continue in this way.
Finally, draw the path $DD_1D_2D_3$ . . . in colour.
Although this is a series of straight lines, it is called a curve of pursuit.

Investigate the paths taken by the dog under different situations.
1   Let the dog start at different distances from *A*.
2   Let the speed of the dog vary from that of the hare, e.g. you could represent the speed of the hare by 0.6 cm steps and the speed of the dog by 1.2 cm steps if you want it to go twice as fast.
3   The hare could start at a different part of the line, perhaps starting at *B* and running towards *A*.
4   The hare could move round a circle. If you make the radius of the circle just larger than your protractor you can mark off equal arcs by using every 10° (or any other angle size) along the edge of the protractor. Again use the ideas of **1**, **2** and **3**. You could try with the dog starting at the centre of the circle.
5   An interesting pattern is formed if you start with four dogs *A*, *B*, *C*, *D* at the corners of a square. *A* is chasing *B*, *B* is chasing *C*, *C* is chasing *D* and *D* is chasing *A*. Where do they all end up ?
    You can repeat this with three dogs at the corners of an equilateral triangle.

You can think of other ideas for yourself.

10. **Using a computer**

You can use your computer to plot straight-line graphs on the screen. You can notice the effect of changing some of the numbers, e.g. changing $y = 2x + 5$ into $y = 2x + 6$, or into $y = 3x + 5$.
You may like to investigate further by plotting graphs which are not straight lines. You could look at the graphs of $y = x^2$, $y = x^3$, etc., and also graphs such as $y = \frac{1}{x}$ and $y = 2^x$. You might also be curious about other functions such as $y = \sin x$ (sine *x*).

With a suitable computer program, a scatter diagram can be plotted on a computer screen. This is very useful if you have a large amount of data, because it is much quicker than drawing your own graph and plotting the points on it. You can see if there seems to be evidence of correlation, and the program will also draw a line of best fit (called a regression line of *y* on *x* in more advanced work).

You can use your computer to do the working out when using trial and error methods in solving quadratic and cubic equations. This saves time, and also means that you can work to more decimal places and get more accurate answers.

A computer is a remarkable invention of our time. Do make good use of it.

PUZZLES

38. How many triangles are there in this figure ?
    If *EA*, *AB*, *BC* are 3 sides of a regular
    pentagon, with *D* as the 5th point, how many
    of the triangles are isosceles ?

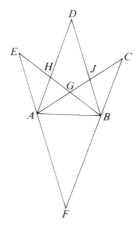

39. A wealthy man owned 100 diamonds of equal value. He said that on his death the
    diamonds should be divided into two parts, one part to give his 5 daughters equal
    numbers of diamonds, and the other part to be shared equally among his 7
    granddaughters. He also said that the share of a daughter and of a granddaughter
    together should total 18 diamonds.
    How should these diamonds be divided ?

40. **Tangrams**
    The 7 pieces for this puzzle are shown on page 200.
    Using all 7 pieces each time, turned over if necessary, make these shapes.

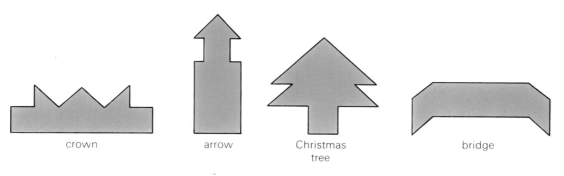

crown   arrow   Christmas   bridge
                              tree

41. The surface areas of 3 sides of this box
    are shown.
    What are its measurements ?
    What is its volume ?

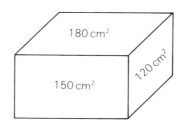

42.   The castle is surrounded by a moat, which is
      10 m wide. At night, the drawbridge was
      raised so that no-one could enter the castle.
      A handsome prince, who wanted to enter the
      castle by night to rescue a princess imprisoned
      there, had 2 planks made, so that he could use
      them to cross the moat.
      Unfortunately, when he arrived at the moat, he
      discovered that the planks, instead of being
      over 10 m long as he had ordered, were only
      9.6 m long.
      How could he use them to get across the moat ?

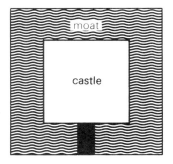

43.   Julian had £22 birthday money to spend. He bought some model trains at £3 each, some
      model coaches at £2 each, and he spent the rest of his money on toy cars at 50p each.
      Altogether he bought 22 items.
      How many of each did he buy ?

44.   **A sliding block puzzle**
      Copy this picture on cardboard, using a
      rectangle 9 cm by 12 cm.
      Cut out the squares and discard the shaded
      square.
      Make a rectangular base to put the squares
      on, of the same size.
      By sliding the pieces into empty spaces, and
      keeping them inside the rectangle of the base,
      you should score a goal by moving the ball
      (the small circle) into the centre of the ring.

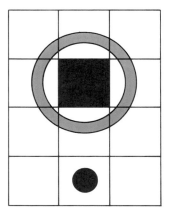

45.   Use 8 playing-cards, 4 Kings and 4 Queens.
      Hold them in a pile, face downwards, and play them in order, 1st card turned up on the
      table, 2nd card put to the bottom of the pile in your hand, 3rd card turned up on the
      table, 4th card put to the bottom of the pile in your hand, and so on until you only have
      1 card left in your hand, which you then put on the table.
      Work out how to pre-arrange the cards in the pile so that as you turn cards up on the
      table, they are alternately Queen and King, in order.
      Maybe you can also arrange them so that they also come in a particular order of suits,
      e.g. Queen then King of hearts, followed by Queen and King of clubs, etc.

46. **The four cubes puzzle**

For this puzzle you need 4 cubes of the same size. You can make them out of cardboard, or you could use 4 dice or similar cubes, with coloured paper stuck on the faces.

The faces should be coloured red (R), yellow (Y), green (G) or blue (B), as is shown on these nets.

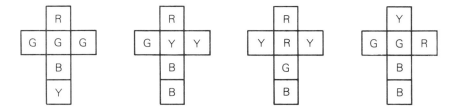

The puzzle is to place the 4 cubes in a row in such a way that all four colours appear on the top faces, all four colours appear on the front faces, all four colours appear on the back faces, and if you turn them over to look at the colours on the bottom faces, all four colours appear there, too. (Do not consider the colours showing on the two ends.)

Index

Answers

Some answers have been given corrected to reasonable degrees of accuracy, depending on the questions.
There may be variations in answers where questions involve drawings or graphs.
Sometimes it will not be possible to give answers to the same degree of accuracy, depending on the scale used.

Page 5   Exercise 1.1

1.   **1** 2^3 **4** $2^2 \times 3^2$
   2 5^2 **5** $2 \times 3^3 \times 5 \times 7^2$
   3 3×7^2

2.   **1** 36   **4** 84
   2 135   **5** 250
   3 100

3.   **1** 2×3^2 **6** 5^2
   2 $2^2 \times 7$ **7** $3^2 \times 5$
   3 2×19 **8** $2 \times 3 \times 7$
   4 $2^4 \times 3$ **9** 7×11
   5 $2^3 \times 11$ **10** 2×7^2

4.   **1** $2^3 \times 3^2$ **6** $2^5 \times 5$
   2 2×3^4 **7** $2 \times 7 \times 11$
   3 $2 \times 3^2 \times 7$ **8** $3^2 \times 5^2$
   4 $5 \times 7 \times 11$ **9** $2^2 \times 3 \times 5^2$
   5 $2^4 \times 3^2$ **10** $3^2 \times 19$

5.   **1** $3^2 \times 7$; 1, 3, 7, 9, 21, 63
   2 $2^3 \times 3 \times 5$; 1, 2, 3, 4, 5, 6, 8, 10, 12, 15, 20, 24, 30, 40, 60, 120
   3 $2^2 \times 5 \times 7$; 1, 2, 4, 5, 7, 10, 14, 20, 28, 35, 70, 140
   4 $2^2 \times 3 \times 7$; 1, 2, 3, 4, 6, 7, 12, 14, 21, 28, 42, 84
   5 $2 \times 3^2 \times 5$; 1, 2, 3, 5, 6, 9, 10, 15, 18, 30, 45, 90

Page 8   Exercise 1.2

1.   **1** 2^6 **5** 7^6 **8** 3^4
   2 3^7 **6** 2^9 **9** $2^3 \times 3^5$
   3 5^3 **7** 3^8 **10** 7^3
   4 5^6

2.   **1** $\frac{1}{11}$ **6** 1
   2 $\frac{1}{2^2}, \frac{1}{4}$ **7** $2^3 \times 5^2$, 200
   3 1   **8** 13
   4 3^4, 81   **9** 2^6, 64
   5 1   **10** $\frac{1}{3^2}, \frac{1}{9}$

3.   **1** 14   **5** 44   **8** 28
   2 55   **6** 35   **9** 18
   3 63   **7** 99   **10** 21
   4 16

4. $2^3 \times 3^3$, 6

Page 10   Exercise 1.3

1.   **1** 2   **8** -2 **15** 2
   2 0   **9** -2 **16** 0
   3 -2 **10** -9 **17** -5
   4 -3 **11** 2   **18** -6
   5 -5 **12** -3 **19** 4
   6 -4 **13** 0   **20** -3
   7 3   **14** 1

2.   **1** 7   **8** 6   **15** -7
   2 2   **9** 3   **16** -1
   3 -1 **10** -4 **17** 1
   4 -3 **11** 7   **18** 5
   5 -8 **12** -7 **19** -5
   6 -2 **13** 0   **20** 1
   7 11   **14** -10

3.   **1** -6 **8** -27 **15** 0
   2 -6 **9** 1   **16** 1
   3 6   **10** -14 **17** -7
   4 10   **11** -2 **18** 6
   5 30   **12** 0   **19** 6
   6 3   **13** 8   **20** 25
   7 0   **14** 2

Page 11   Exercise 1.4

3.
1	4	6	9	11	$\frac{11}{14}$
2	8	7	6	12	$\frac{1}{3}$
3	1	8	15	13	$\frac{3}{4}$
4	5	9	12	14	$\frac{3}{5}$
5	11	10	1	15	$\frac{4}{9}$

4.
1	36	5	72	8	132
2	66	6	150	9	160
3	120	7	84	10	150
4	21				

Page 22   Exercise 2.1

(Answers not given fully.)

1. A rectangle
2. A circle
3. The perpendicular bisector
4. An arc
5. 2 parallel lines and 2 semicircles
6. Angle bisector
7. An arc
8. 2 angle bisectors
9. The perpendicular bisector
10. 3 lines

Page 27   Exercise 2.2

1. PB = 6.1 cm
2. PA = 5.3 cm
3. PD = 9.2 cm
4. PA = 2.6 cm
5. PA = 3.0 cm
6. PA = 3.6 cm, PB = 4.5 cm, PC = 7.2 cm
9. OA = 5.1 cm
10. IX = 2.0 cm

Page 29   Exercise 2.3

9. 50 m
10. 90 m

Page 38   Exercise 3.1

1.
1	$9a$	5	e	8	$5hj$
2	$2b$	6	0	9	$11k$
3	$5c$	7	g	10	$4mn$
4	$6d$				

2.
1	$2a^2$	5	$2g - 2f$	8	$4k^2 + k$
2	$2b + c$	6	$\frac{1}{2}h$	9	$7n - m$
3	$5d^2$	7	j^2	10	$12p - 5q$
4	$4 - 3e$				

3.
1	$6ab$	5	$14fg$	8	$\frac{k}{3}$ (or $\frac{1}{3}k$)
2	$8c^2$	6	$3h$	9	$2n$
3	$8d^3$	7	7	10	$\frac{3p}{2q}$
4	$40e$				

4.
1. $7a$ km
2. $(b - 2c)$ metres
3. $d - 1, d, d + 1$
4. £$(10f - 10e)$ or £$10(f - e)$
5. £$\frac{g}{5}$, $20g$ pence

5.
1	$2a + 10b$	6	$5h - j$
2	$12c - 3d$	7	$4k - 2m$
3	$7e + 3$	8	$2n - 4$
4	$26f - 18$	9	$5p + 61q$
5	$-g - 8$	10	$5r - 1$

6.
1	$x = 3$	5	$x = 4$	8	$x = 0$
2	$x = 4\frac{1}{2}$	6	$x = 4\frac{1}{2}$	9	$x = 3$
3	$x = 2$	7	$x = 1\frac{1}{3}$	10	$x = 8$
4	$x = 1\frac{1}{5}$				

Page 40   Exercise 3.2

1.
1	a^5	5	d^6	8	f^6
2	b^7	6	d	9	g
3	c^8	7	e^2	10	1
4	c^4				

2.
1	a^9	5	e^5	8	$20j^9$
2	b^{12}	6	f^4g^5	9	$24k^7$
3	c^{12}	7	$25h^6$	10	$24m^3n^5$
4	$6d^7$				

3.
1	a^4	5	$4g^3$	8	$6m^2$
2	b	6	$\frac{1}{4}$	9	$2q^2$
3	1	7	$\frac{4j}{3}$	10	$7s^2$
4	$\frac{3f}{2}$				

Page 43   Exercise 3.3

1.
1	$-2a$	5	$3e$	8	$-4h$
2	$-5b$	6	$-4f$	9	$-j$
3	$-c$	7	$-g$	10	0
4	0				

2. **1** $4a$ **5** $5e$ **8** 0
    2 $-3b$ **6** $-f$ **9** $-4j$
    3 $2c$ **7** $-5g$ **10** $-4k$
    4 0

3. **1** $-ab$ **5** $2h$ **8** $-n$
    2 cd **6** $-j^2k$ **9** $-6p^2$
    3 $-e$ **7** 0 **10** -2
    4 -4

4. **1** -1 **5** 14 **8** 2
    2 10 **6** 25 **9** -1
    3 10 **7** -2 **10** 5
    4 -10

5. **1** $x = -3$ **5** $x = -1$ **8** $x = -2$
    2 $x = -1$ **6** $x = -6$ **9** $x = -1$
    3 $x = -\frac{1}{2}$ **7** $x = -1\frac{1}{2}$ **10** $x = -2$
    4 $x = -5$

Page 45   Exercise 3.4

1. **1** $14, 17, 20; 3n - 1$
    2 $50, 40, 30; 100 - 10n$
    3 $29, 34, 39; 5n + 4$
    4 $25 + 1, 36 + 1, 49 + 1; n^2 + 1$
    5 $100\,000, 1\,000\,000, 10\,000\,000; 10^n$
    6 $5 \times 6, 6 \times 7, 7 \times 8; n(n + 1)$
    7 $31, 37, 43; 6n + 1$
    8 $32, 64, 128; 2^n$
    9 $\frac{5}{6}, \frac{6}{7}, \frac{7}{8}; \dfrac{n}{n + 1}$
    10 $125, 216, 343; n^3$

2. **1** $3, 8, 13, 18$ **6** $2, 9, 28, 65$
    2 $16, 15, 14, 13$ **7** $15, 5, -5, -15$
    3 $10, 13, 16, 19$ **8** $0, 2, 6, 12$
    4 $95, 90, 85, 80$ **9** $\frac{1}{3}, \frac{2}{4} (=\frac{1}{2}), \frac{3}{5}, \frac{4}{6} (=\frac{2}{3})$
    5 $1, \frac{1}{2}, \frac{1}{3}, \frac{1}{4}$ **10** $11, 19, 27, 35$

Page 46   Exercise 3.5

1. **1** 2880 **2** 360

2. **1** $(a - 10)$ cm
    2 $10(a - 10)$ cm^2
    3 $\dfrac{a}{2}$ cm
    4 $\dfrac{a^2}{4}$ cm^2

4. **1** sp pence
    2 $(p + r)$ pence
    3 $(xr + yp)$ pence
    4 $8p + 10r = 500$

5. **1** $3x$ years
    2 $(x + 16)$ years
    3 $(3x + 16)$ years
    4 $3x + 16 = 2(x + 16); x = 16$
    5 Alan 48 years, Bill 16 years

6. **1** $x = 36; 36°, 72°, 72°;$ isosceles (acute-angled)
    2 $x = 12; 60°, 60°, 60°;$ equilateral
    3 $x = 28; 32°, 58°, 90°;$ right-angled

7. **1** 855 **4** 2040
    2 325 **5** 5050
    3 5050

Page 54   Exercise 4.1

1. **1** 33.083 6. **1** 1.56
    2 5.931 **2** 0.0163
    3 1.515 **3** 0.007
    4 11.18 **4** 0.0073
    5 21.899 **5** 0.165

2. **1** 12.77 7. **1** 0.36
    2 44.551 **2** 0.014
    3 3.987 **3** 0.32
    4 15.132 **4** 0.0035
    5 0.35 **5** 1.2
                                 6 0.003
3. **1** 15.44 **7** 63
    2 0.156 **8** 0.015
    3 4.15 **9** 0.0008
    4 23.2 **10** 180
    5 6.3

4. **1** 0.165 8. **1** 20
    2 1.957 **2** 0.3
    3 0.01025 **3** 12.5
    4 1.31 **4** 300
    5 0.228 **5** 3
                                 6 0.2
5. **1** 0.76 **7** 50
    2 2830 **8** 8
    3 3020 **9** 130
    4 496 **10** 0.02
    5 0.071

Page 58   Exercise 4.2

1. **1** 134.6
    2 2.004
    3 1199
    4 15.12
    5 495.3
    6 1457
    7 0.2866
    8 19.27
    9 304.1
    10 15.09

2. **1** 51.84
    2 0.125
    3 31.6
    4 3.91
    5 32
    6 50
    7 5.65
    8 19.3
    9 3.30
    10 0.289

3. **1** 19.8
    2 4.71
    3 268
    4 1.91
    5 2.19

4. **1** 20 r 2
    2 4 r 11
    3 248 r 30
    4 16 r 12
    5 52 r 12

Page 60   Exercise 4.3

1. **1** $\frac{1}{5}$
    2 $\frac{1}{21}$
    3 20
    4 $\frac{12}{5}$
    5 $\frac{11}{3}$
    6 $\frac{10}{4}$
    7 $\frac{100}{35}$
    8 $\frac{3}{5}$
    9 $\frac{10}{22}$
    10 $\frac{100}{8}$

2. **1** 0.2
    2 0.048
    3 20
    4 2.4
    5 3.667
    6 2.5
    7 2.875
    8 0.6
    9 0.455
    10 12.5

Page 62   Exercise 4.4

1. **1** 8.45 cm and 8.55 cm
    2 2.345 kg and 2.355 kg
    3 1.15 ℓ and 1.25 ℓ
    4 8 h 15 min and 8 h 25 min
    5 2 h 44.5 min and 2 h 45.5 min
    6 225 kg and 235 kg
    7 67.5 kg and 68.5 kg
    8 345 ml and 355 ml
    9 23.55 m and 23.65 m
    10 £350 and £450

2. **1** 2.95 cm and 3.05 cm
    2 195 g and 205 g
    3 3 min 49.5 s and 3 min 50.5 s
    4 79.5 ml and 80.5 ml
    5 £19.50 and £20.50

3. **1** 156.9 cm, 45.9 cm, 131.1 cm, 2.9 cm, 0.1 cm
    2 70.55 m, 3.29 m, 7.08 m, 0.06 m, 0.05 m
    3 28 kg, 41 kg, 34 kg, 152 kg, 4 kg
    4 46.7 ℓ, 4.1 ℓ, 0.9 ℓ, 8.7 ℓ, 12.1 ℓ
    5 22 min, 9 min, 3 min, 18 min, 28 min

4. **1** 4.0 m   **4** 2000 ℓ
    2 47 s   **5** 16.0 kg
    3 1500 m

Page 63   Exercise 4.5

1. 0.9 deg C

2. 2.54 cm

3. 34.4 cm

4. 0.0075 cm

5. 25.92 guilders

6. 4.2 m

7. £3.10

8. 880 m

9. 108, 6.4 ℓ

10. 27 km

11. **1** 16.5 kg to 17.5 kg, 11.5 kg to 12.5 kg
   2 29 kg
   3 28 kg, 30 kg
   4 5 kg
   5 4 kg, 6 kg

12. **1** 2.04 s
   2 54.6 m

14.

1	30 000	**8**	24	**15**	0.4
2	14	**9**	4.5	**16**	6
3	0.48	**10**	0.1	**17**	8
4	81	**11**	110	**18**	900
5	0.25	**12**	120	**19**	0.9
6	2800	**13**	11	**20**	100
7	0.12	**14**	12		

Page 81   Exercise 6.1

1. **1** 90 cm²   **4** 80 cm²
   2 27 cm²   **5** 144 cm²
   3 77 cm²

2. **1** 150 cm²   **2** 12.5

3. **1** 17.5 cm²
   2 24 cm²
   3 14 cm²

4. 30 cm²

5. 74 cm²

6. 96 cm²

7. 45 cm²

8. **1** 144 cm²
   2 $\triangle ARS$ 21 cm², $\triangle BPS$ 10 cm²,
      $\triangle CPQ$ 12 cm², $\triangle DRQ$ 27 cm²
   3 74 cm²

9. 34.2 cm²

Page 87   Exercise 6.2

1. **1** 440 cm³   **4** 160 cm³
   2 216 cm³   **5** 560 cm³
   3 45 cm³

2. **1** 4 cm   **2** 7 cm

3. **1** 408 cm²   **2** 150 cm²

4. **1** 900 000 cm³
   2 0.9 m³
   3 900 ℓ

Page 87   Exercise 6.3

1. 750 m², 23 m

2. **1** 22 280 m²   **2** 66 800

3. **1** 84 m²
   2 4.2 kg
   3 0.8 kg
   4 60 g

4. **1** 66 m²   **2** 26 400 m³

5. 6 cm

6. **1** 50 m²
   2 600 m³
   3 600 000 ℓ

7. **1** 12 m²
   2 240 m³
   3 600 tonnes

8. 1.5 m²

12. 3.8 cm

Page 92   Exercise A1

1. 85
2. 27 cm³
3. $x + 2y$
4. 0.24
5. 110°
6. 3°
7. 2.4 m
8. 72
9. 160 miles
10. 22 cm
11. $x = 6$
12. £2.10
13. $\frac{2}{7}$
14. 25 (cm)
15. 2500

Page 93   Exercise A2

1. 38, 45
2. 70%
3. 20 m
4. 25p
5. 33
6. $\frac{3}{13}$
7. 4 (km)
8. 6 cm
9. x^5
10. $\frac{1}{5}$
11. rhombus
12. 40 (min)
13. 8
14. 2
15. 5

Page 94   Exercise A3

1. **1** 3×5^2
    2 $2^2 \times 3^3$
    3 $2^2 \times 3 \times 11$

2. $c = 29°, d = 42°, e = 109°, f = 138°$

3. £27.50

4. **1** 1.3   **4** 2.25
    2 0.5   **5** 0.81
    3 0.36

5. **1** D **2** A **3** E

6. 74

7. £12

8. $x = 42$, all 60°, equilateral

10. $88\,cm^2$

11. 43.9 m

12. **1** $3n + 17$ **4** $\dfrac{n}{n+1}$

    2 $50 - n$ **5** $\dfrac{1}{2^n}$

    3 3^n

13. **1** 45°   **2** 70°   **3** 115°

14. B £165, C £75; £450

15. **1** $12a^7$ **4** $\dfrac{1}{3d}$

    2 1   **5** $2e^4$

    3 c^{12}

16. **1** 2 and 3
    2 4
    3 2 and 6

17. 151.5 to 152.5 cm,
    37.5 to 38.5 kg,
    $11\frac{1}{2}$ to $12\frac{1}{2}$ years

18. **1** $(9x - 3)$ cm
    2 $(3x - 1)$ cm
    3 $(4x + 2)$ cm

19. 44°

20. 24 cm

Page 124   Exercise 8.1

1. **1** x is greater than 4
    2 x is less than or equal to 7
    3 x is less than -3
    4 x is greater than 0 but less than 3
    5 x is greater than or equal to -2

2. **1** $x < 5$ **4** $-2 < x < 10$
    2 $x \geqslant -4$ **5** $x \leqslant 6$
    3 $x > 0$

4. **1** $-1, 0, 1, 2, 3, 4, 5$
    2 $-5, -4$
    3 $0, 1, 2, 3, 4, 5$
    4 $-5, -4, -3, -2, -1, 0, 1, 2, 3$
    5 $-5, -4, -3, -2, -1, 0, 1, 2, 3$
    6 no value for x
    7 $-4, -3, -2, -1, 0, 1, 2, 3$
    8 $-5, -4, -3, 5$
    9 $-5, -4, -3, -2, -1, 0, 1, 2, 3, 4, 5$
    10 $-2, -1$

5. **1** $a < c < b$ **4** $a < c < b$
    2 $c < b < a$ **5** $c < a < b$
    3 $c < a < b$

6. **1** $x < 1$ **4** $-2 < x < 2$
    2 $x > -3$ **5** $x \leqslant -2$ or $x \geqslant 3$
    3 $x \leqslant 0$

Page 127   Exercise 8.2

1. **1** $x > 6$ **4** $x < \frac{1}{2}$
    2 $x < 3$ **5** $x \leqslant 9$
    3 $x \geqslant 3$

2. **1** 6, 7, 8, 9, 10
    2 0, 1, 2, 3, 4, 5
    3 5, 6, 7, 8, 9, 10
    4 0, 1
    5 5, 6, 7, 8, 9, 10

3. **1** $-3, -2$
    2 -3
    3 0, 1, 2, 3
    4 3
    5 $-1, 0, 1, 2, 3$

4. **1** $x < 10$ **6** $x > 3$
    2 $x \geqslant -2$ **7** $x > -4$
    3 $x \geqslant 8$ **8** $x \geqslant 0$
    4 $x > -9$ **9** $x < 8$
    5 $x \geqslant 1$ **10** $x \leqslant -6$

Page 128

Example 1
12 litres = 2.64 gallons

Page 129

Example 2
1, 8, 27, 64, 125

Page 130   Exercise 8.3

1. 6.10 m

2. triangular numbers

4. 7

Page 131   Exercise 8.4

1. **1** $10 < x + y \leqslant 18$
    2 $x > y$
    3 $15x + 20y < 300$

2. **1** $x + y > 100$
    2 $7x + 12y > 800$
    3 $x > 2y$
    4 $y \geqslant 20$

3. **1** Mr Archer £$(400 + 5x)$,
        Mr Barton £$13x$
    2 $13x < 400 + 5x$
    3 $x < 50$
    4 Mr Archer

4. **1** $x + y < 30$
    2 $20x + 10y > 300$
    3 $y > 3x$
    4 $x \geqslant 5$

6. **1** 8
    2 4 loaves, 1 bar of chocolate

7. 59°F

8. **1** $4 \leqslant t \leqslant 7$
    2 $c \geqslant 4t, c \leqslant 28$
    3 $50t + 15c \leqslant 600$
    4 5 tables, 23 chairs

Page 139   Exercise 9.1

1. **1** 8, 8.7   **6** 4, 4.7
    2 5, 5.0   **7** 3, 3.3
    3 9, 9.9   **8** 8, 8.2
    4 7, 7.1   **9** 2, 2.9
    5 6, 6.4   **10** 4, 4.1

2. **1** 13.7   **6** 14
    2 14.7   **7** 14.1
    3 21.8   **8** 19.0
    4 15   **9** 22.9
    5 11.0   **10** 37

3. **1** 17 cm   **6** 2.5 cm
    2 10.8 cm   **7** 13.5 cm
    3 13 cm   **8** 16.6 cm
    4 10.8 cm   **9** 12.3 cm
    5 13.9 cm   **10** 6 cm

4. **1** $b = 8.7$ cm   **6** $c = 0.8$ cm
    2 $c = 9$ cm   **7** $b = 9.2$ cm
    3 $c = 7.5$ cm   **8** $c = 11.9$ cm
    4 $b = 24$ cm   **9** $c = 3.9$ cm
    5 $b = 6$ cm   **10** $b = 4.0$ cm

5. $x = 15$ cm, $y = 25$ cm

6. $x = 50$ cm, $y = 40$ cm

Page 142   Exercise 9.2

1. **1** $AB = 8.6$ cm   **4** $BC = 4.5$ cm
    2 $AB = 6.5$ cm   **5** $AB = 23.3$ cm
    3 $AC = 6.6$ cm

2. **1** 5 cm   **2** 16 cm   **3** 21 cm

3. **1** 13 cm   **2** 8 cm

4. 6 cm

5. 13 units

6. 9 cm

7. **1** 4 cm
    2 90°
    3 6.9 cm

8. **1** 7.1 cm   **2** 3.5 cm

9. **1** 40 cm   **2** 12 cm   **3** 15 cm

10. **1** 25 cm
    2 7 cm
    3 66 cm
    4 234 cm^2

Page 144   Exercise 9.3

1. 20 km

2. 10 feet

3. 170 cm

4. 4.12 m

7. **1** a = 4 cm   **6** f = 10 cm
    2 b = 15 cm   **7** g = 17 cm
    3 c = 7 cm   **8** h = 25 cm
    4 d = 5 cm   **9** j = 26 cm
    5 e = 30 cm   **10** k = 2.0 cm

Page 152   Exercise 10.1

1. **1** 10
    2 56
    3 11.8
    4 3.07
    5 110

2. **1** 11
    2 61
    3 12
    4 2.5
    5 105

3. **1** 5
    2 38.5
    3 4.5

4. **1** 2
    2 37
    3 4

5. mean 39 kg, median 37 kg, range 18 kg

6. mean 40.94 m, median 41.8 m,
    range 6.9 m

7. mean 27°C, range 4 deg C

8. mean 13 y 9 m, median 13 y 9$\frac{1}{2}$ m,
    range 1 y 3 m

9. mean 2 h 10 min, range 2 hours

Page 156   Exercise 10.2

1. **1** 2.5
    2 2
    3 2

2. **1** 6.9
    2 7
    3 7

3. **1** 3.7
    2 4
    3 4

Page 160   Exercise 10.3

1. **1** 60 – 69
    2 24.5
    3 64.6

2. **1** 0 – 19
    2 9.5
    3 28.3 (28.25)

3. **1** 7.5 – 8.5 lb
    2 5.0 lb
    3 7.6 lb

4. **1** 5.5 – 6.0 cm
    2 4.75 cm
    3 6.28 cm

5. **1** 1 – 2 hours
    2 0.5 h
    3 1.9 h

6. **1** 7 or 8 years
    2 9.6 years

Page 166   Exercise 10.5

1. **1** 2.5
    2 2
    3 6

2. **1** 6.3
    2 6
    3 6
    4 8

3. **1** 21 – 30 words
    2 5.5
    3 36.3

Page 172   Exercise 11.1

1. $x = 5, y = 3$
2. $x = 1\frac{1}{2}, y = -2\frac{1}{2}$
3. $x = 3, y = 2$
4. $x = 2, y = -1$
5. $x = 13, y = -7$
6. $x = -2, y = 5$
7. $x = 7, y = 5$
8. $x = 2, y = 0$
9. $x = 0, y = 1$
10. $x = 1, y = -1$

Page 175   Exercise 11.2

1. $x = 3, y = 1$
2. $x = -1, y = 3$
3. $x = 4, y = -2$
4. $x = 3, y = 1$
5. $x = 0, y = \frac{2}{3}$
6. $x = 9, y = 1$
7. $x = -2, y = 4$
8. $x = 3, y = -2$
9. $x = 2, y = 1$
10. $x = 3, y = -1$

Page 176   Exercise 11.3

1. $x = 9, y = -5$
2. $x = 5, y = 3$
3. $x = 3, y = -12$
4. $x = -3, y = 2$
5. $x = 4, y = -1$
6. $x = -1, y = -1$
7. $x = 2, y = -3$
8. $x = -1, y = 4$
9. $x = -1, y = 7$
10. $x = 4, y = 0$

Page 177   Exercise 11.4

1. 31 and 12

2. orange 12p, grapefruit 28p

3. 15 of 20p and 8 of 50p

4. $\angle A = 34°, \angle C = 104°, \angle D = 52°,$
    $\angle F = 68°$

5. 36 (£10) and 15 (£20)

6. $x = 7, y = 14; AB = AC = 35$ cm,
    $BC = 14$ cm

7. 42 at £4, 10 at £6.50

8. Adult £25, teenager £20

9. Dad's 8ℓ, Pip's 5ℓ

10. Anne's 7, Barbara's 3

Page 184   Exercise 12.1

1. **1** 37.7 cm
    2 31.4 cm
    3 51.5 cm
    4 28.9 cm
    5 42.1 cm

2. **1** 113 cm^2
    2 78.5 cm^2
    3 211 cm^2
    4 66.5 cm^2
    5 141 cm^2

3. **1** 16.2 cm
    2 12.7 cm
    3 4.37 cm
    4 $r = 4.50$ cm, $A = 63.7$ cm^2

4. **1** 64 cm^2
    2 50.3 cm^2
    3 13.7 cm^2

5. **1** 254 cm^2
    2 162 cm^2
    3 92.5 cm^2

6. **1** 62.8 cm
    2 $\frac{1}{8}$
    3 7.85 cm

Page 188   Exercise 12.2

1. **1** 11 400 cm^3
    2 402 cm^3
    3 2510 cm^3
    4 2040 cm^3
    5 35 300 cm^3

2. **1** 2070 cm^2
    2 101 cm^2
    3 2510 cm^2
    4 679 cm^2
    5 4710 cm^2

3. **1** 251 cm^2
    2 440 cm^2

4. **1** 4.74 cm
    2 2.45 cm
    3 4.27 cm

Page 188   Exercise 12.3

1. 637 m^2

2. 163 cm, 612 revs.

3. 63.7 m

4. 25 400 ℓ/min.

5. 40 cm

6. **1** 350 m³   **2** 471 m²

7. $V = 35\,300\,\text{cm}^3$, weight = 283 kg

8. 471 m², 52.4 ℓ

9. 163 mugs

10. 2210 ℓ

11. square 1600 m², extra 437 m²

13. radius 5.4 cm, height 10.8 cm

Page 192   Exercise B1

1. 67%

2. 1 h 40 min

3. 40

4. 65

5. 400 m

6. 29

7. 4

8. 60 cm³

9. 5 cm

10. x is less than 7

11. 9

12. 3 and 11

13. square

14. 3

15. 25

Page 193   Exercise B2

1. 20

2. £3.60

3. 75°

4. 0.036

5. 3 m

6. $6b^5$

7. 3600

8. 16

9. 0.4

10. $\frac{1}{2}$

11. 25, 16

12. 126 miles

13. x is greater than 4

14. 40

15. 30 cm

Page 194   Exercise B3

1. 8.52

2. **1** 2^9 **2** 5^3 **3** 3^8

3. **1** 0.16 m   **2** 0.0015 m²

4. $x = 8$ or 9

5. **1** 240 cm²
    2 34 cm
    3 14.1 cm

6. **1** 54 y 7 m
    2 66 y 0 m
    3 11 y 0 m

7. **1** $5a$
    2 $c + 12d$
    3 $5e + 9$

8. £5, 14; £20, 4

9. $a = 76°$, $b = 76°$, $c = 28°$

10. **1** 176 cm²
    2 61 600 cm³
    3 492.8 kg

11. **1** $\frac{2}{5}$
    2 $\frac{257}{500}$
    3 44

12. **1** rhombus, square
    2 equilateral triangle
    3 5 cm, right-angled
    4 2.4 cm

13. frequencies in order:
    3, 4, 5, 11, 9, 8, 5, 3, 2
    1 4
    2 5
    3 4.8

14. **1** 48 cm
    2 37.7 cm
    3 10.3 cm

15. **1** 11, 18, 25, 32
    2 7, 4, 1, −2
    3 5, 25, 125, 625
    4 $\frac{1}{3}, \frac{3}{5}, \frac{5}{7}, \frac{7}{9}$
    5 0, 7, 26, 63

16. **1** 11.2 cm   **2** 6.9 cm

17. **1** £2.55
    2 9p, 12p left

18. 6.6 cm

19. **1** £139   **2** £1.39

20. **1** 188 cm²   **2** 198 cm³

Page 216   Exercise 13.1

1. parallelogram

2. **3** (4, 3)

3. **1** $y = x - 1$ **4** $y = \frac{1}{2}x$
    2 $y = -x$ **5** $y = 2 - 2x$
    3 $y = 2x + 1$

4. isosceles right-angled triangle

5. (0.8, 0.4)

Page 219   Exercise 13.2

1. **4** $x = 4, y = 1$

2. $x = 2.8, y = 12.4$

3. $x = 2.7, y = 3.7$

Page 221   Exercise 13.3

1. C (6, 4, 0)
    F (6, 1, 5)
    G (6, 4, 5)
    H (1, 4, 5)

2. B (8, 2, 4)
    C (8, 3, 4)
    D (3, 3, 4)
    E (3, 2, 6)
    F (8, 2, 6)
    G (8, 3, 6)
    H (3, 3, 6)

3. A $(-3, -1, -2)$
    B $(7, -1, -2)$
    C $(7, 8, -2)$
    D $(-3, 8, -2)$
    E $(-3, -1, 5)$
    F $(7, -1, 5)$
    G $(-3, 8, 5)$

Page 222   Exercise 13.4

1. $y = 30x + 40$

2. **1** 26 cm
    2 51 cm
    3 0.37 kg

3. $x + y = 25$,
    $24x + 12y = 480$,
    15 bars of chocolate,
    10 packets of sweets

4. C (5, 8, 3)
    F (5, 5, 15)
    G (5, 8, 15)
    H (1, 8, 15)
    $AB = 4$ units, $BC = 3$, $AC = 5$, $CG = 12$,
    $\angle ACG = 90°$, $AG = 13$

Page 229   Exercise 14.1

2. $1\frac{1}{3}$

3. 14 cm by 10.5 cm

4. **1** 2.5   **2** 4 cm

5. **1** 3.5   **2** 10.5 cm   **3** 2 cm

6. **1** 0.6   **2** 42 cm

Page 230   Exercise 14.2

3. 4.5 m

5. 12 cm, 25 m

Page 241   Exercise 15.2

1. 16 seconds

2. £3 200 000

3. £178

4. **1** 19.4 kg   **2** 365 kg

5. **1** 6.5 mm over 10 m
    2 164°C

Page 248   Exercise 16.1

1. **1** $x = 5$
    2 $x = 6$
    3 $x = 8.94$
    4 $x = 1.48$
    5 $x = 2.23$

2. **1** $x = 2$
   2 $x = 5$
   3 $x = 4$
   4 $x = 6$
   5 $x = 1$
   6 $x = 2$ or $x = 5$
   7 $x = 1$ or $x = 7$
   8 $x = 5$
   9 $x = 7$
   10 $x = 6$

3. **1** $x = 2$
   2 $x = 4$
   3 $x = 3$
   4 $x = 4$
   5 $x = 4$

Page 251   Exercise 16.2

1. $x = 2.4$
2. $x = 3.3$
3. $x = 5.6$
4. $x = 4.8$
5. $x = 2.6$
6. $x = 2.6$
7. $x = 3.3$
8. $x = 5.7$
9. $x = 6.1$
10. $x = 11.5$

Page 251   Exercise 16.3

1. **1** $(x + 8)\,$m
   2 $x(x + 8)\,$m^2, $x(x + 8) = 105$
   3 $x = 7$; $AB = 7\,$m, $BC = 15\,$m

2. **2** 189
   3 7.3 cm

3. 5

4. **1** $3x^3\,$cm^3
   2 500 cm^3
   3 $x = 5.5$

5. **1** 72 m^3
   2 32 m^3
   3 6 min

6. **1** 5 m
   2 9 m
   3 3.2 s

Page 257   Exercise 17.1

1. **1** $\frac{5}{6}$ **2** $\frac{1}{6}$

2. **1** $\frac{23}{100}$ **2** $\frac{77}{100}$

3. **1** $\frac{1}{2}$ **2** $\frac{3}{16}$ **3** $\frac{31}{32}$

4. **1** $\frac{1}{12}$ **2** $\frac{11}{12}$

5. **1** $\frac{4}{13}$ **2** $\frac{9}{13}$ **3** $\frac{5}{13}$

6. **1** $\frac{3}{8}$ **2** $\frac{5}{8}$

7. **1** $\frac{4}{13}$ **2** $\frac{1}{2}$ **3** $\frac{7}{8}$

Page 259   Exercise 17.2

1. **1** 0.3
   2 0.8

2. **1** 0.95
   2 0.05

3. **1** $\frac{2}{5}$ **2** $\frac{3}{10}$ **3** $\frac{7}{10}$ **4** $\frac{3}{10}$

4. **1** 0.13
   2 0.25
   3 0.75

5. **1** 10%
   2 30%

6. **1** 0.26
   2 0.14
   3 0.3
   4 0.7

7. (theoretical probabilities)
   1 0.40
   2 0.60
   3 0.20
   4 0.80

Page 265   Exercise 18.1

1. **4** Mr Gibson, 9.56 am;
   Pauline, 12.05 pm;
   Rajesh, 12.53 pm

2. **1** 4 km
   2 $2\frac{1}{2}$ hours
   3 8 km/h
   4 4 km/h

3. **1** 10 km/h
   2 $\frac{3}{4}$ hour
   3 30 km
   4 40 km/h
   5 $\frac{1}{2}$ hour
   6 $1\frac{1}{4}$ hour
   7 35 km
   8 28 km/h

4. **1** (1) and (4)
    2 (2), 40 km/h
    3 60 km/h

5. **1** 2 km
    2 15 min
    3 24 km/h
    4 8.20 am
    5 $4\frac{1}{2}$ km/h

Page 269   Exercise 18.2

1. **1** £22
    2 £124
    3 4000

2. **1** £1800
    2 £2400
    3 £1670

3. **1** £335
    2 1700 units

Page 270   Exercise 18.3

1. 3.50 pm, 57 km

2. **1** 12.55 pm
    2 20 km

3. 8 days

4. **1** £1700, £7600
    2 £36 000, £7300

6. **1** 1000
    2 £200
    3 625

Page 274   Exercise C1

1. $1\frac{1}{2}$ hours
2. 30 cm
3. 4 m
4. 25, 55
5. $\frac{3}{7}$
6. $y = 2x$
7. 6.5
8. 20
9. 1500 (g)
10. c
11. £2
12. 5 km
13. $x = 3$
14. $\frac{2}{3}$
15. 4.2 m

Page 275   Exercise C2

1. 66p
2. 6300 m^2
3. 4
4. 3
5. 10.20 am
6. 4
7. H A M
8. 10
9. £1.20
10. 3
11. £6
12. yes
13. 1 km
14. 10
15. 0.7

Page 276   Exercise C3

1. **1** 8
    2 9
    3 10
    4 8

2. $1\frac{1}{3}$, 3.6 cm

3. **1** $2 \leqslant x < 6$
    2 $3 < y < 9$
    3 $x + y \leqslant 10$

4. 11, 1.3 m

5. **1** 31°
    2 156 g

6. **1** 706.9 cm^2
    2 2.8 cm

7. B (10, 2, 0)
    C (10, 6, 0)
    D (2, 6, 0)
    E (2, 2, 6)
    F (10, 2, 6)
    G (10, 6, 6)
    H (2, 6, 6)

8. **1** x^5 **4** x^8
    2 x^6 **5** 1
    3 x^3

10. **1** 37 m
    2 228 m

11. $x + y = 25$,
    $2x + y = 45$,
    20 skilled workers, 5 trainees

12. **1** 90 m
     2 1350 m²
     3 trapezium
     4 1340 m²
     5 2690 m²

13. −5

14. **1** frequencies in order:
          10, 7, 8, 4, 1
     2 0
     3 1
     4 1.3

15. 37

16. $a = 144°$, $c = 136°$, $d = 22°$,
     $\angle DAB = 90°$

17. **1** 12 km/h
     2 32 km/h
     3 4.12 pm
     4 9.6 km

18. **1** $x = 5$, $y = 2$
     2 $x = 2$, $y = -1$

19. **1** 0.7
     2 0.3
     3 0.13

20. 15 sides

Page 280   Exercise C4

1. 1.16

2. 54 km/h

3. **1** 201.1 m²
    2 314.2 m²
    3 113.1 m²

4. $2 \times 3^2 \times 5$, 90

5. **1** 50 − 100 g
    2 25 g
    3 129 g

6. **1** $30 - x$
    2 £$(2x + 90)$
    3 $x = 18$
    4 18 adults, 12 children

7. (If VAT at $17\frac{1}{2}$%)
    1 £147
    2 £5.17

8. 35 large, 25 smaller

9. **1** 2 reds, 2 blues
    2 4 blues
    3 0.58
    4 0.42

10. 440

12. **1** 100
     2 1
     3 $\frac{1}{9}$

13. **1** Mr B
     2 Mr A
     3 Mr C

14. **1** $(x^2 + 25x)$ cm²
     2 $x = 4$

16. $1\frac{1}{4}$, 30 cm

17. 4%

18. 50 m

19. $4x + 3y = 240$, $y = x + 10$,
     30 m at £20, 40 m at £15

20. 120 000 m³